THE MAN FROM
MAIN STREET

NOVELS BY SINCLAIR LEWIS

1914 Our Mr. Wrenn
1915 The Trail of the Hawk
1917 The Job
1917 The Innocents
1919 Free Air
1920 Main Street
1922 Babbitt
1925 Arrowsmith
1926 Mantrap
1927 Elmer Gantry
1928 The Man Who Knew Coolidge
1929 Dodsworth
1933 Ann Vickers
1934 Works of Art
1935 It Can't Happen Here
1938 The Prodigal Parents
1940 Bethel Merriday
1943 Gideon Planish
1945 Cass Timberlane
1947 Kingsblood Royal
1949 The God-Seeker
1951 World So Wide

THE MAN FROM MAIN STREET

*Selected Essays and
Other Writings of*

SINCLAIR LEWIS

EDITED BY HARRY E. MAULE AND
MELVILLE H. CANE
Assisted by Philip Allan Friedman

WILLIAM HEINEMANN LTD
MELBOURNE :: LONDON :: TORONTO

FIRST PUBLISHED 1954

PRINTED IN GREAT BRITAIN
AT THE WINDMILL PRESS
KINGSWOOD, SURREY

ACKNOWLEDGMENTS

Grateful acknowledgment for permission to use published material is made to the following:

Newsweek, for "Seeing Red" and "One-Man Revolution", copyright, 1937, by Weekly Publications, Inc.

The United Chapter of Phi Beta Kappa, for "The Artist, the Scientist and the Peace", which appeared in *The American Scholar* in 1945.

The Literary Guild of America, Inc., for "A Note about *Kingsblood Royal*", which appeared in The Literary Guild Review *Wings*.

Richard R. Smith Publisher, Inc., for "A Letter on Religion", from *The Meaning of Life*, edited by Will Durant, copyright, 1932, by Will Durant.

The New Yorker, for "My First Day in New York", copyright, 1937, by the New Yorker Magazine, Inc.

New Colophon, for "Breaking into Print", copyright, 1937, by Pynson Printers.

The New York Sun, Inc., for "Two Yale Men in Utopia", copyright, 1906, by The New York Sun, Inc.

Hearst Magazines, Inc., for "Is America a Paradise for Women?" published in *Pictorial Review*; "This Golden Half-Century, 1885–1935", published in *Good Housekeeping*; and "I'm an Old Newspaperman Myself", published in *Cosmopolitan*. Copyright, 1929, 1935, 1947, by The Hearst Corp.

The George Macy Companies, Inc., for "A Note on Book Collecting" from *Samples*, copyright, 1935, by the Limited Editions Club, Inc.; "Introductory Remarks" from *The Three Readers*, copyright, 1934, by the Press of The Readers Club; Preface to *Fathers and Sons* by Ivan Turgenev, copyright, 1941, by The Heritage Press; Preface to *Main Street*, The Limited

Editions Club edition, copyright, 1937, by The Limited Editions Club, Inc.

Esquire, Inc., for "The Death of Arrowsmith", published in *Coronet*; "Gentlemen, This Is Revolution", and "Obscenity and Obscurity", published in *Esquire*, copyright, 1941, 1945, by Esquire, Inc.

Yale Literary Magazine, for "Rambling Thoughts on Literature".

New York Herald Tribune, for "A Pilgrim's Progress", "The American Scene in Fiction", and "Our Friend, H. G.", copyright, 1924, 1929, 1936 and 1946, by the New York Herald Tribune, Inc.

Harper & Bros., for "A Letter on Style", from *Types and Times in the Essay*, selected and arranged by Warner Taylor, copyright, 1932, by Harper & Bros.

The Saturday Review, for "Fools, Liars and Mr. DeVoto", copyright, 1939, 1944, by The Saturday Review Associates, Inc.

The New York Post, for "A Hamlet of the Plains", copyright, 1922, by The New York Post, Inc.

The American Peoples Encyclopedia, for "No Flight to Olympus", copyright, 1951, by Spencer Press, Inc.

Doubleday & Co., Inc., for "My Maiden Effort", copyright, 1921, by Doubleday, Page & Co., Introduction to *Selected Short Stories of Sinclair Lewis*, copyright, 1935, by Sinclair Lewis; and quotations from *Sinclair Lewis: A Biographical Sketch* by Carl Van Doren, with a Bibliography by Harvey Taylor, copyright, 1933, by Doubleday, Doran & Co., Inc.

The Crowell-Collier Publishing Co., for "How I Wrote a Novel on Trains and Beside the Kitchen Sink", published in the *American*, copyright, 1921, by The Crowell-Collier Publishing Co.

Harcourt, Brace & Co., for "The Art of Dramatisation" from *Dodsworth*, dramatised by Sidney Howard, copyright, 1933, 1934, by Sinclair Lewis and Sidney Howard.

The New York Times, for "Novelist Bites Art", copyright, 1941, by The New York Times Co.

The Nation, for "Minnesota, the Norse State", copyright, 1923, 1924, by The Nation, Inc.

Liveright Publishing Corp., for "Minnesota, the Norse State", from *These United States* edited by Ernest Guening, copyright renewed 1950 by Ernest Gruening.

Current History, for "Back to Vermont", copyright, 1936, by Form Publishing Co., Inc.

The Bell Syndicate, Inc., for "Americans in Italy", taken from a series of newspaper articles, copyright, 1949, by The Bell Syndicate, Inc.

United Feature Syndicate, for "Cheap and Contented Labour", copyright, 1929, by United Feature Syndicate, Inc.

The Nobel Foundation, for quotations from *Nobel: The Man and His Prizes,* 1950.

The editors wish to express their special appreciation to the following individuals:

To Mr. James T. Babb, Librarian, Yale University Library, for making available material from the Lewis Collection at the Yale Library;

Mrs. Marian H. Christensen, Principal Librarian, Archives, University of Minnesota, for bibliographical research;

Mr. Philip Allan Friedman, for aid in research;

Miss Leah Gadlow, for research, invaluable suggestions and criticism and for her unflagging efforts on behalf of this book;

Mr. Donald C. Gallup, Curator of the Yale Collection of American Literature, for making available material from the Lewis Collection at the Yale Library;

Mr. Joseph Henry Jackson of the *San Francisco Chronicle,* for research on matters pertaining to the period when Sinclair Lewis lived in San Francisco;

Mrs. Matthew Josephson of The American Academy of Arts and Letters, for her co-operation and for making available the Sinclair Lewis material from the Academy's collection;

Mr. George Macy, for furnishing needed bibliographical data;

Mrs. Christine Pollard, for aid on bibliographical matters.

CONTENTS

INTRODUCTION

ON THE DEATH OF SINCLAIR LEWIS AT ROME ON JANUARY 10, 1951, it became the duty of his executors to make an inventory of his writings, both published and still in manuscript. In the process, and with the aid of existing bibliographies, they discovered articles in the files of magazines and newspapers long defunct; regular contributions to many national periodicals on a wide range of subjects; unknown autobiographical reminiscences; reviews of current books which often served as the springboard for extended essays; manuscript outlines for his projected novels, such as the one for *Babbitt,* reprinted herein; and a miscellaneous assortment of unclassified literary notations of abiding value and interest.

The vitality and variety of this material at once convinced the executors that it should be made available to the general public in a selected volume of Lewis's non-fiction pieces. The suggested project met with instant enthusiastic response, and the sympathetic co-operation between editors and publisher has resulted in the present collection.

The discussion of the place of Sinclair Lewis in the literary history of America will continue for many years. It is not the aim of this book to take a position on that subject, but rather to illuminate it by bringing together in one volume the cream of the material mentioned above. This covers every period of the author's life from college days to the year of his death.

Of the many persons who could rightly claim intimate friendship with Sinclair Lewis at some time or other, not one ever knew all the eddies and cross-currents of that torrent of living and writing. Not that he was reticent. No man ever carried on his life more publicly than Lewis. But he was so immersed in the current project that he was impatient of any attempts to bring him back to reminiscence or explanation of past events. It will be many years before the whole being—man and artist—can be captured and presented on the printed page. Meanwhile, this collection may spread a searchlight over some hidden areas.

Few of his readers ever considered Lewis an essayist; yet this book, culled from nearly a million words of material, shows that his entire life was devoted to such writing, on every subject which captured his restless, all-embracing spirit. From the imitative theme papers written for Chauncey Tinker and William Lyon Phelps at Yale, through days of stormy radicalism, news jaunts over the face of America and Europe, residence in Vermont, Minnesota, New York, Massachusetts, up to his last days in Italy, we see here a volcanic energy at work. Here is the record of a many-sided man. We hope that this collection will be useful and instructive, but we know too much of Red Lewis to believe that here, or in a book of ten times the length, we could present him whole.

We believe that it does hold intimations of one outstanding fact, that Sinclair Lewis perhaps exerted a more profound influence upon the United States of America than any other writer of his time. The critics may debate the niceties of his style; the literary historians may place him in an orderly niche. The fact remains that Lewis's books roused the world to a better understanding of America and affected the course of our national thinking about America and Americans. We venture to prophesy that, a century from now, literate people will look to Sinclair Lewis to tell what his country was like in those amazing four decades from 1910 to 1950.

As Carl Van Doren said of Lewis in a biographical sketch published by Doubleday, Doran & Company in 1933: "Not one of them [Lewis's contemporaries] has kept so close to the main channel of American life as Mr. Lewis, or so near to the human surface. He is a part of channel and surface. To venture into hyperbole, not only is he an American telling stories, but he is America telling stories."

Relieved of the iron discipline of fiction-writing, Mr. Lewis is at his free-wheeling best in many of these pieces. His opinion of the moment always seemed the most important thing in the world to him, and, of course, he had opinions on everything. In stating them he resorted to the slashing wit, satire and caricature of his novels. Some pieces are like Red talking with a group of congenial friends—an unforgettable experience for those who have heard him. He was a superb mimic, and used this talent freely to develop an idea. In controversy he was a ruthless opponent, and he did not hesitate to use sarcasm, exaggeration, scorn and ridicule. We have included one or two such controversial pieces. Not to have done so would be to ignore an important facet of the man's literary personality.

Also, we think the material in this book emphasises Lewis's importance as a literary bridge. Entering the scene in the early 1900s—remember that he started the embryonic novel which became *Main Street* in 1905—he broke down the polite tradition represented by William Dean Howells and prepared the world for a freer, more critical, more realistic appraisal of American life. Lewis has had very few imitators and none successful, but we think it can be demonstrated that the authors of the 1920s and '30s owe him a debt for breaking ground. As Carl Van Doren said, he was a seismograph recording the changing moods and attitudes of the American public even before they themselves were conscious of them.

In selecting the material which appears here, two standards were followed. Sometimes they ran along together; sometimes they did not. First, of course, was the literary quality of the writer's output at the particular period of his life from which the article was drawn. Second was the historical importance of any given essay to Lewis's work as a whole. A corollary, or third standard, was the choice of pieces which revealed the man and the conditions of his life. The arrangement is topical rather than chronological, and the pieces are placed loosely under the subjects treated. In many instances, the grouping is arbitrary because of Lewis's habit of starting off with one theme and branching out into other matters to make his point.

Because magazine articles are invariably cut or edited, we have followed the author's complete text when it was available in original manuscript or in a carbon copy corrected by him. When such text could not be found in Lewis's papers, we have used the printed version. Likewise, when he himself gave a title to a piece, we have used that. When he did not, we have used the magazine title or, if it was unpublished, a simple, descriptive caption. With the exception of three essays, all have been used complete, either as Mr. Lewis wrote them or as the magazines published them. In three instances we have made some cuts to conserve space and to permit the publication of more items.

We can only wish the readers of this book the same pleasure of rediscovery that was ours in compiling it.

HARRY E. MAULE

MELVILLE H. CANE

I

DECLARATIONS

THE AMERICAN FEAR OF LITERATURE

An address by Sinclair Lewis, December 12, 1930, on receiving the Nobel Prize in Literature

¶ *Sinclair Lewis was the first American to receive the Nobel Prize in Literature. The award was made at the Nobel Festival in the Stockholm Concert House on December 10, 1930. He received the prize from the hands of King Gustav and his address was delivered two days later in a ceremony before the Swedish Academy, held at the Stock Exchange Hall.*

Some of the reasoning of the judges who made the award is set forth in the book, Nobel: The Man and His Prizes, *written by various authors and published in 1950 by The Nobel Foundation, Stockholm. The following quotation is taken from the section on The Literary Prize, written by Andres Österling:*

"The 1930 prize was awarded to Sinclair Lewis (b. 1885) 'for his vigorous and graphic art of description and his ability to create, with wit and humour, new types of people.' On the final phrase special emphasis should be laid, because when the Academy agreed in favour of his nomination, it was influenced, among other things, by a desire to recognise a vigorous trend in modern literature—high-class American humour, the best traditions of which had been continued with such marked success by Sinclair Lewis.

"Against him was weighed another wholly different painter of American reality, the ponderous and solemn Theodore Dresier, the pioneer American writer of novels criticising social conditions. Against Lewis's gay virtuosity and flashing satire could be set Dreiser's all-embracing sympathies and his affec-

3

tion for the productive chaos of existence, but the future alone can decide which is the more significant."

The text of the address used here is a second edition revised by the author. It was printed in a little book issued by Harcourt, Brace and Company in May, 1931, entitled Why Sinclair Lewis Got the Nobel Prize, *by Erik Axel Karlfeldt, permanent secretary of the Swedish Academy. The edition was only 2,000 copies, according to the Harvey Taylor Bibliography. Of the first, unrevised edition, 3,000 copies were printed, of which 2,000 were destroyed and 1,000 distributed.*

MEMBERS OF THE SWEDISH ACADEMY; LADIES AND GENTLEMEN: Were I to express my feeling of honour and pleasure in having been awarded the Nobel Prize in Literature, I should be fulsome and perhaps tedious, and I present my gratitude with a plain "Thank you."

I wish, in this address, to consider certain trends, certain dangers, and certain high and exciting promises in present-day American literature. To discuss this with complete and unguarded frankness—and I should not insult you by being otherwise than completely honest, however indiscreet—it will be necessary for me to be a little impolite regarding certain institutions and persons of my own greatly beloved land.

But I beg of you to believe that I am in no case gratifying a grudge. Fortune has dealt with me rather too well. I have known little struggle, not much poverty, many generosities. Now and then I have, for my books or myself, been somewhat warmly denounced—there was one good pastor in California who upon reading my *Elmer Gantry* desired to lead a mob and lynch me, while another holy man in the State of Maine wondered if there was no respectable and righteous way of putting me in jail. And, much harder to endure than any raging condemnation, a certain number of old acquaintances among journalists, what in the galloping American slang we call the 'I Knew Him When Club', have scribbled that since they know me personally, therefore I must be a rather low sort of fellow and certainly no writer. But if I have now and then received such cheering brickbats, still I, who have heaved a good many bricks myself, would be fatuous not to expect a fair number in return.

No, I have for myself no conceivable complaint to make, and yet for American literature in general, and its standing in a country where industrialism and finance and science flourish and the only arts that are vital and respected are architecture and the film, I have a considerable complaint.

I can illustrate by an incident which chances to concern the Swedish Academy and myself and which happened a few days ago, just before I took ship at New York for Sweden. There is in America a learned and most amiable old gentleman who has been a pastor, a university professor, and a diplomat. He is a member of the American Academy of Arts and Letters and no few universities have honoured him with degrees. As a writer he is chiefly known for his pleasant little essays on the joy of fishing. I do not suppose that professional fishermen, whose lives depend on the run of cod or herring, find it altogether an amusing occupation, but from these essays I learned, as a boy, that there is something very important and spiritual about catching fish, if you have no need of doing so.

This scholar stated, and publicly, that in awarding the Nobel Prize to a person who has scoffed at American institutions as much as I have, the Nobel Committee and the Swedish Academy had insulted America. I don't know whether, as an ex-diplomat, he intends to have an international incident made of it, and perhaps demand of the American Government that they land Marines in Stockholm to protect American literary rights, but I hope not.

I should have supposed that to a man so learned as to have

5

been made a Doctor of Divinity, a Doctor of Letters, and I do not know how many other imposing magnificences, the matter would have seemed different; I should have supposed that he would have reasoned: "Although personally I dislike this man's books, nevertheless the Swedish Academy has in choosing him honoured America by assuming that the Americans are no longer a puerile backwoods clan, so inferior that they are afraid of criticism, but instead a nation come of age and able to consider calmly and maturely any dissection of their land, however scoffing."

I should even have supposed that so international a scholar would have believed that Scandinavia, accustomed to the works of Strindberg, Ibsen, and Pontoppidan, would not have been peculiarly shocked by a writer whose most anarchistic assertion has been that America, with all her wealth and power, has not yet produced a civilisation good enough to satisfy the deepest wants of human creatures.

I believe that Strindberg rarely sang the 'Star-Spangled Banner' or addressed Rotary Clubs, yet Sweden seems to have survived him.

I have at such length discussed this criticism of the learned fisherman not because it has any conceivable importance in itself, but because it does illustrate the fact that in America most of us—not readers alone but even writers—are still afraid of any literature which is not a glorification of everything American, a glorification of our faults as well as our virtues. To be not only a best-seller in America but to be really beloved, a novelist must assert that all American men are tall, handsome, rich, honest, and powerful at golf; that all country towns are filled with neighbours who do nothing from day to day save go about being kind to one another; that although American girls may be wild, they change always into perfect wives and mothers; and that, geographically, America is composed solely of New York, which is inhabited entirely by

6

millionaires; of the West, which keeps unchanged all the boisterous heroism of 1870; and of the South, where everyone lives on a plantation perpetually glossy with moonlight and scented with magnolias.

It is not today vastly more true than it was twenty years ago that such novelists of ours as you have read in Sweden, novelists like Dreiser and Willa Cather, are authentically popular and influential in America. As it was revealed by the venerable fishing Academician whom I have quoted, we still most revere the writers for the popular magazines who in a hearty and edifying chorus chant that the America of a hundred and twenty million population is still as simple, as pastoral, as it was when it had but forty million; that in an industrial plant with ten thousand employees, the relationship between the worker and the manager is still as neighbourly and uncomplex as in a factory of 1840, with five employees; that the relationships between father and son, between husband and wife, are precisely the same in an apartment in a thirty-storey palace today, with three motor-cars awaiting the family below and five books on the library shelves and a divorce imminent in the family next week, as were those relationships in a rose-veiled five-room cottage in 1880; that, in fine, America has gone through the revolutionary change from rustic colony to world-empire without having in the least altered the bucolic and Puritanic simplicity of Uncle Sam.

I am, actually, extremely grateful to the fishing Academician for having somewhat condemned me. For since he is a leading member of the American Academy of Arts and Letters, he has released me, has given me the right to speak as frankly of that Academy as he has spoken of me. And in any honest study of American intellectualism today, that curious institution must be considered.

Before I consider the Academy, however, let me sketch a

fantasy which has pleased me the last few days in the unavoidable idleness of a rough trip on the Atlantic. I am sure that you know, by now, that the award to me of the Nobel Prize has by no means been altogether popular in America. Doubtless the experience is not new to you. I fancy that when you gave the award even to Thomas Mann, whose *Zauberberg* seems to me to contain the whole of intellectual Europe, even when you gave it to Kipling, whose social significance is so profound that it has been rather authoritatively said that he created the British Empire, even when you gave it to Bernard Shaw, there were countrymen of those authors who complained because you did not choose another.

And I imagined what would have been said had you chosen some American other than myself. Suppose you had taken Theodore Dreiser.

Now to me, as to many other American writers, Dreiser more than any other man, marching alone, usually unappreciated, often hated, has cleared the trail from Victorian and Howellsian timidity and gentility in American fiction to honesty and boldness and passion of life. Without his pioneering, I doubt if any of us could, unless we liked to be sent to jail, seek to express life and beauty and terror.

My great colleague Sherwood Anderson has proclaimed this leadership of Dreiser. I am delighted to join him. Dreiser's great first novel, *Sister Carrie,* which he dared to publish thirty long years ago and which I read twenty-five years ago, came to house-bound and airless America like a great free Western wind, and to our stuffy domesticity gave us the first fresh air since Mark Twain and Whitman.

Yet had you given the Prize to Mr. Dreiser, you would have heard groans from America; you would have heard that his style—I am not exactly sure what this mystic quality 'style' may be, but I find the word so often in the writings of minor critics that I suppose it must exist—you would have heard that

8

his style is cumbersome, that his choice of words is insensitive, that his books are interminable. And certainly respectable scholars would complain that in Mr. Dreiser's world men and women are often sinful and tragic and despairing, instead of being for ever sunny and full of song and virtue, as befits authentic Americans.

And had you chosen Mr. Eugene O'Neill, who has done nothing much in American drama save to transform it utterly, in ten or twelve years, from a false world of neat and competent trickery to a world of splendour and fear and greatness, you would have been reminded that he has done something far worse than scoffing—he has seen life as not to be neatly arranged in the study of a scholar but as a terrifying, magnificent and often quite horrible thing akin to the tornado, the earthquake, the devastating fire.

And had you given Mr. James Branch Cabell the Prize, you would have been told that he is too fantastically malicious. So would you have been told that Miss Willa Cather, for all the homely virtue of her words concerning the peasants of Nebraska, has in her novel, *The Lost Lady,* been so untrue to America's patent and perpetual and possibly tedious virtuousness as to picture an abandoned woman who remains, nevertheless, uncannily charming even to the virtuous, in a story without any moral; that Mr. Henry Mencken is the worst of all scoffers; that Mr. Sherwood Anderson viciously errs in considering sex as important a force in life as fishing; that Mr. Upton Sinclair, being a Socialist, sins against the perfectness of American capitalistic mass-production; that Mr. Joseph Hergesheimer is un-American in regarding graciousness of manner and beauty of surface as of some importance in the endurance of daily life; and that Mr. Ernest Hemingway is not only too young but, far worse, uses language which should be unknown to gentlemen; that he acknowledges drunkenness as one of man's eternal ways to happiness, and asserts that a soldier may find love more significant than the hearty slaughter of men in battle.

Yes, they are wicked, these colleagues of mine; you would have done almost as evilly to have chosen them as to have chosen me; and as a chauvinistic American—only, mind you, as an American of 1930 and not of 1880—I rejoice that they are my countrymen and countrywomen, and that I may speak of them with pride even in the Europe of Thomas Mann, H. G. Wells, Galsworthy, Knut Hamsun, Arnold Bennett, Feuchtwanger, Selma Lagerlöf, Sigrid Undset, Werner von Heidenstam, d'Annunzio, Romain Rolland.

It is my fate in this paper to swing constantly from optimism to pessimism and back, but so is it the fate of anyone who writes or speaks of anything in America—the most contradictory, the most depressing, the most stirring, of any land in the world today.

Thus, having with no muted pride called the roll of what seem to me to be great men and women in American literary life today, and having indeed omitted a dozen other names of which I should like to boast were there time, I must turn again and assert that in our contemporary American literature, indeed in all American arts save architecture and the film, we—yes, we who have such pregnant and vigorous standards in commerce and science—have no standards, no healing communication, no heroes to be followed nor villains to be condemned, no certain ways to be pursued and no dangerous paths to be avoided.

The American novelist or poet or dramatist or sculptor or painter must work alone, in confusion, unassisted save by his own integrity.

That, of course, has always been the lot of the artist. The vagabond and criminal François Villon had certainly no smug and comfortable refuge in which elegant ladies would hold his hand and comfort his starving soul and more starved body.

He, veritably a great man, destined to outlive in history all the dukes and puissant cardinals whose robes he was esteemed unworthy to touch, had for his lot the gutter and the hardened crust.

Such poverty is not for the artist in America. They pay us, indeed, only too well; that writer is a failure who cannot have his butler and motor and his villa at Palm Beach, where he is permitted to mingle almost in equality with the barons of banking. But he is oppressed ever by something worse than poverty—by the feeling that what he creates does not matter, that he is expected by his readers to be only a decorator or a clown, or that he is good-naturedly accepted as a scoffer whose bark probably is worse than his bite and who probably is a good fellow at heart, who in any case certainly does not count in a land that produces eighty-storey buildings, motors by the million, and wheat by the billions of bushels. And he has no institution, no group, to which he can turn for inspiration, whose criticism he can accept and whose praise will be precious to him.

What institutions have we?

The American Academy of Arts and Letters does contain, along with several excellent painters and architects and statesmen, such a really distinguished university president as Nicholas Murray Butler, so admirable and courageous a scholar as Wilbur Cross, and several first-rate writers: the poets Edwin Arlington Robinson and Robert Frost, the free-minded publicist James Truslow Adams, and the novelists Edith Wharton, Hamlin Garland, Owen Wister, Brand Whitlock and Booth Tarkington.

But it does not include Theodore Dreiser, Henry Mencken, our most vivid critic, George Jean Nathan, who, though still young, is certainly the dean of our dramatic critics, Eugene O'Neill, incomparably our best dramatist, the really original and vital poets, Edna St. Vincent Millay and Carl Sandburg,

Robinson Jeffers and Vachel Lindsay and Edgar Lee Masters, whose *Spoon River Anthology* was so utterly different from any other poetry ever published, so fresh, so authoritative, so free from any gropings and timidities that it came like a revelation, and created a new school of native American poetry. It does not include the novelists and short-story writers, Willa Cather, Joseph Hergesheimer, Sherwood Anderson, Ring Lardner, Ernest Hemingway, Louis Bromfield, Wilbur Daniel Steele, Fannie Hurst, Mary Austin, James Branch Cabell, Edna Ferber, nor Upton Sinclair, of whom you must say, whether you admire or detest his aggressive Socialism, that he is internationally better known than any other American artist whosoever, be he novelist, poet, painter, sculptor, musician, architect.

I should not expect any Academy to be so fortunate as to contain all these writers, but one which fails to contain any of them, which thus cuts itself off from so much of what is living and vigorous and original in American letters, can have no relationship whatever to our life and aspirations. It does not represent literary America of today—it represents only Henry Wadsworth Longfellow.

It might be answered that, after all, the Academy is limited to fifty members; that, naturally, it cannot include everyone of merit. But the fact is that while most of our few giants are excluded, the Academy does have room to include three extraordinarily bad poets, two very melodramatic and insignificant playwrights, two gentlemen who are known only because they are university presidents, a man who was thirty years ago known as a rather clever humorous draughtsman, and several gentlemen of whom—I sadly confess my ignorance—I have never heard.

Let me again emphasise the fact—for it is a fact—that I am not attacking the American Academy. It is a hospitable and generous and decidedly dignified institution. And it is not altogether the Academy's fault that it does not contain many of the men who have significance in our letters. Sometimes it is the fault of those writers themselves. I cannot imagine that grizzly-bear Theodore Dreiser being comfortable at the serenely Athenian dinners of the Academy, and were they to invite Mencken, he would infuriate them with his boisterous jeering. No, I am not attacking—I am reluctantly considering the Academy because it is so perfect an example of the divorce in America of intellectual life from all authentic standards of importance and reality.

Our universities and colleges, or gymnasia, most of them, exhibit the same unfortunate divorce. I can think of four of them, Rollins College in Florida, Middlebury College in Vermont, the University of Michigan, and the University of Chicago—which has had on its roll so excellent a novelist as Robert Herrick, so courageous a critic as Robert Morss Lovett —which have shown an authentic interest in contemporary creative literature. Four of them. But universities and colleges and musical emporiums and schools for the teaching of theology and plumbing and sign-painting are as thick in America as the motor traffic. Whenever you see a public building with Gothic fenestration on a sturdy backing of Indiana concrete, you may be certain that it is another university, with anywhere from two hundred to twenty thousand students equally ardent about avoiding the disadvantage of becoming learned and about gaining the social prestige contained in the possession of a B.A. degree.

Oh, socially our universities are close to the mass of our citizens, and so are they in the matter of athletics. A great college football game is passionately witnessed by eighty thousand people, who have paid five dollars apiece and motored anywhere from ten to a thousand miles for the ecstasy of watching twenty-two men chase one another up and down a curiously marked field. During the football season, a capable player ranks very nearly with our greatest and most admired heroes—even with Henry Ford, President Hoover, and Colonel Lindbergh.

And in one branch of learning, the sciences, the lords of business who rule us are willing to do homage to the devotees of learning. However bleakly one of our trader aristocrats may frown upon poetry or the visions of a painter, he is graciously pleased to endure a Millikan, a Michelson, a Banting, a Theobald Smith.

But the paradox is that in the arts our universities are as cloistered, as far from reality and living creation, as socially and athletically and scientifically they are close to us. To a true-blue professor of literature in an American university literature is not something that a plain human being, living today, painfully sits down to produce. No; it is something dead; it is something magically produced by superhuman beings who must, if they are to be regarded as artists at all, have died at least one hundred years before the diabolical invention of the typewriter. To any authentic don there is something slightly repulsive in the thought that literature could be created by any ordinary human being, still to be seen walking the streets, wearing quite commonplace trousers and coat and looking not so unlike a chauffeur or a farmer. Our American professors like their literature clear and cold and pure and very dead.

I do not suppose that American universities are alone in this. I am aware that to the dons of Oxford and Cambridge it would seem rather indecent to suggest that Wells and Bennett and Galsworthy and George Moore may, while they commit the impropriety of continuing to live, be compared to anyone so beautifully and safely dead as Samuel Johnson. I suppose that in the universities of Sweden and France and Germany there exist plenty of professors who prefer dissection to understanding. But in the new and vital and experimental land of America one would expect the teachers of literature to be less monastic, more human, than in the traditional shadows of old Europe.

They are not.

There has recently appeared in America, out of the universities, an astonishing circus called 'the New Humanism'. Now of course 'humanism' means so many things that it means nothing. It may infer anything from a belief that Greek and Latin are more inspiring than the dialect of contemporary peasants to a belief that any living peasant is more interesting than a dead Greek. But it is a delicate bit of justice that this nebulous word should have been chosen to label this nebulous cult.

In so far as I have been able to comprehend them—for naturally in a world so exciting and promising as this today, a life brilliant with Zeppelins and Chinese revolutions and the Bolshevik industrialisation of farming and ships and the Grand Canyon and young children and terrifying hunger and the lonely quest of scientists after God, no creative writer would have time to follow all the chilly enthusiasms of the New Humanists—this newest of sects reasserts the dualism of man's nature. It would confine literature to the fight between man's soul and God, or man's soul and evil.

But, curiously, neither God nor the devil may wear modern dress, but must retain Grecian vestments. Œdipus is a tragic figure for the New Humanists; man, trying to maintain himself as the image of God under the menace of dynamos, in a world of high-pressure salesmanship, is not. And the poor comfort which they offer is that the object of life is to develop self-discipline—whether or not one ever accomplishes anything with this self-discipline. So this whole movement results in the not particularly novel doctrine that both art and life must be resigned and negative. It is a doctrine of the blackest reaction introduced into a stirringly revolutionary world.

Strangely enough, this doctrine of death, this escape from the complexities and danger of living into the secure blankness of the monastery, has become widely popular among professors in a land where one would have expected only boldness and intellectual adventure, and it has more than ever shut creative writers off from any benign influence which might conceivably have come from the universities.

But it has always been so. America has never had a Brandes, a Taine, a Goethe, a Croce.

With a wealth of creative talent in America, our criticism has most of it been a chill and insignificant activity pursued by jealous spinsters, ex-baseball-reporters, and acid professors. Our Erasmuses have been village schoolmistresses. How should there be any standards when there has been no one capable of setting them up?

The great Cambridge–Concord circle of the middle of the nineteenth century—Emerson, Longfellow, Lowell, Holmes, the Alcotts—were sentimental reflections of Europe, and they left no school, no influence. Whitman and Thoreau and Poe and, in some degree, Hawthorne were outcasts, men alone and despised, berated by the New Humanists of their generation. It was with the emergence of William Dean Howells that we first began to have something like a standard, and a very bad standard it was.

Mr. Howells was one of the gentlest, sweetest, and most honest of men, but he had the code of a pious old maid whose greatest delight was to have tea at the vicarage. He abhorred not only profanity and obscenity but all of what H. G. Wells has called "the jolly coarseness of life". In his fantastic vision of life, which he innocently conceived to be realistic, farmers and seamen and factory-hands might exist, but the farmer must never be covered with muck, the seaman must never roll out bawdy chanties, the factory-hand must . thankful to his good employer, and all of them must long for the

opportunity to visit Florence and smile gently at the quaint-
ness of the beggars.

So strongly did Howells feel this genteel, this New Human-
istic, philosophy that he was able vastly to influence his contemporaries, down even to 1914 and the turmoil of the Great
War.

He was actually able to tame Mark Twain, perhaps the
greatest of our writers, and to put that fiery old savage into
an intellectual frock-coat and top hat. His influence is not
altogether gone today. He is still worshipped by Hamlin Garland, an author who should in every way have been greater
than Howells but who under Howells's influence was changed
from a harsh and magnificent realist into a genial and insignificant lecturer. Mr. Garland is, so far as we have one, the
dean of American letters today, and as our dean he is alarmed
by all of the younger writers who are so lacking in taste as to
suggest that men and women do not always love in accordance
with the prayer-book, and that common people sometimes use
language which would be inappropriate at a women's literary
club on Main Street. Yet this same Hamlin Garland, as a
young man, before he had gone to Boston and become cultured
and Howellised, wrote two most valiant and revelatory works
of realism, *Main-Travelled Roads* and *Rose of Dutcher's
Coolly*.

I read them as a boy in a prairie village in Minnesota—just
such an environment as was described in Mr. Garland's tales.
They were vastly exciting to me. I had realised in reading
Balzac and Dickens that it was possible to describe French and
English common people as one actually saw them. But it had
never occurred to me that one might without indecency write
of the people of Sauk Centre, Minnesota, as one felt about
them. Our fictional tradition, you see, was that all of us in
Mid-Western villages were altogether noble and happy; that
not one of us would exchange the neighbourly bliss of living

on Main Street for the heathen gaudiness of New York or Paris or Stockholm. But in Mr. Garland's *Main-Travelled Roads* I discovered that there was one man who believed that Mid-Western peasants were sometimes bewildered and hungry and vile—and heroic. And, given this vision, I was released; I could write of life as living life.

I am afraid that Mr. Garland would not be pleased but acutely annoyed to know that he made it possible for me to write of America as I see it, and not as Mr. William Dean Howells so sunnily saw it. And it is his tragedy, it is a completely revelatory American tragedy, that in our land of freedom men like Garland, who first blast the roads to freedom, become themselves the most bound.

But, all this time, while men like Howells were so effusively seeking to guide America into becoming a pale edition of an English cathedral town, there were surly and authentic fellows—Whitman and Melville, then Dreiser and James Huneker and Mencken—who insisted that our land had something more than tea-table gentility.

And so, without standards, we have survived. And for the strong young men it has perhaps been well that we should have no standards. For, after seeming to be pessimistic about my own and much beloved land, I want to close this dirge with a very lively sound of optimism.

I have for the future of American literature every hope and every eager belief. We are coming out, I believe, of the stuffiness of safe, sane, and incredibly dull provincialism. There are young Americans today who are doing such passionate and authentic work that it makes me sick to see that I am a little too old to be one of them.

There is Ernest Hemingway, a bitter youth, educated by the most intense experience, disciplined by his own high standards, an authentic artist whose home is in the whole of life; there is Thomas Wolfe, a child of, I believe, thirty or younger, whose one and only novel, *Look Homeward, Angel,* is worthy to be compared with the best in our literary production, a Gargantuan creature with great gusto of life; there is Thornton Wilder, who in an age of realism dreams the old and lovely dreams of the eternal romantics; there is John Dos Passos, with his hatred of the safe and sane standards of Babbitt and his splendour of revolution; there is Stephen Benét, who to American drabness has restored the epic poem with his glorious memory of old John Brown; there are Michael Gold, who reveals the new frontier of the Jewish East Side, and William Faulkner, who has freed the South from hoop-skirts; and there are a dozen other young poets and fictioneers, most of them living now in Paris, most of them a little insane in the tradition of James Joyce, who, however insane they may be, have refused to be genteel and traditional and dull.

I salute them, with a joy in being not yet too far removed from their determination to give to the America that has mountains and endless prairies, enormous cities and lost farm cabins, billions of money and tons of faith, to an America that is as strange as Russia and as complex as China, a literature worthy of her vastness.

LETTER TO THE PULITZER PRIZE COMMITTEE

¶ *Of all the sensational and controversial actions credited to Mr. Lewis in the 1920s, his refusal of the Pulitzer Prize in 1926 probably aroused stormiest comment.*

The letter itself was written from the Hotel Ambassador, Kansas City, Missouri, and an abstract of it was issued by his publishers, Harcourt, Brace and Company, on May 4. It produced a wave of opinion pro and con from the press. The

Literary Digest *of May 29 quoted editorials by five major newspapers.*

The Philadelphia Record *said in part: "He has a perfect right to express his personal aversion to accept the judgment. Not quite so happy is his assumption that any writer who does accept such a tribute thereby debases his profession and expresses a paltry subservience to arbitrary authority for the sake of gain. . . . We think his passionate fears for literary freedom are a little neurasthenic."*

The Minneapolis Tribune *in his home state said: "Essentially a somewhat futile institution, the Pulitzer Prize award is dignified too much when Mr. Lewis proceeds to wax so spectacular and melodramatic about it."*

The Outlook, The Nation *and* The Survey *all opened their pages to heated discussion of the author's action. William E. Harmon, president of the Harmon Foundation, attacked Mr. Lewis's position, while Agnes Repplier, Zona Gale and Carl Van Doren supported it. Some years later, in his biographical sketch published by Doubleday, Doran and Company in 1933, Mr. Van Doren wrote in regard to Lewis's refusal of the prize: "He gave serious reasons for his stand. . . . Hardly any attention was paid to what he said. His true reasons were found for him by all the gossips. . . . Simplicity and originality are more than strategy. They are unpredictable, inimitable essentials. No matter what may happen, Adam must remain the first man. And Mr. Lewis must remain the first man who ever made a literary prize a nine-days' tempest in the American press. His craft was pure nature. He was simply and originally himself, and the endless argument flowed from that mysterious fact."*

The complete text of the published letter follows.

SIRS:— I WISH TO ACKNOWLEDGE YOUR CHOICE OF MY NOVEL

Arrowsmith for the Pulitzer Prize. That prize I must refuse, and my refusal would be meaningless unless I explained the reasons.

All prizes, like titles, are dangerous. The seekers for prizes tend to labor not for inherent excellence but for alien rewards: they tend to write this, or timorously to avoid writing that, in order to tickle the prejudices of a haphazard committee. And the Pulitzer Prize for novels is peculiarly objectionable because the terms of it have been constantly and grievously misrepresented.

Those terms are that the prize shall be given "for the American novel published during the year which shall best present the wholesome atmosphere of American life, and the highest standard of American manners and manhood". This phrase, if it means anything whatever, would appear to mean that the appraisal of the novels shall be made not according to their actual literary merit but in obedience to whatever code of Good Form may chance to be popular at the moment.

That there is such a limitation of the award is little understood. Because of the condensed manner in which the announcement is usually reported, and because certain publishers have trumpeted that any novel which has received the Pulitzer Prize has thus been established without qualification as *the best* novel, the public has come to believe that the prize is the highest honor which an American novelist can receive.

The Pulitzer Prize for novels signifies, already, much more than a convenient thousand dollars to be accepted even by such writers as smile secretly at the actual wording of the terms. It is tending to become a sanctified tradition. There is a general belief that the administrators of the prize are a pontifical body with the discernment and power to grant the prize as the ultimate proof of merit. It is believed that they are always guided by a committee of responsible critics, though in the case both of this and other Pulitzer Prizes, the administrators can, and sometimes do, quite arbitrarily reject the recommendations of their supposed advisers.

If already the Pulitzer Prize is so important, it is not absurd to suggest that in another generation it may, with the actual terms of the award ignored, become the one thing for which any ambitious novelist will strive; and the administrators of the prize may become a supreme court, a college of cardinals, so rooted and so sacred that to challenge them will be to commit blasphemy. Such is the French Academy, and we have had the spectacle of even an Anatole France intriguing for election.

Only by regularly refusing the Pulitzer Prize can novelists keep such a power from being permanently set up over them.

Between the Pulitzer Prizes, the American Academy of Arts and Letters and its training-school, the National Institute of Arts and Letters, amateur boards of censorship, and the inquisition of earnest literary ladies, every compulsion is put upon writers to become safe, polite, obedient, and sterile. In protest, I declined election to the National Institute of Arts and Letters some years ago, and now I must decline the Pulitzer Prize.

I invite other writers to consider the fact that by accepting the prizes and approval of these vague institutions we are admitting their authority, publicly confirming them as the final judges of literary excellence, and I inquire whether any prize is worth that subservience.

> I am, Sirs,
> Yours sincerely,
> (Signed) SINCLAIR LEWIS

UNPUBLISHED INTRODUCTION TO *BABBITT*

Intro—1.

¶ *This is the only heading to what Donald C. Gallup, Curator, Collection of American Literature of the Yale University Library, refers to as the "possible introduction to* Babbitt". *It appears in Mr. Lewis's voluminous note-book for that novel, and so far as known was never published. The note-book is a part of the Yale collection of Lewis material left in his will to the University Library. The position in the note-book of this introduction would indicate that it was written towards the end of the period of gathering material for the book.*

At the time this was written, it will be noticed, the protagonist's name was G. T. Pumphrey, not Babbitt, and the place was Monarch City, not Zenith. Interesting as an example of Mr. Lewis's scrupulous care, there is an added sheet of exceptions to his rather sweeping list of American cities where the G. T. Pumphreys dwell. These exceptions, in order of his notation, and in his spelling, are "N.Y., Chi., Boston, Phila., Washn., N. Orleans, Charleston, Victoria, S. Francisco."

THIS IS THE STORY OF THE RULER OF AMERICA.

The story of the Tired Business Man, the man with tooth-brush moustache and harsh voice who talks about motors and prohibition in the smoking-compartment of the Pullman car, the man who plays third-rate golf and first-rate poker at a second-rate country club near an energetic American city.

Our conqueror, dictator over our commerce, education, labour, art, politics, morals, and lack of conversation.

There are thirty millions of him, male and female, and his

autocracy is unparalleled. No czar controlled the neckwear and dice-throwing of his serfs; no general in the most perilous climax of war has codified his soldiers' humour or demanded that while they engage the enemy they admire narratives about cowpunchers and optimistic little girls. But this completeness our ruler has attained.

Though English morals and French politics and German industry have been determined by the Sound Middle-Class, the Bourgeoisie, the Pumphreysie, have never dared also to announce standards in sculpture and table-manners. For in those lands there are outcasts and aristocrats who smile at the impertinence of the unimaginative. But in America we have created the superman complete, and the mellifluous name of the archangelic monster is Pumphrey, good old G. T. Pumphrey, the plain citizen and omnipotent power.

Note: Above too much hints of another Main St. Most of this and all of "pos. part of Intro". cd be used, say, as Chapter [word indistinct] in Part III or IV.

Though this is the individual romance of one G. T. Pumphrey and not the breviary of his community, that community enters his every moment, for it is himself, created in his varnished image. Monarch City is every "progressive, go-ahead, forward-looking, live, up-to-date" city of more than eighty thousand in the United States and Western Canada, with 8 or 10 venerable exceptions.

These exceptional cities Pumphrey visits with frequency, and stirs their theatres, hotels, books, and wholesalers to emulate the perfection of Monarch City, that even we who faint may win at the last to purity, efficiency, and ice water.

Distinctly, however, Pumphrey is not a satiric figure, nor a Type.

24

He is too tragic a tyrant for the puerilities of deliberate satire. And he is an individual, very eager and well-intentioned, credulous of pioneering myths, doubtful in his secret hours, affectionate towards his rebellious daughter and those lunch-mates who pass for friends—a god self-slain on his modern improved altar—the most grievous victim of his own militant dullness—crying in restless dreams for the arms of Phryne, the shirt of Jurgen and the twilight sea that knows not purity nor efficiency nor 34 x 4 casings.

As a PART OF INTRODUCTION, or in the story, or just implied in the story, or in an appendix *on Main Street vs. the Boulevard vs. Fifth Ave.*

They are complex phenomena, these American cities of from 80,000 to 1,000,000. They are industrially magnificent. They supply half the world with motor-cars, machine tools, flour, locomotives, rails, electric equipment—with necessities miraculous and admirable. They are provided with houses more elaborate than any palaces, with hotels and office buildings as vast as and more usable than any cathedral. Their citizens are not unaccustomed to Fifth Avenue, to Piccadilly, to the Champs Élysées. Hither comes Galsworthy to lecture, Caruso to sing, Kreisler to play (even though they do beg him always to play the Humoresque), and here, in a Little Theatre, a Schnitzler play may have a hearing as soon as Vienna, long before London. Yet they are villages, these titanic huddles. They import Kreisler as they import silks—not because they passionately love music or silks, but because those obvious symbols of prosperity give social prestige. To attend a concert is almost as valuable a certificate of wealth as to be seen riding in a Pierce-Arrow car. It is not an elegant and decorous listening to a great violinist which attests musical understanding; it is a passionate playing of one's own music—though the playing may be very bad indeed; may be nothing but the agitated scratching of four old 'cellists in a beery cellar. Since there is—as yet—no instrument which measures ergs of spiritual energy, the matter cannot be neatly and statistically proven, but one suspects that there is not one of these cities with a million, or half a million, people which has one-tenth of the joyous mental activity of little Weimar, with its 35,000—among whom once moved no Crackajack Salesmen, perhaps, but only Goethe and Schiller.

And those glorious Little Theatres—those radiant and eager Little Theatres—indeed they do revel in Glaspell and Eugene O'Neill and Ervine—for one season or two; and then the players who have gone into this new sport for social prestige grow weary; the professional producer grows yet wearier of begging for funds, and of seeing newspapers which give a column to a road company in a musical comedy, and two columns to a wedding between patent medicines and steel, present a brilliant performance of Shaw in two paragraphs with four solecisms; he goes his ways, and the Little Theatre is not.

Villages—overgrown towns—three-quarters of a million people still dressing, eating, building houses, attending church, to make an impression on their neighbours, quite as they did back on Main Street, in villages of two thousand. And yet not villages at all, the observer uneasily sees, as he beholds factories with ten thousand workmen, with machines more miraculous than the loaves and fishes, with twice the power and ten times the skill of a romantic grand duchy. They are transitional metropolises—but that transition will take a few hundred years, if the custom persists of making it a heresy punishable by hanging or even by ostracism to venture to say that Cleveland or Minneapolis or Baltimore or Buffalo is not the wisest, gayest, kindliest, usefullest city in all the world. So long as every teacher and journalist and workman admits that John J. Jones, the hustling sales manager for the pickle factory is the standard in beauty and courtesy and justice—well, so long will they be sore stricken with a pest of J. J. Joneses.

It is not quite a new thought to submit that though admittedly Mr. Jones somewhat lacks in the luxuries of artistic taste and agreeable manners, yet he is so solid a worker, so true a friend, and so near to genius in the development of this astounding and adventurously new industrial system that he is worthier, he is really more beautiful, than any Anatole France or [word omitted]. Are his pickle machines with their power and ingenuity a new art, comparable to *vers libre,* and is there not in his noisiest advertising, his billboards smeared across tranquil fields, a passion for achievement which is, to the unprejudiced discernment, a religious fervour, an æsthetic passion, a genius such as inspired the crusader and explorer and poet? Is not his assailant a blind and reactionary fellow who demands in this rough glorious pioneer outworn standards and beauties dead and dry?

Only it happens that these generous inquirers who seek to make themselves comfortable by justifying their inescapable neighbour, Mr. Jones, give him somewhat too much credit. Mr. Jones, the sales manager, Mr. Brown, the general manager, Mr. Robinson, the president—all the persons in the pickle hierarchy most to be accredited with passion and daring and new beauties—are nothing in the world but salesmen, commercial demagogues, industrial charlatans, creators of a demand which they wistfully desire to supply. Those miraculous, those admittedly noble machines—they were planned and built and improved and run by very common workmen, who get no credit whatever for pioneering. Those astounding pickle formulæ, they were made by chemists, unknown and unglorified. Even those far-flung billboards, the banners of Mr. Jones's gallant crusade—their text was written by forty-a-week copywriters, their pictures—their very terrible pictures—painted by patient hacks, and the basic idea, of having billboards, came not from the passionate brain of Mr. Jones but was cautiously worked out, on quite routine and unromantic lines, by hesitating persons in an advertising agency.

And it is these workmen, chemists, hacks, who are likely to be eager about beauty, courageous in politics—Moon-Calves—children of the new world. Mr. Jones himself—ah, that rare and daring and shining-new creator of industrial poetry, he votes the Republican ticket straight, he hates all labour unionism, he belongs to the Masons and the Presbyterian Church, his favourite author is Zane Grey, and in other particulars noted in this story his private life seems scarce to mark him as the rough, ready, aspiring, iconoclastic, creative, courageous innovator his admirers paint him. He is a bagman. He is a pedlar. He is a shopkeeper. He is a campfollower. He is a bag of aggressive wind.

America has taken to itself the credit of being the one pioneering nation of the world; it has thereby (these three hundred years now) excused all flabbiness of culture and harshness of manner and frantic oppression of critics. And, strangely, Europe has granted that assertion. Never an English author descends upon these palpitating and grateful shores without informing us that from our literature one expects only the burly power and clumsiness of ditch-diggers. We listen to him, and are made proud of the clumsiness and burliness—without quite going so far as to add also the power.

It is a national myth.

England has, in India, Africa, Canada, Australia, had quite as many new frontiers, done quite as much pioneering—and done it as bravely and as cruelly and as unscrupulously—as have we in pushing the western border from the Alleghenies to Honolulu. Thus France in Africa, Holland in the West Indies, Germany all over the world. And England has quite as many Rough Fellows as America. Lord Fisher criticising the British Navy in the tones of a tobacco-chewing trapper—is he so much less of a Rough Fellow and Pioneer and Innovator than the Harvard instructor reading Austin Dobson by candle-light? The silk salesman, crossing the Arizona desert —in a Pullman—is he so much bolder a ditch-digger than Ole Bill, the English Tommy?

A myth! America is no longer an isolated race of gallant Indian-slayers. It is a part of the world. Like every other nation, it is made up of both daring innovators and crusted crabs. Its literature and its J. J. Joneses are subject to the same rules as the literature and the bustling innumerous J. J. Joneses of England or Spain or Norway. Mr. Henry van Dyke is no newer or more pioneering than Mr. H. G. Wells—and subject to no more lenient rules or more provincial judgments.

Of this contradiction between pioneering myth and actual slackness, these Monarchs, these cities of 300,000 or so, are the best examples. Unfortunately American literature has discerned as types of communities only the larger or older cities—as New York, San Francisco, Richmond—and the villages, with nothing between. Yet there is a sort of community in between, an enormously important type—the city of a few hundred thousand, the metropolis that yet is a village, the world-centre that yet is ruled by cautious villagers. Only Booth Tarkington, with his novels flavoured by Indianapolis, and a few local celebrities eager to present the opulence of their several Monarchs, have dealt with these cities which, more than any New York, produce our wares and elect our presidents—and buy our books. Yet they are important enough to quarrel over—they are great enough to deserve the compliment of being told one's perception of the truth about them.

Just use "city man & country girl" How dif from N.Y.

To say that they are subject to the same rules as Munich or Florence does not at all mean that they are like Munich or Florence. They have grown so rapidly, they have been so innocent and so Republican and so Presbyterian and so altogether boosting and innocent, that they have produced a type of existence a little different from any other in the world. It may not continue to be so different—it some time may be subject also to fine tradition and the vision of quiet and honest work as against noisy selling of needless things—but this fineness it will not attain without self-study, and an admission that twenty-storey buildings are not necessarily nobler than Notre Dame, and that the production of 19,000 motor-cars a day does not of itself prove those cars to be better built than cars produced at one a day.

This foreshadowing of a future adoption of richer traditions does not, of course, mean at all that in the future these Monarchs are to be spiritually or physically like Munich or Florence. It is a paradox of psychology that it is precisely the richest philosophies, with the largest common fund of wisdom from all ages, which produce the most diverse and lovely products, while it is the thinner and hastier philosophies which produce the most standardised and boresomely similar products.

German Munich and Italian Florence are vastly and entertainingly different in all that counts—in passions, wines, aspirations, and furniture—for the reason that they have both digested and held and brilliantly changed a common wisdom of Plato and Shakespeare and Karl Marx. But German Milwaukee and Italian Hartford are uncomfortably alike because they have cast off all the hard-earned longings of mankind and joined in a common aspiration to be rich, notorious, and One Hundred Per Cent American.

It is this fact which is the second great feature of the American cities of 300,000—and as important as their other feature of unconquerable villageness. It is this fact which makes a novel that chanced to be local and concrete and true in regard to Omaha equally local and concrete and true regarding twenty other cities. Naturally, they are not all precisely alike. There is a difference resulting from situation—from a background of hills or plain, of river or sea coast; a difference from the products of the back country—iron, wheat, cotton; a distinct difference from the various ages—the difference between Seattle and Charleston.

But these differences have for a long time now tended to decrease, so powerful is our faith in standardisation. When a new hotel, factory, house, garage, motion-picture theatre, row of shops, church, or synagogue is erected in grey Charleston, rambling New Orleans, or San Francisco of the '49ers, that structure is precisely, to the last column of reinforced concrete and the last decorative tile, the same as a parallel structure in the new cities of Portland or Kansas City. And the souls of those structures—the hospitality of the hotels, the mechanical methods in the garages, the minutest wording of the sermons in the churches—are increasingly as standardised as the shells.

It would not be possible to write a novel which would in every line be equally true to Munich and Florence. Despite the fundamental hungers equally true to all human beings, despite the similarity of manners and conversation in the layer of society which contentedly travels all over the world, despite the like interest of kissing at Fiesole and at Gansedorf, so vast and subtle are the differences in every outward aspect, every detail of artistic aspiration and national pride and hope, that the two cities seem to belong to two different planets.

But Hartford and Milwaukee—the citizens of those two distant cities go to the same offices, speak the same patois on the same telephones, go to the same lunch and the same athletic clubs, etc., etc., etc.

Novel unlike M. St. cf Carol [Kennicott] on standardised life in U.S.

The test of the sameness is in the people. If you were by magic taken instantly to any city of over 80,000 in the United States and set down in the business centre, in a block, say, with a new hotel, a new motion-picture theatre, and a line of newish shops, not three hours of the intensest study of the passing people—men on business errands, messenger-boys, women shopping, pool-room idlers—would indicate in what city, indeed in what part of the country, you were. Only by travelling to the outskirts and discovering mountains or ocean or wheat-fields, and perhaps negro shanties, Mexican adobes, or German breweries, would you begin to get a clue—and these diverse clues lessen each year. They know it not but all these bright women and pompous men are in uniforms, under the discipline of a belligerent service, as firmly as any soldier in khaki. For those that like it—that is what they like; but there are those of us who hesitated about being drafted into the army of complacency.

SEEING RED (ON COMMUNISM)

From *Newsweek,* November 29, 1937.

¶ *In the following review of* The Writer in a Changing World, *a report of the Second American Writers' Congress, published by the Equinox Press, Mr. Lewis showed that he saw clearly just what Communism meant to writers and the world at large. This was written at a time when many intellectuals— not to say government officials—were following the Party line and the results bore their bitter fruit years later in the Hiss– Chambers Case, as well as other investigations of subversive activity.*

For a man who at the very time of this review was arguing the reasons why he should live in an ivory tower and was play-

ing with the idea of a novel to be called The Quiet Mind, *it is
something of a foray into the arena.*

IS IT FUNNY OR A LITTLE TRAGIC? MANY WOULD-BE AUTHORS WHO
long to produce honest fiction will be influenced by *The Writer
in a Changing World,* the just-published report of the Second
American Writers' Congress, held in New York in June. The
youngsters will seek here guidance to nobility, but find only a
summons to submit themselves to Stalinist Communism.
Comrade Earl Browder says: "They (the Communists) call
for a common discipline for the whole democratic camp . . .
Is that regimentation, is it intolerance, is it crushing the free
spirit of truth?" Why, yes, Comrade, it is, when the discipline
originates in the Kremlin.

It's an old trick of the Communists, and a good one, to coax
an illustrious innocent to serve as show-window dummy. They
were able to use Dreiser so, until he murmured, with unexpected sincerity, that he disliked the Jews, whereupon he
was heaved out of Zion.

There is no excuse for anyone to swallow the Bolshevik
claim to be the one defence against Fascism. There are too
many dependable accounts of what, actually, the Communists
have done in their own private laboratory. It is not necessary
to listen to hacks for reactionary magazines, so large a store is
there of scrupulous books by men who went to Russia with
every hope, and returned in disgust.

Recently published are Eugene Lyons's *Assignment in
Utopia,* the tale of a radical East Sider who in Russia found
all his ideals cynically betrayed; *Russia Twenty Years After,*
in which Victor Serge, once a leader of the Communist International, uncovers the intellectual racketeering and ruthless-
ness of the Russian bureaucracy; and, especially annoying to the
pint-sized replicas of Stalin on Union Square, André Gide's

Return from the U.S.S.R. Max Eastman's 'Artists in Uniform' was so revelatory of what Communist discipline actually does do to writers that *New Masses* prophets would answer it only by a characteristic "All lies—all Fascist lies", and the two most recent books of William Henry Chamberlin, greatest of Anglo-American correspondents in Russia, *Collectivism: A False Utopia,* and *Russia's Iron Age,* are the final pillorying of the Communist dictatorship.

Rather neglected has been *Proletarian Journey,* the exciting story of Fred Beal, once a Communist leader in textile strikes. Read it! He was charged, probably falsely, with murder in the Gastonia strike; he escaped to Russia, and found that workers' paradise a little worse than any Southern mill town. He also presents a noble portrait of American Communist leaders on vodka-jazzed junkets in Moscow—at the expense of American workers. He paints Mike Gold, the Lucius Beebe of Communist journalism:

"Gold is a sentimental revolutionist who has been very successful in exploiting his sentiments. He is undoubtedly sincere in his feeling for the working classes and will do anything to help them—*from a safe distance.* Gold was followed by the intellectuals among the American Communists, each of whom expected to write a 'best seller' or a popular play about the coming revolution and settle down on a farm in Pennsylvania."

THE ARTIST, THE SCIENTIST AND THE PEACE

First given as a radio broadcast from the Metropolitan Opera House, New York, on December 16, 1944, as a part of the

34

Opera Victory Rally Series. Reprinted by *The American Scholar* in its summer issue in 1945

¶ *Here Mr. Lewis states with customary vigour the choice before the artist-scientist in a world facing totalitarian rule. While this address was presented at a time when mankind's deliverance from the Nazi-Fascist menace seemed assured, it can be read today in the context of the present Communist threat to free nations. It is another example of the author's prescience.*

IT IS POSSIBLE—IT IS AT LEAST POSSIBLE—THAT NO ARTIST AND NO scientist has ever been able to carry out half his plans to make mankind more cheerful and decent, and possible that this failure has been due less to the illness or laziness of the artist than to the fact that, since history began, all creative talents have been cramped by the insecurity of a world insane with war and tyranny. Yet it has been the artist-scientist himself who has least acknowledged this, who has most tried to hide himself from the age-long conflict for a more reasonable world.

But a strange thing about the present war-time is the number of artist-scientists who *have* realised that their work, no matter how detached from commerce or political ambition it may be, is still dependent on the universal struggle for and against democracy; who have come out of the studio or the laboratory or the theatre to stand with their fellow-workers; who are listening to the question: "*Which side are you on*—isolation or world-control—*which side are you on?*"—and who are now answering it.

The old-fashioned type of artist-scientist—the Pasteurs and Whistlers and Walter Paters—felt that their creative work was so superior that they could live in plush-lined clouds *above* the human struggle. Here and there a Voltaire or a Dickens or a physician like Vesalius knew that he could have no private light to work by if the whole world elsewhere was in darkness, and he cried "Let there be universal light!" even if, in so crying, he lost his respectable reputation or his very life. Then, during the last war, so timid and retired an etcher of society as Henry James saw that he and his work were meaningless unless he came out and rejoined the human race, and at last, rather timidly, he did so, and took his stand against Germany.

All along, people like Bernard Shaw and Professor Einstein and Carl Sandburg have seen that their little desks were nothing unless they were joined to all the other little desks in the world, and that not least, but most of all men, the artist, the scientist, must know and somewhat loudly state whether he is for tyranny and cruelty and machine discipline, or for the people, for all the people.

In this war, among the German writers the renowned Gerhart Hauptmann, once the darling, almost the Frank Sinatra, of all revered German novelists and dramatists, decided on just which side *he* belonged. He belonged with safety and a handsome new farm and obsequiousness to all the goose-stepping lords of the revised Germany. So, even in war-time, he got these luxuries—he lost nothing but his self-respect, and the love of every decent man. That's excellent—he openly took his side—he didn't hide his shamefulness.

But certain Germans and Austrians, like Franz Werfel, Bruno Walter, Stefan Zweig, Freud, Bela Schick, Thomas Mann, Lion Feuchtwanger, decided that new houses and new coats and the hoarse cheering of *schmalz*-headed drill-sergeants weren't enough to make up for the loss of honour, the loss of that quiet satisfaction with your work which is life itself, and they went into exile, gave up every neighbour, every title, even the sweet sound of their own accustomed language, that the world might know on which side they were.

But it's time to stop all that, isn't it? It's cosmic idiocy that an honest and competent man should have to lose even his own tongue and his beloved citizenship because he *is* too honest and too competent to stand for the botched tyrannies of gangster rulers. The world has always allowed that sort of thing, since long before the exile of Dante, and it is time, it always has been time, for a new kind of world organisation which won't merely yearn for but actually produce security for the competent and honest, and not permit them again to be smashed by incessant and senseless wars. Public murder has become a little too costly—there are people who are really thinking about some sort of a law against it!

Everybody suffers from the usurpation of wars, whether lawyer or garage mechanic or farmer or housewife, but the problem of the scientist or the artist—and consequently the problem of such citizens as want to enjoy the product of the artist and to benefit by the discoveries of the scientist—is two-fold. Like everybody else, he must think about that interesting task, making a living, a diversion extremely cramped by war, but his supreme interest has little to do with a mere living. The ordinary workman, whether he is a carpenter or a senator, works best when he scrupulously follows the best standards of the day. When a surgeon takes out an appendix, we don't think more highly of him if he tries the experiment of getting at the appendix through the right elbow. But the creator in the arts and the researcher in the laboratory and the inventor in the workshop have a value exactly as their work is a little different from anything that has been done before. And they can never develop that differentness in a world of insecurity, where they know that anything they do, trivial or important, is judged not by its significance to mankind but by the way in which it tickles a gang of gorillas. Their native land is truth, but no artist or scientist in history has yet dwelt utterly and continuously in that land of truth, because it always has been stormed by the lovers of power.

But it is not important merely for the artists and the scientists themselves to see how their truth has been corrupted, to see where they stand; it is just as important for their admirers. When the Nazis burned the books in Berlin—or, for that matter, when a certain handsome old city in these United States flops back into medievalism and bans books that do not seem to do much injury to the other cities—then it is the would-be readers of the books that suffer more than the writers; and when the Nazis decide that the music of Mendelssohn is Jewish and not at all the sort of thing that Dr. Goebbels would care to write, then it is the lovers of symphonies and not the ghost of the great master that are robbed. If people really want great music, great poetry, great painting, if they really want medical discoveries which will save their babies from death, instead of wanting to live either in a Fascist slaughter-house or a comic strip of world triviality, then they must give the artists and the scientists a civilisation in which they can show what they really can do—as none of them has ever yet had the chance to show.

It isn't that the artist needs softer beds or more food, and as for publicity, in these days of radio and tabloids, he probably gets too much of it! It is a spiritual thing that he needs—an assurance that what he is doing is not futile, a sense that it profits him to produce what will demand of him the labour of years, that will demand a whole lifetime of the most honest devotion, instead of quickly turning out something that will please the fickle vanity of Fascist playboys whose toys are not only the machine-gun and the rope but pretty propaganda.

But the artist will never do his possibly magnificent best if there is going to be a patched-up world in which the prospects for an unending peace are just a *little* better than in 1936—if there are to be merely a few more pleasant fictions called treaties and tea-parties called conferences. I am not at all sure but that the most mulish kind of complete isolationism is not preferable to playing at world government, because it is at least honest: you know what and where it is. By the way, I imagine that this will be the only time during this series of broadcasts when confirmed isolationism is going to have such ardent praise!

In the matter of civilisation for the artist or scientist, it has been all or nothing, and usually it has been nothing. However great his talent, if it is at all corrupted by the cynicism that spreads in an insecure and dishonest world, then that one germ of despair will flourish until it rots the whole, and the artist or scientist, along with all his followers, will have a shining brilliance, but it will be the autumnal colour of decay.

Consider the science of genetics, the science of birth and the production of better children. So long as that science is devoted to producing more and stronger little Nazis, it is evil, and the more skilful it may become, the more evil it will be. That knowledge will not even begin to be valuable until it is devoted to producing not better little Germans—yes, or better little Americans or Englishmen—but universally, everywhere in the world, regardless of uniforms, better human beings. The scientist, the artist, can ultimately contribute to making a world fit to live in, only *in* a world that is fit to live in—not a city or a state or a nation, but a *world* that is fit to live in. That fact he must know, and must proclaim.

A NOTE ABOUT *KINGSBLOOD ROYAL*

Published in *Wings,* The Literary Guild Review, issued in June of 1947. Reprinted in condensed form in the *Negro Digest*

¶ *According to custom of The Literary Guild, in choosing a book for distribution to their subscribers, Mr. Lewis was asked to write a piece about his novel for their magazine. He had come to New York from Thorvale Farm to make final preparations for a trip to Europe and was staying briefly at the Hotel Algonquin. He made it a point in his latter years not to be in America when a book was published. "If I refuse to give interviews," he said, "I'm a crab. If I do, some reporter will ask questions which I will have to answer in a way that will be misinterpreted. Yes, the only course is to be away."*

AFTER EVERYTHING WILL HAVE BEEN SAID ABOUT MY TWENTIETH novel, some of it with considerable heat, a voice here and there may announce the revolutionary tidings that the story itself is the important thing. My own conviction that one of the most amusing, exasperating, exciting and completely mysterious peoples in the world is the Americans may well be ignored. My delight in watching the small Middle Western cities grow, sometimes beautifully and sometimes hideously, and usually both together, from sod shanties to log huts to embarrassed-looking skinny white frame buildings to sixteen-storey hotels and thirty-storey bank buildings, may be commented on casually. There is a miracle in the story of how all this has happened in two or three generations. Yet, after this period, which is scarcely a second in historic time, we have a settled civilisation with traditions and virtues and foolishness as fixed as those of the oldest tribe of Europe. I merely submit that such a theme is a challenge to all the resources a novelist can summon.

This innocent conviction may be overlooked. What will be cried from the house-tops is that I have written a novel which is so frantically devoted to racial controversy that it will entail a new attack on Fort Sumter. Actually, the 'race question' is only a small part of *Kingsblood Royal,* but it is the part which will stand out. And as old a hand at writing as myself remembers sadly, in the long winter evenings on my Massachusetts farm, how many times one airy opinion or unfortunate wise-crack in a book has swamped all the rest of the vast store of household recipes, curious facts about the domestic life of the kings of Bengal and the Eleventh Dynasty, baseball records, notes on the conjugation of Italian verbs, cracks at the English, cracks at the Russians, especially violent cracks at the people who don't like Rotary, and carefully worked-out jokes which, as is notorious, have constituted the main contents of my books.

It is probably perfectly safe in a novel to attack simultaneously the Archbishop of Canterbury, the Chief Rabbi of Jerusalem and the Grand Mufti of the same salubrious town, but he would be a heroic man who should dare to say publicly that dogs are frequently nuisances and loving mothers sometimes talk too much. Never, never would I venture even to suggest either of these violent thoughts, and perhaps next to them in peril is to suggest that a final and complete solution of all racial questions is to hint that maybe negroes are nothing more nor less than human beings. They have the same motorcycles, admiration for Ingrid Bergman, and hatred of getting up in the morning that characterise the rest of the human race—white, pink, tan, yellow, green and office colour.

I don't think the Negro Problem is insoluble because I don't think there is any Negro Problem. The races of mankind in every country run through a gradation of colour from intense black to the almost pure white which is to be found only in alarming cases of anæmia. No one has ever determined just where the line in this shading is to be drawn.

There are no distinctive coloured persons. The mad, picture-puzzle idiocy of the whole theory of races is beautifully betrayed when you get down to the question of 'negroes' who are white enough to pass as Caucasians. In several states of the Union, the definition either by judicial decision or by legal statute is that a negro is a person who has one drop of African blood.

Manifestly, a fair percentage of negroes do look different from the average American, who is a combination of English, Scotch, Irish and German stocks. So do Sicilians look different. So do Assyrians look different. So do Chinese look different. And there was a time in our history, and ever so short a time ago, when the Scotch–English in New England thought all the Irish were fundamentally different and fundamentally inferior. And then these same conceited Yanks (my own people) moved on to the Middle West and went through the same psychological monkey-shines with the Scandinavians and the Bohemians and the Poles. None of the profound and convincing nonsense of race difference can be made into sense.

I do think, however, it makes sense to see and try to understand a young man like my hero, kindly, devoted to bridge and hunting, fond of his pleasant wife and adorable daughter, who flies off the handle and suddenly decides that certain social situations, which he had never even thought of before, were intolerable. In order to fight those situations, with a grimness and a valour probably greater than that of any fancy medieval knight, not hysterically but with a quiet and devastating anger, he risks his job, his social caste, his good repute, his money, and the father and mother and wife and child whom he loves. When we find him, as we have found several millions of him—or her—in each of our wars, we realise that the banal slickness of electric refrigerators and tiled bathrooms and convertible coupés have no more lessened his romantic and rather terrifying courage than did the dirty, reed-covered floors and snarling dogs and dinners of gnawed beef bones coarsen the Knights of the Crusade. And probably the Knights of the Crusade no more sang poetry about themselves than does my hero, the young banker of Grand Republic, Minnesota. It is only centuries later that the epic poet comes along and finds them elevated and given to speaking in blank verse. It will be a sufficient reason for a lifetime of writing if my notes on my hero's refrigerator and electric razor will serve the purpose of some future Mr. Homer or Milton (born in North Dakota) who will make ringing heroic couplets out of him. The ring and the heroism are there all right, and I hope they are implicit in my own sardonic cataloguing.

Besides those 'typical fine Young Americans'—as they are frequently called and as sometimes, I regret to say, they call themselves—there are one or two negro characters whose learning and charm will be sharply questioned by critics who just haven't met that kind of people. There is one Dr. Ash Davis, chemist, Doctor of Science, tennis player, musician who prefers Bach. There is another doctor among the coloured brethren also—the Baptist preacher in a tiny chapel whom I present as a Doctor of Philosophy from Columbia. I am going to be told that there are no such animals except in the rarest cases, and the teller is going to be sure of it because he hasn't met them. But he must not blame me because he has travelled so little. I refer him to some hundreds of negroes, easily to be found now, who are fit companions to Bill Hastie—His Excellency, the Honourable Dr. William Hastie, Governor of the Virgin Islands, former Federal Judge of the United States of America, former Dean of Howard University Law School, Harvard man, scholar, a man known for his wit and charm

43

and scholarship in London and Paris as he is in Washington and New York. Or to the eminent New York 'coloured' surgeon, Dr. Louis T. Wright.

These are distinguished and charming men, but you don't meet them in the daily press, which gives most Americans what they consider information about negroes. If a poor drug-ridden negro shoots a white woman, that is News. If his cousin, a competent negro doctor, saves her life—that isn't News.

Strangely enough—is it another sign of their inferiority?—the negroes seem to prefer men of education and training as their leaders instead of politicians distinguished for the amount of brass in their oratory and in their consciences, and Ph.D.s are as common in the great negro organisations as they are rare in Tammany Hall or the Union Club. Yes, it is certainly an odd and therefore undoubtedly inferior trait that they actually take seriously the education that all the rest of us praise so heartily in prospect and laugh at so convulsively when we run into it.

Another question that is going to be debated is whether my young banker hero would actually do certain dangerous things which he feels called upon to take up, although it is only his own conscience that calls him, while all common sense is against it. And then I think of the story of Count Milhály Karolyi. Before World War One he was the richest man in Hungary, with a million or so acres, enormously fertile, and enormously profitable in their cattle and sugar beets. On his estates, solely in his possession, were a score of towns and villages and sugar factories, and a hundred people would drop in for one of the more casual and intimate luncheons. When the old régime was overthrown, Mike Karolyi decided that the ways of his ancestors for a dozen generations were gone for ever, and knowing perfectly that it would mean that he would lose everything, that he would be impoverished, and that he would be lucky if the Ultra Whites on the one side and the Ultra Reds on the other did not kill him—with torture —he headed the first Hungarian Republic that campaigned bravely and tragically against everything for which the great families like the Karolyis had always stood. And his chief cabinet minister was Baron Hatvany, whose story was precisely the same. Quite casually, these two men said: "God help me, I can do no other."

And in little American cities, in quite respectable circles with quite respectable golf scorers, there are young men and women who give Luther's heroic saying a little differently: "I could do no other—thank God!"

That's the story.

A LETTER ON RELIGION

From *On the Meaning of Life,* edited by Will Durant and published in 1932 by Ray Long and Richard R. Smith, Inc.

¶ *Readers who remember the sensational newspaper accounts of the brash young man who stood in a pulpit in Kansas City and defied God to strike him dead will be impressed by the objectivity and mildness of tone of this brief statement on religion by the author of* Elmer Gantry.

IT IS, I THINK, AN ERROR TO BELIEVE THAT THERE IS ANY NEED OF religion to make life seem worth living, or to give consolation in sorrow, except in the case of people who have been reared to religion, so that, should they lose it in their adult years, they would miss it, their whole thinking having been conditioned by it. I know several young people who have been reared entirely without thought of churches, of formal theology, or any other aspect of religion, who have learned ethics not as a divine commandment but as a matter of social convenience. They seem to me quite as happy, quite as filled with purpose and with eagerness about life as anyone trained to pass all his troubles on to the Lord, or the Lord's local agent, the pastor.

Their satisfaction comes from functioning healthily, from physical and mental exercise, whether it be playing tennis or tackling an astronomical problem.

Nor do I believe that most of them will even in old age feel any need of religious consolation, because I know also a few old people who have been thus reared all their lives and who are perfectly serene just to be living. A seventy-four-year-old agnostic like Clarence Darrow is not less but more cheerful and excited about life's adventure—yes, and 'spiritual minded' —than an aged bishop whose bright hopes of Heaven are often overbalanced by his fears of Hell.

If I go to a play I do not enjoy it less because I do not believe that it is divinely created and divinely conducted, that it will last for ever instead of stopping at eleven, that many details of it will remain in my memory after a few months, or that it will have any particular moral effect upon me. And I enjoy life as I enjoy that play.

II

S.L. REMEMBERS

SELF-PORTRAIT (BERLIN, AUGUST, 1927)

¶ *Simply nothing is known by the executors of the Lewis Estate, by the Yale Library or by the writer of these lines of the origin of or reason for the composition of this comprehensive autobiographical sketch. It is dated Berlin, 1927, and a carbon copy of it was found among his papers at Thorvale Farm after his death. At a guess, it was written for his German publisher. There is no record of its ever having been printed.*

Granted this sketch repeats facts stated in other items of this section, its tone is typical of Lewis in a self-critical mood. As such, it presents an interesting sidelight on the man.

It must be borne in mind that this sketch was written in 1927. In later years Lewis developed several interests and hobbies not entirely connected with his work. He discovered music and acquired a magnificent library of records of the world's finest compositions. Never a poseur about music, he rarely talked much about it, but played records endlessly to find out what he liked. He became a passionate chess player— how good the writer cannot testify, but visitors to Thorvale Farm were rated by their ability to play. Another hobby was the study of the Italian language, along with the history and art of Italy.

No comment need be made upon the candid self-analysis revealed in this fugitive piece.

MR. JOSEPH HERGESHEIMER, AN AMERICAN AUTHOR WHOM I peculiarly recommend to Europe because he is free of that sociological itch which afflicts so many writers like myself, said once in a brief autobiography that there was really nothing to recount of Hergesheimer the man which had not already been exhibited in the characters of his novels. And that is true of every novelist who, whether he be capable or lacking, is a serious workman.

It is not true of the hack writer. In private life the hack is often a charming fellow, a seer and a companion to his children, tolerable to his wife, an excellent poker-player, and a great camp cook, despite the sapless virgin heroines and the pompously patriotic heroes whom he has created.

Mr. Hergesheimer's contention I may claim for myself. Whether or no there is any merit in my books, I do not know and do not vastly care, since I have had the somewhat exhausting excitement of writing them. But, good or not, they have in them everything I have been able to get from life or to give to life.

There is really no Sinclair Lewis about whom even that diligent scribbler himself could write, outside of what appears in his characters. All his respect for learning, for integrity, for accuracy, and for the possibilities of human achievement are to be found not in the rather hectic and exaggerative man as his intimates see him, but in his portrait of Professor Max Gottlieb, in *Arrowsmith*. Most of the fellow's capacity for loyalty to love and friendship has gone into Leora in that same novel, and into the account of George F. Babbitt's affection for his son and for his friend Paul—most, but, thank Heaven, not quite all, since it is one of the few virtues of Lewis, in *propria persona,* that he remains fond and almost childishly admiring of a few friends, men and women. And whatever potentialities for hard, lean, Lindbergh-courage this Lewis, this product of the pioneer forests and wheat-fields of Minnesota, may once have had, it has seemingly all gone into the depiction of such characters as 'Hawk' Ericson (that aviator so curiously like Lindbergh, though created a dozen years ago) in *The Trail of the Hawk* or the resolute country doctor, Will Kennicott, in *Main Street,* or Frank Shallard, quakingly but unyieldingly facing the bloody Fundamentalist fanatics in *Elmer Gantry*. In his private life, the fellow himself has no drop of such courage. He trembles on the funiculars of the Swiss mountains, in automobiles speeding on wet pavements, on ships moaning terror in the mid-sea fog.

I am assuredly not indulging in that pretended modesty which is a reversed and irritating egotism—that "See me, I'm so noble that I can even admit that I am not noble". Nor am I hinting that here is a case interesting in its peculiarity. It's very common. I know a novelist who, in that real and uninhibited portion of him which is his novels, depicts with authentic impressiveness a high, free, passionate, winged love between men and women, but who in private life is always creeping and peeping around corners as pitifully as any clerk starving for romance in his boarding-house. I know another who is all strength and soaring beauty in his books, yet privately sits by his fireside, puffy, pudgy, fussing over little bibelots. And I know a good many writers who find that the best inspiration for their accounts of austere self-rule is to he had in a bottle of whisky.

No! If the ordinary lay reader were wise, he would flee desperately from meeting most of his favourite authors. And this ecclesiastical secret which I am so unprofessionally giving away explains why the biographies of authors would be achingly dull if they were but written honestly.

Take the subject of this particular biography—Sinclair Lewis.

There was never in private life a less attractive or admirable fellow—except to a few people who like him from perversity or because they find his conversation amusing. Of that one thing, talk, he is a master, in certain of its minor and more flippant and hysterical phases. He imitates an American Babbitt boasting about his motor-car, a Swede or a Yankee speaking German, a college professor lecturing ponderously on nothing in particular.

An occasional auditor is delighted and exclaims: "This Lewis is giving us the very soul of a character, and through him of a civilisation."

But they overpraise the fellow. When they know him well enough, they find him repeating these parlour tricks over and over, as childishly as the village clowns described in his own *Main Street*. And anyway, he is really only practising, only making a sketch, for the next character he is to paint. When he is in such almost vaudeville-like moods, he is intolerably inconsiderate of the fact that others in the company might now and then like to talk. He rides them down, bewilders them and buries them in the flood of his boisterous comedy. Only thus, apparently, can he impress them. In the profundities of scientific conferences, in the delicate give and take of well-bred worldly chatter, in really earnest and scholarly consideration of the arts—even of his own novel-writing—the fellow is as dumb as a fish.

Besides a certain amount of lasting affection for his friends and this pyrotechnical conversation, the man seems to me to have no virtues whatever save a real, fiery, almost reckless hatred of hypocrisy—of what the Americans call 'bunk', from the older word 'buncombe', and this may not be a virtue at all, but only an envy-inspired way of annoying people by ignoring their many excellent qualities and picking out the few vices into which they have been betrayed by custom and economic necessity.

He hates, equally, politicians who lie and bully and steal under cover of windy and banal eloquence, and doctors who unnecessarily and most lucratively convince their patients that they are ill; merchants who misrepresent their wares, and manufacturers who pose as philanthropists while underpaying their workmen; professors who in war-time try to prove that the enemy are all fiends, and novelists who are afraid to say what seems to them the truth. Why, this man, still so near to being an out-and-out Methodist or Lutheran that he would far rather chant the hymns of his boyhood evangelicism than the best drinking song in the world, is so infuriated by ministers who tell silly little jokes in the pulpit and keep from ever admitting publicly their confusing doubts that he risks losing all the good friends he once had among the ministers by the denunciations in *Elmer Gantry*.

But aside from these three virtues—if they be such—the man is a most dingy and unstimulating recluse. Tall, awkward, rusty of hair, long-nosed, dressed neither handsomely nor with picturesque disarray, a Yorkshire yeoman farmer with none of the farmer's strength and horsey dash, he is a figure altogether unromantic. He has no hobbies save rather unimaginative travel to obvious and uninterestingly safe tourist centres. And he has no games. He has never in his life played bridge, golf, mah jong, or billiards; he plays tennis like an eight-year-old boy—quite definitely and literally so; his swimming is confined to a timorous paddling near shore; and even in motoring, though he comes from a land in which there must be at least 60,000,000 proficient drivers, he has as much dash and speed as an archdeacon of eighty, with false teeth and rheumatism.

He detests polite dinner parties. As he listens to the amiable purring of nice matrons, he is afflicted with ennui as with disease. And years in Europe, even Paris, have given him none of the charming tastes of the gourmet. He is (yet without any of the barbarian's virility) a barbarian in the arts of the table. He prefers whisky and soda to the most delicate vintage; he is often known to commit that least excusable of American atrocities—smoking cigarettes between courses at a perfect dinner. And he boasts. He may seem modest enough in writing, but when he is gabbling and off his guard, he tells at tedious length what fools are all the critics who criticise him.

The man is now forty-two. He looks, when he hasn't stayed up too late (as he is likely to do, talking, for ever talking) slightly younger, because of his thinness. He was born, son and grandson of country doctors, in the sort of shambling prairie village which he has described in *Main Street*; a village of low wooden shops, of cottages each set in its little garden, of rather fine trees, with the wheat a golden sea for miles about.

His boyhood was utterly commonplace—lessons in school, swimming in summer, hunting ducks in the autumn, skating in winter, with such household tasks as sawing stove-wood and cleaning from the sidewalk the deep snow of the far-northern land. It was a boyhood commonplace except for a love of reading not very usual in that raw new town. He revelled in Dickens, Walter Scott, Washington Irving.

Doubtless this habit of reading led to his writing. He began as a wild romanticist. His first efforts were entirely in verse—banal and imitative verse, all about troubadours and castles as sagely viewed from the eminence of a Minnesota prairie village. It is ironical that later in regions where castles and the memory of troubadours really did exist—in Kent and Cornwall, Fontainebleau and London and Rome—he should sit writing of Minnesota prairie villages!

Lewis had a singularly easy youth. No picturesque chronicle of gallant fighting against poverty and inappreciation was his. His father sent him to Yale University; afterwards he became a newspaper reporter, a magazine editor, and literary adviser to publishers. In between there were a few adventures and a few lean years, but they were only amusing incidents of youth. He went to a radical co-operative colony as a janitor, and was titanically a failure at the job. He ventured to Panama, during the time when the great canal was being excavated, in the hope of a job in that picturesque jungle. He sailed to Panama in the steerage and came back stow-away—without the job! For a year and a half he lived in California; partly in a cottage near the beach of the Pacific, existing on borrowed money and trying to write short stories, in company with the American poet, William Rose Benét; partly doing (and doing very badly) newspaper work in San Francisco.

But from 1910 to December, 1915, he was a very prosaic and unenterprising editor in New York, acquiring a wife, and a conviction that he never would, never could, learn to compose anything more imaginative than advertisements for bad novels —though in America such advertisements can be very imaginative indeed. He did, with difficulty, manage to write two novels, *Our Mr. Wrenn* and *The Trail of the Hawk,* during evenings after days of editorial work, but they were financial failures and at first critically unnoticed.

A humorous story, written as a lark and without expectation that it would ever be published, opened for him the doors of the *Saturday Evening Post,* and in a few months he had enough money saved to be able to leave his position and start free-lancing.

That was in December, 1915, and ever since then he has wandered, by train, motor, steamer, on foot. Naturally he is always being congratulated for thus scouring the world for information, and naturally he travels for no such estimable reason but only because he is afflicted with Wanderlust, which is one of the most devouring of diseases. In these eleven and a half years, the longest time he has spent in any one place was nine months in London. He has motored through nearly every state in America. He has seen Europe from Berlin down to Seville and Athens. He has spent weeks in Northern Canada, two hundred miles from any railroad or even wagon road. He has drifted through the West Indies to Venezuela and Colombia. But meantime he has written eleven books and some scores of short stories and articles, because he is able to settle down in a strange room in a strange city, and be serenely at work within three hours. During his hours of writing he is indifferent as to whether his typewriter is beside a window looking on Fifth Avenue, a London fog, or a silent mountain.

He is vaguely thinking now of the Orient—of India, Java, Japan—from which it is to be judged that his Wanderlust is incorrigible.

A dull fellow, and probably unimaginative. Otherwise he would stay home and be inspired by his own vision instead of having to be aroused by new streets, new hills, new faces.

A dull fellow whose virtue—if there be any—is to be found only in his books.

SINCLAIR LEWIS

SELF-PORTRAIT (NOBEL FOUNDATION)

Written for the Nobel Foundation in 1930. Not published in the United States

¶ *The autobiographical note which follows necessarily repeats the facts set down in the previous one. Its use here seems justified, if not imperative, because of the difference in tone and emphasis. Also, since it was written at the request of the Nobel Foundation, the author himself considered it important.*

TO RECOUNT MY LIFE FOR THE NOBEL FOUNDATION, I WOULD LIKE to present it as possessing some romantic quality, some unique character, like Kipling's early adventures in India, or Bernard

Shaw's leadership in the criticism of British arts and economics. But my life, aside from such youthful pranks as sailing on cattle-ships from America to England during university vacations, trying to find work in Panama during the building of the canal, and serving for two months as janitor of Upton Sinclair's abortive co-operative colony, Helicon Hall, has been a rather humdrum chronicle of much reading, constant writing, undistinguished travel à la tripper, and several years of comfortable servitude as an editor.

I was born in a prairie village in the most Scandinavian part of America, Minnesota, the son of a country doctor, in 1885. Until I went East to Yale University I attended the ordinary public school, along with many Madsens, Olesons, Nelsons, Hedins, Larsons. Doubtless it was because of this that I made the hero of my second book, *The Trail of the Hawk,* a Norwegian and Gustaf Sondelius, of *Arrowsmith,* a Swede— and, to me, Dr. Sondelius is the favourite among all my characters.

Of Carl Ericson of *The Trail of the Hawk*, I wrote—back in 1914, when I was working all day as editor for the George H. Doran Publishing Company, and all evening trying to write novels—as follows:

"His carpenter father had come from Norway, by way of steerage and a farm in Wisconsin, changing his name [to Americanise it] from Ericsen. . . . Carl was second-generation Norwegian; American-born, American in speech, American in appearance save for his flaxen hair and china-blue eyes. . . . When he was born the 'typical Americans' of earlier stocks had moved to city places or were marooned on run-down farms. It was Carl Ericson, not a Trowbridge or a Stuyvesant or a Lee or a Grant, who was the 'typical American' of his period. It was for him to carry on the American destiny of extending the western horizon; his to restore the wintry Pilgrim virtues and the exuberant, October, partridge-drumming days of Daniel Boone; then to add, in his own or another generation, new American aspirations for beauty."

My university days at Yale were undistinguished save for contributions to the *Yale Literary Magazine*. It may be interesting to say that these contributions were most of them reeking with a banal romanticism; that one who was later to try to present livingly ordinary pavements trod by real boots should through university days have written nearly always of Guinevere and Lancelot—of weary bitterns among sad Irish reeds—of story-book castles with troubadours vastly indulging in wine, a commodity of which the author personally was singularly ignorant. What the moral is, I do not know. Whether imaginary castles at nineteen lead always to the sidewalks of Main Street at thirty-five, and whether the process might be reversed, and whether either of them is desirable, I leave to the psychologists.

I drifted for two years after college as a journalist, as a newspaper reporter in Iowa and in San Francisco, as—incredibly— a junior editor on a magazine for teachers of the deaf, in Washington, D.C. The magazine was supported by Alexander Graham Bell, inventor of the telephone. What I did not know about teaching the deaf would have included the entire subject, but that did not vastly matter, as my position was so insignificant that it included typing hundreds of letters every week begging for funds for the magazine and, on days when the negro janitress did not appear, sweeping out the office.

Doubtless this shows the advantages of a university education, and it was further shown when at the age of twenty-five I managed to get a position in a New York publishing-house at all of fifteen dollars a week! This was my authentic value on the labour market, and I have always uncomfortably suspected that it would never have been much higher had I not, accidentally, possessed the gift of writing books which so acutely annoyed American smugness that some thousands of my fellow-citizens felt they must read these scandalous documents whether they liked them or not.

From that New York position till the time five years later when I was selling enough short stories to the magazines to be able to live by free-lancing, I had a series of typical white-collar, unromantic, office literary jobs with two publishing-houses, a magazine (*Adventure*), and a newspaper syndicate, reading manuscripts, writing book-advertising, writing catalogues, writing uninspired book-reviews—all the carpentry and plumbing of the city of letters. Nor did my first five novels rouse the slightest whispers: *Our Mr. Wrenn, The Trail of the Hawk, The Job, The Innocents,* and *Free Air,* they were called, published between 1914 and 1919, and all of them dead before the ink was dry. I lacked sense enough to see that, after five failures, I was foolish to continue writing.

Main Street, published late in 1920, was my first novel to rouse the embattled peasantry and, I have already hinted, it had really a success of scandal. One of the most treasured American myths had been that all American villages were peculiarly noble and happy, and here an American attacked that myth. Scandalous! Some hundreds of thousands read the book with the same masochistic pleasure that one has in sucking an aching tooth.

Since *Main Street,* the novels have been *Babbitt,* 1922; *Arrowsmith,* 1925; *Mantrap,* 1926; *Elmer Gantry,* 1927; *The Man Who Knew Coolidge,* 1928; and *Dodsworth,* 1929. The next novel, yet unnamed, will concern idealism in America through three generations, from 1818 till 1930—an idealism which the outlanders who call Americans 'dollar-chasers' do not understand. It will presumably be published in the autumn of 1932, and the author's chief difficulty in composing it is that after having received the Nobel Prize he longs to write better than he can!

I was married, in England, in 1928, to Dorothy Thompson,

an American who had been the Central European correspondent and chef de bureau of the *New York Evening Post*. My first marriage, to Grace Hegger, in New York in 1914, had been dissolved.

During these years of novel-writing since 1915 I have lived a quite unromantic and unstirring life. I have travelled much; on the surface it would seem that one who during these fifteen years has been in forty states of the United States, in Canada, Mexico, England, Scotland, France, Italy, Sweden, Germany, Austria, Czechoslovakia, Jugoslavia, Greece, Switzerland, Spain, the West Indies, Venezuela, Colombia, Panama, Poland, and Russia must have been adventurous. That, however, would be a typical error of biography. The fact is that my foreign travelling has been a quite uninspired recreation, a flight from reality. My real travelling has been sitting in Pullman smoking-cars, in a Minnesota village, on a Vermont farm, in a hotel in Kansas City or Savannah, listening to the normal daily drone of what are to me the most fascinating and exotic people in the world—the Average Citizens of the United States, with their friendliness to strangers and their rough teasing, their passion for material advancement and their shy idealism, their interest in all the world and their boastful provincialism —the intricate complexities which an American novelist is privileged to portray.

And nowadays, at forty-six, with my first authentic home— a farm in the pastoral state of Vermont—and a baby born in June, 1930, I am settled down to what I hope to be the beginning of a novelist's career. I hope the awkward apprenticeship with all its errors is nearly done!

MY FIRST DAY IN NEW YORK

¶ The following article appeared in The New Yorker *of January 2, 1937, under the title of 'That Was New York and That Was Me.' Since the text here printed follows the author's original manuscript, we have used his own title 'My First Day in New York.' It was written at his Vermont home, Twin Farms, South Pomfret, during the summer of 1936. Aside from its value as an autobiographical fragment, it will wring a pang of sweet sadness from the heart of anyone who can remember his or her first entry into New York with aspirations to conquer the world.*

IT WAS A THIRD OF A CENTURY AGO, IN SEPTEMBER OF 1903, THAT I first came to New York, on my way to college. The Pacific cable had just been opened and Roosevelt I. had sent a message to Governor Taft of the Philippines; Whistler had just died; Carrie Nation was pre-imitating Badoglio; the Wright brothers were three months later to make the first aeroplane flight; and, to crib from Mr. Mark Sullivan, in August for the first time an automobile had crossed the continent under its own power. It was the entering edge, then, of the new world of gasoline, and I should have found New York, which (except for trolleys and the elevated) was as horsified as it had been in 1700, a serene and provincial old town, to be remembered with nostalgia in these days of taxis.

I didn't find it anything of the kind.

Born in Minnesota, I had never been east of Chicago except for a couple of months at Oberlin College, Ohio, an institution which singularly failed to resemble Columbia or the Sorbonne. Smoking was forbidden, and class parties were opened with a powerful prayer by some student in training as a Y.M.C.A. secretary.

From Minnesota to Albany, there was nothing sensational in my journey, though later I found that the youth to whom I had confided, on a station platform, that proudly I was a "Yale man" was also going East to enter the business of being a "Yale man". But, having attended a prep school instead of a Western high school, he knew that there was nothing more boorish, nothing that, in the cant of that day, would so throughly 'queer' you, as to call yourself a Yale man. . . . He let me learn all about it, afterward, in New Haven, with the beneficent result that to this day, if anyone demands, "Aren't you the author?" I protest, "Certainly not. The fellow who you prob'ly saw his picture, he's my cousin, they say he looks like me, on account of because we're both skinny. But *me*, thank God, I'm in the wholesale grocery racket. Why say, brother, my territory. . . ." By that time, the interested one has usually fled. Try it.

With my trunk sent on to New Haven, I debarked at Albany, and came down to Manhattan by the Hudson River Day Boat. That's the sort of thing one has the sense to do, at eighteen, and never in the duller years thereafter; to swim into New York on a tide of history. There were my first mountains, the Catskills; there were Ichabod Crane and Rip Van Winkle visible on the blue uplands or in the mountain gorges; George Washington rode all over the place; and there were stone houses that, compared with the frame cottages of a prairie village, seemed to me coeval with the Acropolis—and in considerably better repair. This, I decided, oh, this was *good*; I was simply going to love the East, particularly New York; love it and dominate it. Give me twenty years and I would be a literary fellow there, with an income of at least two thousand dollars a year—prob'ly twenty-two hundred, by the time I was fifty—and a fine four-room flat, decorated with

Japanese prints and Della Robbia plaques, in which I would entertain all the great artists of the day: Richard Le Gallienne and Maxfield Parrish, and James Huneker—the last of whom I prized, I imagine, not because he was a sound appraiser but because he furnished to the young pretender so many lovely names of Czech etchers and Finnish trioletists. (I had in the puerility of college prep only nibbled at the really enduring craftsmen: Hamlin Garland, Booth Tarkington, George Ade, Finley Peter Dunne, William Gillette; while William Dean Howells wasn't romantic enough for me. Le Gallienne's *Quest of the Golden Girl* and *The Idylls of the King* were my meat; chicken à la king was tastier than lamb chops. That is as it should be—Freshmen should be romantics, Sophomores should be Socialists, Juniors should be bums, and after that it doesn't matter.)

I was coming into New York an emperor on a barge. It wasn't the skipper who was taking the boat in, but my will to conquer; and I was almost sorry for New York, that would have to yield so humbly to my demands.

It was early dusk when the boat docked. I don't know whether the same pier served ferries also, or there were ferry houses hard by, but from the safe deck of the river-boat I was cast out into a riot of fiends.

I know now that they were only Jersey commuters with their little hearts as white as snow, scampering home with Italian sausage and shin-guards for Junior and copies of *The Century,* thinking of nothing more alarming than an evening of Five Hundred or crochinole, and if they looked agitated, it was because they were afraid they would miss the 6.07. But to me, then, they were out of Inferno by Doré. In that smoky darkness, on the rough floor of the pier and the rougher pavement outside, pushed, elbowed, jabbed by umbrellas, my suitcase banging my legs, I saw them as the charging army of Satan himself, their eyes hateful, their mouths distorted with fury, their skinny hands clutching at me. From provincial embarrassment I turned to utter panic fear. I wailed at a policeman, asking what trolley I should take for the Grand Central. Another dozen hussars of hell had shouldered me, bumped me and turned me about before the policeman took time to indicate a trolley with a jerked thumb.

God knows where the street-cars took me in Manhattan that night—from the Harlem River to the Battery and back again, I should think. I know I changed cars several times, and each time desired to weep upon the shoulder of some exceedingly unsympathetic conductor or cop. The golden streets of the dream city were not merely tarnished; they were greasy. Everywhere, people bumped along the shadow-lurking streets as viciously, as threateningly, as they had at the ferry house. Their eyes seemed full of a passion of malice and every manner of crime, and in their deft dodging at street corners there was a surly, defiant, urban competence which the young man from Minnesota could surely never emulate. (Yes, and he never has; it's only moral cowardice that keeps him from taking a taxi to cross Madison Avenue.) Dominate the city? He was beaten before he started by this dirty-grey, hoarse, leaping dinosaur of a city; he would never drive it. (Nor ever has!)

On that erratic trolley-journey, I saw, but was too overpowered to enjoy seeing, real live Italians and Chinamen and negroes. I think—possibly I dreamed it afterward, but I think I gawked up from the trolley window at the fabulous Flatiron Building, highest business structure in the whole world—seven or eight times as high as the building in Sauk Centre which housed the *Weekly Avalanche,* the Masonic lodge, and the town photographer. But I know that miraculously, without merit, I did come to the red brick barn that then was the Grand Central Station, and to a dirty day-coach for New Haven.

Even if it had not been dark, I doubt if, in my exhausted

disillusion, I could really have seen the Connecticut apple orchards and the little hilly fields, pointed with stone walls, to which I had been looking forward these five years. I was simply hiding in that day-coach, which brought me, rather surprisingly I thought, to New Haven.

It was quiet enough in New Haven, as with my suitcase I plodded out of the station, looking for a hotel. I remember that the hotel I found wasn't much of a hotel. In fact, it was probably a thundering bad hotel, lacking air, respectable pillows, and running water. But its quiet, the gentility of its walls in not rising up and crushing me to death, as that New York crowd had so resolutely tried to do, were heavenly.

So I had started my thirty-three years of New York and the East.

Seven years later I came to New York to stay. I was twenty-five then—not quite so young and promising—and I had a job at fifteen dollars a week with the promise that if I stayed on the job for five or ten years, I might possibly rise to twenty-five a week. And that wasn't so enticing a New York, either, that fifteen-a-week New York where, pay-day being Saturday noon, we underlings in the business—including George Soule, now of the *New Republic*—never had breakfast on Saturday morning.

London, Paris, Berlin, Rome, Vienna—I had found them to be comfortable and easily familiar cities. If no citizen talks to you in London, the bobbies do give you directions. If in Paris on a wet day the taxis skid three times to the block, no one is ever hurt save in his vocabulary. But New York is still to me very much what it was on that September evening in 1903. Ogden Nash can have it; as for me, I would not take a taxi from Ninetieth Street to the Village even to go to a party at which the presence was guaranteed, under heavy penalty, of Gandhi, Frank Sullivan, Phyllis McGinley, Dr. Harvey Cushing, General Göring, F.P.A., Bernarr McFadden, and

J. Edgar Hoover, complete with sawed-off shot-gun. My first day in New York has never quite ended. And eighty cents seems too much to pay for orange juice.

TWO YALE MEN IN UTOPIA

From *The New York Sun,* December 16, 1906

¶ *Most of the biographical sketches of Sinclair Lewis have mentioned his sojourn at Helicon Hall, Upton Sinclair's experiment in communal living. None of them has given as complete and colourful an account as Lewis does here. As Carl Van Doren said in* A Biographical Sketch, *published by Doubleday, Doran in 1933: "He looked for an intenser, richer life at Helicon Hall in New Jersey as Hawthorne had looked for it in an earlier communistic experiment at Brook Farm, and found himself as dissatisfied as Hawthorne."*

Lewis's stay at Helicon Hall as furnace tender and man-of-all-work lasted about a month during the winter of 1906. (In his Nobel Prize 'Self Portrait' Mr. Lewis stated that he worked at Helicon Hall for two months.) So far as known, the following piece is the author's sole account of this experience. As noted in the introduction, this is one of three items which we have taken the liberty of cutting. In each instance the deletions were made solely for reasons of space.

The writer of these lines can attest the amusing truth of Mr. Lewis's picture of Helicon Hall in its brief and stormy existence, because he often visited the place and there first met Mr. Lewis.

The account recalls one of the fragments of verse which Hal (as he was then called) used to rattle off without copying. This

66

particular bit of nonsense referred to Professor William and Mrs. Anna Noyes of Teachers College, Columbia University, who enjoyed a supervisory post in charge of fellow-workers. One day after a gruelling bout with a refractory furnace and immovable bed-spring, Lewis declaimed a verse reciting his woes. It ran, if memory serves, something like this:

> *Each genius to his menial task*
> *To honoured labour, and at eve*
> *To sit and dream as girls and boys*
> *Except, that is,*
> *The bloodless ones called Noyes.*

Did any reader, present on that occasion, copy down the verse?

Although the diary dates are out of sequence, this is precisely the way the piece appeared in The Sun.

SATURDAY, NOVEMBER 3.—AS CÆSAR ONCE NEARLY REMARKED, I'VE come, seen and been conquered.

Helicon Hall, near the summit of the Palisades, in Englewood, N.J., as the prospectus puts it, is a great old establishment. In spite of the bed-springs in the main hall and the remains of packing-boxes in the wooded court, which, I understand, is called the patio; in spite of the fact that I'm to be an ordinary janitor, whereas I have always yearned to be something more elevated, I've promised to join the colony.

The author of *The Jungle* did it. For three solid hours I sat in his office while language flowed from him in a scintillating stream. It took him thus long to explain that my duty was to be firing a furnace. But after he had told how the cook was a Cornell M.A., the laundress a well-known assistant muckraker, the scullion a Tennessee lawyer and Poe critic, the other janitor a wealthy Providence wholesaler, it made my objections to janiting seem weak and unnatural.

"I have always wanted to work with my hands," declared the *Jungle* man, displaying a large blister on his thumb. "See that? I got that chopping down a tree this morning."

Then he took me down to see the swimming-pool, which he cheerfully characterised as 'bully'. A 'jolly' bowling-alley also shook my orthodox notions of the man who had baited the meat trust and written the poetic soul-writhings of Arthur Stirling. Also I saw the engine with its bewildering array of valves and things, all of which, I understand, minister to the general purpose of keeping the house warm.

During our tour of inspection Mr. Sinclair kept up a running fire of conversation in explanation of his plans. He had put up most of the money necessary to secure an option on the house, he said, so firm was his faith in his project. He expected to do away with regular servants altogether; the work was to be done wholly by socially 'possible' people, who would earn enough to support themselves by a working day of six or seven hours and devote their leisure time to science, philosophy, art and literature.

Budding young geniuses, in which class I was placed, were especially to receive encouragement. Here they will have quiet and a congenial atmosphere. I am enthusiastic about the plan.

But one small cloud, not even of the proverbial man's hand bigness, mars the prospect. Upon my introduction to the housekeeper, who will be *in loco Sinclairis* as far as the actual running of the establishment is concerned, she looked at me critically, I may almost say piercingly, and asked:

"Does he know that he will have to do sweeping?"

"Yes, oh, yes," interrupted Mr. Sinclair, as I was just about to ask for further information.

"And window-washing?" pursued the housekeeper mercilessly.

"Oh, yes," repeated Mr. Sinclair, wriggling still farther down into his chair—he is accustomed to sit, in a truly remarkable manner, upon the nape of his neck.

I am glad that Mr. Sinclair answered these questions for me; they gave me a sort of shock, and I might not have been able to answer them so readily.

Tuesday, November 13.—This is certainly an intellectual joint. This afternoon the cook, the scullion, the chambermaid, and the Columbia instructor in philosophy got into a calorific discussion of the decadence of George Moore, with side-lights on Max Nordau.

"Why, take *Esther Waters*," exclaimed the cook, forgetting the cocoa she was watching. "Is that degenerate? It's the essence of genuine realism; and you know the exposition of the necessity of realism in the first chapter of *Diana of the Crossways*."

"Nietzsche says . . ." began the philosophical one, when he was interrupted by the chambermaid.

"Fudge!" she snorted. "Everyone knows that *Esther Waters* is a $1.08 reprint of Zola. It's . . ."

So we fought until it was decided to refer the matter to James Huneker, via The Editor, a colonist who knows the critic. Our discussion was merging into animadversions on the influence of the same set of ideas on Turgenev, and on the music of Tschaikowsky, when an unlovely odour from the stove made the cook exclaim:

"I'm forgetting the cocoa."

"And I the furnace," I moaned. "Twenty-three for *moi*." Which latter remark was to indicate that I am one of these real college boys, don't you know, and not one of the common or garden muckers, who could be blamed if they let the furnace go out occasionally.

69

Friday, November 16.—Sat two feet from Upton Sinclair, reading his *Arthur Stirling,* this evening. Personally, I think it's excellent; sort of prolegomenon to the future *Keith Rickman;* but Sinclair regards it impersonally as a mistake because of its erroneous views on social subjects. The Upton Sinclair of the newspapers he regards quite impersonally also, saying correctly that there has been set up a hypothetical figure which has nothing to do with the real Sinclair.

Arthur Stirling was supposed to be autobiographical, yet the poet is extravagantly emotional, wildly impractical; while Sinclair is the opposite—logical, non-emotional. True, both are inclined to solitude, both thinkers, readers of Nietzsche and the poets; but Sinclair is a broad man, an economist, and optimist (H. G. Wells presented a book to Sinclair as "To the most optimistic from the next most.") Stirling cowers in poetry as a refuge, as Pater would have men do.

Assistant laundressing is another merry game. Instead of a washboard they use a patent business, which 'works by suction'. One stands there by the fiery-tempered little laundry stove pumping away on the handle of the thing. The only solace is to quote the 'Ballad of East and West', whose metre is excellent for punctuation by the 'um-hum, um-hum' of the handle.

Then comes the wringing, one fishing semi-clean clothes from the water and sticking them into the wringer. It's no harder than gymnasium work, but that 'mouse grey' water, as Yeats calls it—ashen grey, rather—is a most slimy, sweet thing to thrust one's fingers into . . . !

Finally it's out of doors with a large gingham apron, to hang up socks and towels, while some haughty delivery-boy scorns me from his aristocratic grocery wagon. One of his ilk made me so sore that I attached my Chi Delta Theta triangle to my watch-chain, to make myself, at least, feel some of the comforting fact that I am a true scholar and a Yale man.

I had finished the job, under the instructions which Mike roared at me above the buzzing of the boiler and noise of the machinery. While I was wet with perspiration from head to foot and gasping for breath, I was forced to join Mike in a mad scramble for kindling wood in order to build up the fire which I had nearly put out. When I had finally finished, and the gauge was slowly creeping up with its gladsome tidings that steam was again generating in the boiler, Mike took occasion to remark that he had heard that mental work was much more laborious than physical. Gently but firmly I upheld the negative.

Right here allow me to remark that Mike is a true gentleman. Although he didn't know he was to be replaced, didn't know that Mr. Sinclair had decreed that he was quite impossible, nevertheless he had a strong suspicion of it. But this didn't keep him from showing me every courtesy; nay, kindliness.

I should feel sorry for him if I hadn't a sort of sneaking suspicion that he will be needed on that furnace job long, long after it is generally supposed. The dismissal of one who can work that engine, with its complication of hot-water pump, hot-air fan, steam-heating apparatus, automatic traps, which don't always automat, is not to be lightly considered.

Sunday, November 25.—This morning the lawyer-Poe-critic scullion got off the job with great suddenness, and departed, bag and baggage, for New York. I've been taking his place.

I'd often pitied that intellectual scull, but never adequately. He used to work from fourteen to seventeen hours a day and do rather less than the average woman scull can do in five.

It was pathetic almost to see him peeling apples and potatoes in the lulls of sculling. He had such difficulty in getting the outsides off these things, and it took such an awful lot of them to supply the thirty or forty residents of the hall.

The direct cause of his going was a difficulty with the cook regarding something which got burned. But I guess, as in the case of the Revolutionary War, there was a good deal in the indirect causes. They are going to get a regular scull woman from the village tomorrow. It will not be strictly in accord with the social idea of the colony, but I'm not kicking on a little thing like that.

Tuesday, November 27.—The assistant housekeeper went this afternoon. She said she didn't like to make beds and fill water pitchers and empty slops. It hurt her wrists.

She held some sort of business position in New York before she turned to the delights of Helicon and regretfully she has to go back to it—on account of her wrists. My wrists are a bit on the bum also. I spent the day digging a ditch for a drainpipe. It was better than sculling. The new scull woman certainly beats me hollow, anyway.

However, I suppose even Elysium must have a reverse side; and from the formidable appearance of the furnace, I think it will require most of my time.

Monday, November 5.—I've been very much on the job all day. I expected to work only seven hours a day, which is to give me an income of $35 a month, with expenses for board and room of about $24, but until things get settled I'll probably have to work nearer seventeen.

My principal employment has been the carrying of countless bed-springs, iron bedsteads and mattresses from their purely decorative position in the main hall to the various living-rooms on the second floor, where they may be useful as well as ornamental. This day's work has given me an insight into the true nature of bed-springs which I probably would never have acquired otherwise.

Wednesday, November 7.—This morning the housekeeper casually asked me whether I was accustomed to the use of tools; there was a set of shelves to be made for the kitchen, she said. The thought of more bed-springs exaggerated my real ability scarcely to distinguish between saw and hammer and their uses into quite respectable craftsmanship, and so I was started at the shelves.

After several trials I was able to saw a twelve-inch board very nearly straight across, and in the course of the afternoon I produced a set of shelves which really gave me some pride. I discovered, however, upon attempting to put them in that I had miscalculated in the measurements to such an extent that they wouldn't fit in the place for which they had been intended. But by knocking them to pieces again and sawing off the boards, I got them into place a little before dark. I trust no carpenter will ever have occasion to look at them.

This evening I played billiards with the Columbia instructor, and there was a dance late in the evening. The instructor and I danced with the two maids who were imported today.

Tuesday, November 20.—This is a mighty pleasant place some ways. Take the evenings when I am not working.

From the third-storey gallery one looks down through the jungle of palm and rubber trees to the leaping flames of the great fireplace. It has an appealing, exotic charm.

Once I saw the shadow of a palm tree cast above the niche at the end of the patio, where stood a Venus of Milo, a glory in the moonlight. They have talked of dedicating the four sides of the fireplace to science, philosophy or politics, the arts —and loafing. In reality it is all dedicated to the last, and to business.

The fire-bed is like a large brazier, hung from four pillars which support the chimney. On one side sit three of us, the Loafers' Club, congratulating ourselves on knowing the science of contentedly doing nothing, lolling in our big wicker chairs and staring into the fire. On another side, even until 11, sits the tireless housekeeper, talking purchases or adding accounts, or planning work.

On another side is perhaps the remains of an adjourned

mothers' meeting discussing soulfully whether the institutionalised children should be allowed to drink six or seven times a day. Loafing and business only. The arts and sciences are in their rooms, pinkling (Helicon term for typewriting) articles for the magazines, which they do in such quantities here that it is unsafe to criticise any popular writer lest that writer be some resident of the colony in *nom de plume*.

When all the diligent ones have gone to bed, when the lights have been turned out and the fire has almost died, the Loafers' Club still sits dreaming. A weird grey bat who inhabits the patio whirrs past and the moon gleams strangely through the big skylight over the court. A good place, say I, and redolent of dreams. But think of getting at that shoulder-and back-breaking ditch-digging again, first thing tomorrow! And seventeen million filthy rugs waiting to be beaten!

Wednesday, November 21.—During the beating of those rugs this afternoon a fine young forest fire sprang up, and Irish Mike, the Columbia instructor, the veteran of the Civil War, and I went out to fight it with brooms and gunny-sacks.

Real pioneering, this. Forest fires are a danger here, for there is a walk from the Hall to the Palisades of a mile and a half through virgin woods. From the Palisades there is a glorious view of the Hudson.

At night the lights of upper New York look like the lights in stage scenery. Also, it is worth living and janiting for to be able to stand at the dining-room window beside a man of the finest sympathies and watch the rich sunset across the sweep of valley to the Jersey hills.

There are rugs to beat instead of carpets, because simplification is one theory here. They use paper napkins, for example.

Saturday, November 24.—My introduction to the furnace occurred today. Mike, who officiates in capacity of attendant at present and whom the wealthy Providence wholesaler and I are expected to replace, served as introducer.

74

He kindly allowed me to clean the thing as a sort of starter.

Today a new system was inaugurated with me. I'm to work whenever called upon—that is to say, be sort of continually on the job, with such leisure as comes between.

I don't like this arrangement. Think of being in the middle of a gentle lyric and having to go to hitch up Dobbin. This morning I was called to build a grate fire in the middle of an octave on 'Faustus'. Beastly bore.

Also I hear rumours that the management, which consists of the housekeeper and the wealthy wholesaler, who displays abilities too signal for a plain janitor, thinks my arrangement with them as to remuneration too much my way. They got a boy today who works all day (about twelve hours usually) for his board and $10 a month. As I work only seven hours and am rather less handy than the boy, it will be readily seen that I am a bad investment. The rumour comes pretty straight, too.

Wednesday, November 28.—Cook left today. Laundress, who has been elected one of the board of directors, has been transferred to kitchen, and two regular washerwomen, one coloured, imported to take care of laundry. More knocks at social idea. Cook took her M.A. to Newark for a teacher's job, I understand. I feel almost like a lone survivor.

Another maid imported today, and a man named O'Grady, to assist in kitchen. Also another boy to do about the work I've been doing, apparently. More interesting.

Man imported last night to help with furnace left very suddenly this morning before breakfast. He merely asked me to tell the superintendent of buildings that he feared he couldn't fit into the place.

Mr. Sinclair took out his long unused axe today and chopped down a tree and a half while he interviewed a *Sun* reporter. The *Sun* reporter will probably write about it in his article.

P.S.—Later—The reporter wrote a lot about it in his article.

Friday, November 30.—Here's where I get through. While

I was in the Columbia instructor's room this evening, after banking the furnace fire for the night, telling him that the extreme manualness of the labour is too much for me, there came an uproar from below. Voices called my name, and yelled "Where's Mike?" anxiously.

Saturday, December 1.—Quit. Left for a visit in New Haven.

Sunday, December 2.—In New Haven. It's pleasant to be among class-mates, instead of being of the mass for a while. Took particular pains to patronise my old dormitory sweep— a mere janitor! He seemed not to recognise me as of his craft.

New York tomorrow. Though I can't janit properly, and though I received only $6 wages above my expenses for a month's work, yet a taste for real life has been awakening. Manual work has been hard, yet good for me. It has been a joy to live among real men and women, not schoolboys.

Taking it by and large, where else than at Helicon Hall could I have learned so many new things every minute; or of how little worth I am in manual labour, seen so many novel yet vital things and have met in intimacy and equality so many thoroughly worth-while people?

BREAKING INTO PRINT

From *The Colophon,* a periodical dedicated to fine printing, book-making and the interests of connoisseurs and collectors. Published in No. II of the New Series in the Winter of 1937.

¶ *This article covers the continuity and details of Mr. Lewis's writing career more completely than other sketches available.*
Lewis was the least reticent of men in conversation about

himself, other people or anything that interested him, but he exhausted his own personal experiences so quickly, so intensely, that later he rarely found them as interesting to talk about as ideas, events, people. Small talk drove him to maniacal fury and one suspects that in his mind personal reminiscences came under the head of small talk.

It is interesting to note that Mr. Lewis here credits to Mary Heaton Vorse a formula for successful writing which for many years had been ascribed to him. It is: 'The art of writing is the art of applying the seat of the pants to the seat of the chair.'

ONE OF THE MOST CURIOUS QUESTIONS ABOUT A WRITER, AND ONE least often answered in biographies, is why he ever became a writer at all; why, instead of the active and friendly career of a doctor or a revolutionist or an engineer or an actor or an aviator (stage-driver it would have been in my early day), he should choose to sit alone, year after year, making up fables or commenting on what other and livelier citizens actually do. There is no problem about it when the writer's family circle is 'artistic'—as with Hugh Walpole, collateral descendant of the great Horace and son of a brilliant bishop. He goes into his father's business somewhat as the grocer's son takes in his turn to the appalling existence of handing ketchup and cornstarch across a counter all day long. But how the devil did a Wells, a Bennett, a Howells, a Whitman ever, in their dreary middle-class boyhood homes, happen on writing as a desirable thing to do?

And how did a Harry Sinclair Lewis, son of an average doctor in a Mid-Western prairie village who never—but never! —heard at table any conversation except "Is Mrs. Harmon feeling any better?" and "Butter's gone up again" and "Mrs. Whipple told me that Mrs. Simonton told her that the Kellses have got a cousin from Minneapolis staying with them"—a youth who till he was ready to enter university had never seen any professional writer except the local country editors—how came it that at eleven he had already decided to become a short-story writer (an ambition, incidentally, that he never adequately carried out), and that at fourteen he sent off to *Harper's Magazine* what he believed to be a poem?

A good many psychologists have considered that in such a case the patient has probably by literary exhibitionism been trying to get even with his school-mates who could outfight, outswim, outlove, and in general outdo him. Of me that explanation must have been partly true, but only partly, because while I was a mediocre sportsman in Boytown, I was neither a cripple nor a Sensitive Soul. With this temptation to artistic revenge was probably combined the fact that my stepmother (since my father remarried when I was six, she was psychically my own mother) read to me more than was the village custom. And my father, though he never spoke of them, did have books in the house, and did respect them, as one who had been a school-teacher before he went to medical school.

Anyway, cause or not, there was, at eleven or earlier, the itch for scribbling. I must have been about ten when I regularly wrote a newspaper with the most strictly limited clientèle in the world—myself. It had 'departments', with not only a by-line but a portrait of the department editor. And at fifteen or so I had a vacation-time job on the Sauk Centre *Herald,* setting type, running a hand-press, and writing items (usually ending "A good time was voted by all") at the combined salary of nothing at all. Toward the end of summer, when I asked for a rise, I was fired on the reasonable grounds that I wasn't worth what I had been getting. But I first had, that summer (perhaps in 1899 or 1900), the ecstasy of thus Breaking into Print.

By the time I had wriggled doubtfully into Yale, the itch was beyond prophylaxis. To writing, then, I devoted more eagerness than to any study, any sport, and on the *Yale Literary Magazine* and the *Yale Courant* I showered long medieval poems, with (O God!) ladies clad in white samite, mystic, won-der-ful; tales about Minnesota Swedes; and even two lyrics in what must have been terrible German. Perhaps half of them were accepted. The *Lit* was solemn, awesome, grammatical, traditional, and completely useless as a workshop; the *Courant* was frivolous, humble, and of the greatest use. . . . There was also a class in short-story writing in which the teacher, later author of a couple of fifth-rate novels, might have been pretty harmful if he had only been brighter.

During Yale I had my first acceptance by a real magazine—and it was critical, slightly scandalous, and, I can now see, inclined to make any number of worthy persons uncomfortable. It was the time when Katherine Cecil Thurston's *The Masquerader* was the book of the hour, receiving as much quivering adulation as now lays itself before *Gone with the Wind*. At that time (end of my Sophomore year, I remember) I happened on an old novel, *The Premier and the Painter,* by Israel Zangwill but published under a pseudonym, and this tale was in general scheme and a good many separate scenes precisely like *The Masquerader.* I reported this in an article published in the now perished *The Critic*. . . . And that was the first of the many happy times that I have been damned, been put in my place, by the New York editorial writers.

My next adventure in what is termed 'letters' was even more dubious. Having a natural distaste for children and an inability to communicate with them which has persisted to this day, I naturally took to writing 'children's verse', of which a litter appeared in the women's magazines. As I remember these finger exercises, compared with them A. A. Milne's pranks are Miltonic. And it was during college or just afterwards that I sold my first short story—to a California magazine called *The Blue Mule,* and for the very satisfactory price of seven dollars. Commercially, at least, I had come on an impressive way since reportage on the Sauk Centre *Herald.*

But all through college, with all this nonsense about Guinevere and Launcelot (a dumb hero if ever there was one), about the Little Ones and the gas-stove that was really a beastie, I was trying to try to plan a serious, a respectable novel. It was to be called *The Children's Children,* and it was an early guess at the four-generation novel that would, years later, with my having nothing at all to do with it, become only too ponderously plentiful. In my scheme, each generation was to revolt against the earlier, and move—from New Haven to Minnesota to California and then (in this I did a little anticipate a paradoxical migratory movement which then had only begun) rebound against the wall of the Pacific Ocean and back East again. I doubt if I ever wrote so much as ten pages of this opus, but out of planning it, seeing its distressing problems, I probably got more sense of writing than in all my spawn of scribbling for the magazines.

So out of college, out West as secretary to Grace Macgowan Cook—William Rose Benét and I shared a shack in Carmel when it was only a clearing among the pines—back East to work in a publishing-house, and, all the years from 1908 to 1914, trying to write my first actually completed novel, *Our Mr. Wrenn. Main Street,* which is always put down as my first book, happens to have been my seventh.

Wrenn, published in 1914, was a fair piece of light fiction; its soundest virtue that it did have an authentic sympathy with a very little Little Man; a New York clerkling, lonely and timid, who longed to 'see the world', as we used to say in those days before the world became suicidal and dishevelled and generally not worth seeing. He inherited a fortune of a few hundred dollars; he started off world-seeing by cattle-boat to Liverpool and on foot through England; he became as retchingly home-sick as I had been on just the same sort of trip after Freshman year in college; and he wisely returned to clerkship and littleness.

The book sold well enough—perhaps 3,000 copies—and even had two or three cordial reviews. That, naturally, was enough to make the disease chronic and incurable.

So 1920, and *Main Street* and the damned photographs, interviews, invitations to lecture, nibbles (still resisted) from Hollywood, and all the rest of the clamour with which the world tries, inevitably, to keep a writer from his one job— which is writing. It has been a good job and, even when it has been rather sweaty and nerve-jangling, I have enjoyed it more than I would have enjoyed anything except pure research in a laboratory. Mind you, the writing itself has been as important to me as the product, and I have always been somewhat indifferent as to whether I have been working on a solemn novel or an impertinent paragraph for the *New Yorker*. I have never been a propagandist for anything, nor against anything save dullness. A good job—and not for gold would I recommend it as a career to anyone who cared a hoot for the rewards, for the praise, for the prizes, for the embarrassment of being recognised in the restaurants, or for anything at all save the secret pleasure of sitting in a frowsy dressing-gown before a typewriter, exulting in the small number of hours when the words (noble or ribald, it doesn't matter) come invigoratingly out in black on white, and the telephone doesn't ring, and lunch may go to the devil.

And as the recipe for writing, all writing, I remember no high-flown counsel but always and only Mary Heaton Vorse's jibe, delivered to a bunch of young and mostly incompetent hopefuls back in 1911: "The art of writing is the art of applying the seat of the pants to the seat of the chair." As for the others—let them go to Hollywood or to the 'studios' of the

N.B.C., and everything will be idealistic, and the literary caravan will march gaily on.

I'M AN OLD NEWSPAPERMAN MYSELF

From *Cosmopolitan*, April and May, 1947

¶ *An autobiographical memoir of great value written at the author's Massachusetts place, Thorvale Farm, near Williamstown, in late 1946 or early '47.*

The carbon copy of the original typescript shows that it was written as a three-part piece. Mr. Lewis's own sub-title calls it a 'Series of Three Story Articles'. The parts bore the following titles:

> *I: Harry, the Demon Reporter*
> *II: You Meet Such Interesting People*
> *III: You Get Around so Much*

Here will be found the amusing account of the author's journalistic career in which the established author draws himself as a typical character in a Sinclair Lewis novel. Even more interesting is the light thrown upon the author's childhood.

But no matter how much ridicule he may heap upon his early literary efforts, there was at the time he was first breaking into print a sort of general agreement among his detractors as well as his friends that Hal Lewis was something special, was headed for greater things. We couldn't have put it in words then, but we all felt it about him as we did not feel it about the others in the group.

82

HARRY, THE DEMON REPORTER

TO THE UNFORTUNATE NEWSPAPERMEN OF THE LATE 1940S, WHO never have any headlines to write except 'Molotov Says No,' I want to give a vision of the golden era from 1890 to 1910, when news was news and reporters were hairy-chested heroes continuously engaged in chartering special locomotives, rescuing ladies from opium-dens—where, today, is there one single first-class horrible opium-den?—and attending fires which, in the good old days, were never smaller than Conflagrations. In fact, everyone is urged to return at once to 1899, a particularly shining year, since it was marked by my joining the staff of the Sauk Centre *Weekly Herald,* in June. It was also marked by my being fired from the same, in July, the first of the four times when I was thus picked out as a Man of Promise.

In 1899, if you had coursed through Stearns County, Minnesota, plaintively searching for young Mr. Sinclair Lewis, you would not have found him. To this day, indeed, in Stearns County, only a few learned school-teachers know him by that name. But there was, in Sauk Centre, a skinny, perpetually complaining small boy named 'Ole Doc Lewis's youngest boy, Harry', or, more intimately, 'Claude Lewis's red-headed kid brother'.

My older brother, Fred, was given to fishing and meditation, but Claude was a hustler, the leader of his gang into such improving pursuits as hooking mushmelons (not stealing muskmelons), communal study of very fine little books about Deadeye Dick, the Daring Desperado of Deadwood, and, on Hallowe'en, moving small buildings up on the porch of the Superintendent of Schools, who was known as the Prof. Claude is a surgeon now, and a natural leader still. I might be indifferent to what George Bernard Shaw, George Jean

Nathan, and George the Seventh might say, but for sixty years I have tried to impress my brother Claude.

It has been my chief object and my chief failure. Some day, I shall go to Hollywood and make a million dollars, and buy a house with a private night-club and a helicopter landing-field, solely to conquer his admiration. He will come out and look at it genially, and ask: "What direction does it face, and how many square feet of radiation has it, and what's the tax rate?" and I shall not know any of the answers, and shall again have failed.

When I was ten or so, Claude's gang, composed of old, seasoned scouts of fifteen, were masters of the woods, the lake, and the swimming-hole in Hoboken Crick (not Creek), up by the Arch. When I tried to swim there, getting no farther than bubbling and choking, Claude's more meticulous vandals tied my clothing in knots and painstakingly soaked it. When I climbed out of the mud and found my knotted costume, I rose to a precocious eloquence which received from Jim Hendryx, Claude's lieutenant, my only compliment: "Gee, Harry musta swallowed the dictionary!" He was generously indicating that I might become a Prof or a state representative or even a Minneapolis auctioneer. Poor Jim! He wanted to be a great trapper in Saskatchewan, but he is merely a novelist!

Despite such rebuffs and disasters, I insisted on tagging after the gang, and Claude had to assign none other than his commando-chief, Charley McCadden, expert purloiner of chickens and rutabeggies (*sic*), to regularly losing me. And he never failed, never.

Charley would confide to me: "Ah, gee, I'm sore on the gang! Lez just you and me go chase around."

Who would not ignore even the gang for the honour of intimacy with a man of the world like Charley, who could chin himself seventeen times and who had bummed on the blind baggage clear to Osakis, not less than fifteen miles away?

We strolled down to Main Street, engaged in sophisticated conversation about brakies on the G.N. and the catching of sunfish in Sauk Lake. As though I were his own age, not a mere child five years younger, Charley told me the inside secrets of local Society: that Horace Alden, the jeweller, was going to get up a new game called Tennis and had bought a striped red and black jacket for it; and that Prof Stanton had licked Bill Keller for sassing his teacher. We ambled along Main Street like the Prince of Wales and the Duke of Aosta on Piccadilly, and I felt that life was full of promise, and some day I would live in Minneapolis and be a reporter on the *Tribune* and own a sulky with red wheels.

In front of S. P. Hansen's Grocery, Charley said carelessly: "Jus' second, got to see uh," and darted in. I waited. I looked at the wonder of oranges and pineapples in the window, and tried to charm the store cat, a haughty and public cat. Five minutes, which to a small boy are five hours, half a day, must have passed before I suspected that Charley had ditched me— again.

He had. He had skipped out by the back door of S.P.'s and was fleeing like a highwayman to join Claude's gang at their rendezvous, and I went home heartbroken, to read Grote's *History of Greece,* a vast and horrible opus in many volumes with fine print, which I stoutly went on plodding through, not because I enjoyed the thing but because I hoped, vainly, thus to impress Claude, Jim Hendryx, and the other young intelligentsia of Sauk Centre.

When I saw Charley that evening, upon certain matters relative to playing prisoner's-base under the arc-light at Capser's corner, he demanded: "Where did you go safternoon? Old Mr. Norris, the deepo agent, ast me to help him lug a package and," piously, "I was glad to help the old gentleman, and when I hustled back to S.P.'s you was gone. Why, Harry, that ain't a nice way to treat a friend, to run out on him!"

If I wept, it was less in grief over my thoughtlessness than from relief that I had, after all, not been betrayed by Claude's top sergeant.

The next time was even easier for Old Sleuth McCadden. On a baking day of summer vacation, when the gang had decided to tramp out to Cedar Lake, to prepare those exquisite boyland baked potatoes, black outside and raw within, Charley whispered to me that they were really going up to Ashley Crick, and he and I would fool 'em—walk up the N.P. tracks and catch 'em!

In front of a large willow by the tracks, Charley screamed: "Lookit! Lookit the flying fox! There! Up in the tree!"

Certain, from my extensive reading of the *Youth's Companion* or *Yousumpanion,* that we were making a portentous discovery, because flying foxes were oftener to be found in Tasmania than on the Minnesota prairie, I rushed round and round the tree, encouraged by Charley's cries of "Up higher!" which grew more and more faint. When I glanced down, Charley just wasn't there, he wasn't anywhere in sight. Big Chief McCadden had vanished up a gulley like a Chippewa, and there was nothing to be seen but the twin rails of the N.P. on the gravel embankment, like two streaks of fire.

I had always failed to startle Claude's gang at skating, diving, shooting prairie chickens, or bobbing for fish through the ice, so I would have to overwhelm them with strictly high-class intellectual feats. All right, then, I'd become a reporter, and *then* they'd be sorry!

But it was another three or four summers before I coaxed Mr. Hendryx to give me a job on the Sauk Centre *Weekly Herald.* He was the father of Jim, and of the golden Myra with whom I was in love. Was it before or after Myra that I cherished an adoration for Nellie Hansen which was chilled when, trying to kiss her at a nice refined game of Post Office, I landed only on her nose, and she ran out giggling and told the whole party?

Mr. Hendryx was unusually literate for a country editor on the prairie in 1900, and he was not at all certain that Harry would be useful.

"What makes you think you can become a reporter?" he wanted to know, and when I explained, "Oh, I wrote a short story for Miss Cooper for the Friday exercise in our grade," he sniffed, "How are you on sweeping the floor?"

I quite understood that this would be one of my major literary achievements, and my mother would have been astonished by my enthusiasm over my gifts as a sweeper. I doubt if Mr. Hendryx was convinced, but he took me on—at a salary of nothing a week.

Those were the high days, and I could—anyway, I thought I could—look down on Charley McCadden and even Claude. I was a licensed reporter. I dashed up to Banker Lucius Kells at the G.N. Depot and, just as he got on the train for the Twin Cities, I craftily probed: "Are you thinking of taking a train for the Twin Cities?" Venerable old matrons of forty, who had never much noticed Claude's red-headed brother Harry, now called me up on their porches, bribed me (so early!) with cup cakes, and handed me the list of newly elected officers of the Kaffee-klatsch Klub. And once a new father gave me a cigar, which I took home to Claude, who said: "I don't want to see you with these poisonous things, Harry. You bring 'em right to me."

While I was investigating the secrets of society and big business, I was also learning type-setting. I have doubts now about my speed, but I could pick up a piece of type and wave my arm in a figure of eight as ritually as any tramp printer.

And, as a technical triumph, I did not write out my news items, but set them in type. You may see the young adventurer composing in metal such lyrics as:

"George O'Gara and Eddie Hansen was to the Cities last week they took in a theater show and while there they seen W. O. P. Hilsdale, Judge Barto, Doc DuBois, John McGibbon, sr. and several other of our esteemed fellow townsmen they had a good time and went to a chop sooey restaurant but when interviewed on return they said they was real pleased to be back home there is no place like Sauk Centre. St. Paul is a lovely metropolis and etc. to make a visit to but they would not take it as a gift, give me Sauk Centre to live in every time they said."

Now I submit that this was a ringing report, replete with ascertained fact, poetic emotion and human motives, but Mr. Hendryx so blue-pencilled it on the proof that I had to re-set the whole thing. I knew that school-teachers were fanatics about commas and "they was", but you could not expect a man to be so fussy when he was busy giving the world his Message and trying to keep ink off his blouse.

With my very first item, Mr. Hendryx shocked me. I had feverishly written something like this:

"Mrs. Pike entertained the ladies of the Congregational Church last Thursday afternoon. Delicious cocoa and doughnuts were served and a good time was reported by all."

"Harry," sniffed Mr. Hendryx, "did you specifically inquire of each lady incriminated whether she had a good time?"

"Huh?"

"How many of the ladies there present *did* you ask whether they had a good time?"

"Well, gee, I guess I didn't ask any of 'em."

"Yet you so far gamble with the truth as to state, in this moral family gazette, that each of them asseverated that she had a good time—on cocoa!"

"Well, gee, that's just the way they write—even in the *Herald!*"

"Only in the country correspondence, which I endeavour never to correct. My son, the first rule of writing is that if you have always seen a statement made in a certain way, that is itself a reason for not saying it that way." He seized his calamitous blue pencil; he drained out all of my heart's blood after "delicious cocoa and doughnuts were served". He snapped: "I'll bet they weren't so delicious, at that," and slammed the copy on the hook, whence it would be taken by the regular printer, a man who was always glancing at me and puzzling me by unexplained laughter.

With singulars and plurals tamed, I became the romantic reporter, solving mysteries, and now it was I who was followed by Charley McCadden! Ah, that triumph of the great creative brain over such vulgar gifts as whistling between your teeth! With Charley as my Dr. Watson, I pushed boldly into the Menace of the Signal Lights at Stabler's Grove.

From my bedroom I noted lights appearing and vanishing in a regular pattern in the cottonwood grove just this side of Indian Mound, two miles away across lake and prairie. Lights! Popping out and vanishing! In a code! Way late at night—after nine o'clock! This was an era too early for German spies, too late for organised horse-thieves, but after reasonable and profound thinking, I was certain that something criminal was afoot, and I gravely permitted my one-time superior officer, Charley, to have a look.

We stood up there in my room, in the summer dusk, and, sure enough, there was the terrifying signal light—flash, dark, flash, dark, flash.

"What would you think," I said calmly to Charley, in my office at Scotland Yard, "if I told you that operating out there, signalling their confederates, are the worst gang of

D*

international counterfeiters in all of Stearns County? Do you want to join me in detecting them?"

Ye-es, *maybe* he would, quaked Charley.

It was comforting to have behind me a man with the physical prowess of Sergeant-Major McCadden, who would even pick up garter snakes. I was not sure just what counterfeiters do, when they get detected. They might yell at you very loud, or even slap you, but the Sergeant-Major would yell right back—I hoped.

Now, naturally, you could capture criminals only by night. Who ever heard of closing in on Professor Moriarty on a prairie afternoon, with meadow-larks piping? But at Doc Lewis's you went to bed before nine-thirty. How would Sherlock Holmes have liked it if, when he had just put on a dress suit, a mask, and a crimson-lined opera cloak, to go out and rescue the King of Bohemia, Old Dr. Lewis had said to him: "Sherry, it's ten minutes after nine and time to get ready to go up to bed, and no arguing now"?

But came a night when the Doctor was out on a case and Mother spending a hectic evening at the Eastern Star Membership Committee meeting. Charley and I fled out to Stabler's Grove. We hooked a ride on a farm wagon, slipped off at the edge of the cottonwoods—and Colonel Lewis suddenly was scared to death.

"Sssssssuppose they catch us catchin' 'em, Charley?"

"Wwwwwwwwe'll run like the devil!" said that practical man.

We crawled a perilous distance, at least ten feet, among the cottonwood trunks to a space from which we could see the farmyard. It was so disastrously still, as we crouched, that we could hear all those terrifying noises that do not exist. From the farm-house kitchen a low light came with a calm and matter-of-fact steadiness that was the more threatening. What was the gang doing in there? Carving out lawless gold eagles with their jack-knives? . . . Watching us through spy-glasses?

Then, "Look!" hissed Charley. Critics like F.P.A. sneer that you cannot hiss a word with no S's in it. Charley did. He hissed it. And not till then had I perceived that one trouble with dangerous adventure is that sometimes there is danger in it.

Out of the house came the familiar Mr. Stabler, carrying a lantern. He headed for the barn. As he walked, the trees in the barnyard cut off the light of his lantern in a clear pattern of flash, dark, flash, dark, flash.

Sergeant McCadden remarked bitterly: "Counterfeiters! Charley Bennett always did say you were the dumbest boy in the West End of town! Signalling! Look what Mr. Stabler's doing now!"

So far as I could see, Mr. Stabler was merely patting a horse, but I trembled, "H-how d'you mean, Charley?"

But Charley was not there, he just wasn't there at all, and I walked home alone through a darkness filled with counterfeiters, spooks, grizzly bears, and two-toed sloths.

Next morning, in the *Herald* office, Mr. Hendryx inquired: "Did you get any news about the Eastern Star membership from your mother this morning?"

"Gee, I forgot to ask her."

"That's all right. That's perfectly all right. Let me see, Harry. How much am I paying you now?"

Wild expectations leaped in young hopeful. "Why, just now, you're paying me nothing a week."

"Well, my boy, I'm afraid you aren't worth that much. You're fired, and I hope this will be only the first of many such journalistic triumphs."

It was.

YOU MEET SUCH INTERESTING PEOPLE

MY SECOND NEWSPAPER JOB WAS ON THE OTHER WEEKLY IN THE fair city of Sauk Centre, Minnesota, the next summer vacation, and my rise in salary was one of the largest in journalistic history—three hundred infinities per cent. Match that, Horace Greeley! That is, I rose from nothing a week to three dollars a week, for merely sweeping, reporting, setting type, running the hand-press, and rushing the growler, and if I was overpaid by perhaps one hundred infinities, yet I was an earnest scribe (sure, I said 'scribe') who had learned to worry less about libel than about getting the middle initials of all subscribers right whenever we mentioned them—which was once a week or so.

The name of the paper was the Sauk Centre *Weekly Avalanche.*

Then, when I went East to college, I toyed . . . one evening a week on the New Haven *Journal and Courier,* a sheet remarkable for the fact that the editors really liked reporters, even when they were young gentlemen from Yale who piped to Art Sloan, the telegraph editor: "I realise it's just my good luck that I'm studying Homer, while you fellows never had a chance to get educated. Eh?"

" 'Eh,' Greek particle derived through Sanskrit from the primitive Iranian," said Art gravely.

"Huh?" said the bewildered young gent.

My first full-dress newspaper job was on the Waterloo, Iowa, *Courier,* and it demonstrated the financial value of a university education. For filling only three separate jobs at the same time—editorial writer, telegraph editor, and proofreader—I received eighteen dollars a week, which is six dollars per job. . . . That is, I received it till I was fired.

In my editorials I was expected to deal chiefly with local

Iowa politics. Now I sat ready to inform the citizens of
Waterloo about the ethnological variations between Nigeria
and Uganda or the day-by-day proceedings of the Council of
Trent, but I did not know that the Hon. Member from
Cattarincktus County was a fine judge of corn and a candi-
date for the Supreme Bench and a low dog in general, and
without such knowledge my editorials were worthless. Papers
in Davenport and Mason City began to refer to the Immigrant
Editor of Waterloo, and my Boss stared at me with growing
speculation.

I began to make not-very-difficult puns about Waterloo, and
to save eight dollars a week out of my eighteen. If I could
last ten weeks, I would have enough to take me to New York,
where the managing editors would all be waiting for me at
the Grand Central. I dined at a bakery where, with nice stale
rolls, you could get by for fifteen cents, and for romantic
recreation I walked the evening streets. Sometimes I walked
north, out on the prairie, and then, for variation, I walked
south—out on the prairie, and went back to my furnished
room, to sleep on a granolithic bed. Once I recklessly ventured
into a Recreation Park, just throwing twenty cents into the
air, and a very nice-looking young woman looked at me
smilingly—and I fled. I could see that young Delilah getting me to spend twenty cents more just as though it were
water.

Oh, those rare mad hours of the young poet, when you
roister all night long!

To make sure that I would be a rapidly climbing failure, I
got into a row with the composing-room. As dramatic critic
(that was my fourth job, but I don't think I was paid for it)
I covered the one musical show that came to town that
summer, and in my review, a pretty high and serious piece
of work, I used the word 'rococo'. The foreman of the
chapel came to me in my capacity as proof-reader, pointed

out that odd collection of O's surrounded by consonants, and grumbled: "There's no such a word."

The proof-reader, the editorial writer and the telegraph editor, all of them looked at him intolerantly and, with a nice combination of Yale and Sauk Centre in their communal voice, they snarled: "And have you taken the trouble to look it up in the dictionary?" The "my good man" was implied.

No, he hadn't. But from then on I was in the position of a second-lieutenant who has been sniffy to the sergeant who runs the colonel.

On Thursday morning of my tenth week, the Boss came in cheerily with: "Well, he's just wired me—your successor. He'll be on the train in half an hour, so you get through this evening. But," in a debauch of generosity, "I'll pay you right through to Friday evening!"

That was the first I had heard of my successor and of being more succeeded than success, but with the eighty dollars, minus two or three, that I had saved, I was on the train for Chicago on Friday morning. Ahead were New York and glory—quite a way ahead. I had a suitcase containing three extra shirts, the extra pair of trousers, and my Roget's *Thesaurus*.

There is nothing to these voluptuous Pullmans. You see a lot more of Ohio scenery when you ride the day-coach from Iowa to New York, and when you look at Ohio scenery, you can forget that out of four newspaper positions so far, you have been fired from two.

What jobs youngsters do get, and how lucky they are for them! If I had been President of the First National, I would never, when the eighty-minus dollars were about gone in New York, have become Night Agent of the Joint Application Bureau of the Charity Organisation Society and the Association for the Improvement of the Condition of the Poor. (Their condition still seems pretty unimproved, for all my efforts.)

94

That welter of uplift words meant that I sat at a desk from early evening to midnight, while ingratiating hoboes, to whom worthy citizens had given little cards with the address of the Bureau instead of giving them a quarter which might have been wasted on strong drink, came in and told me glorious lies about beachcombing in Samoa and construction gangs in the Raton Pass. They breathed on me—and that was as good as a two-day drunk—and begged: "Now, Mister, I ain't no panhandler, so don't send me to no MooniCIPal Lodging House tonight—they steam your close—grrr!" I then fulfilled my mission towards Society by giving them a ticket to the Municipal Lodging House, to which they could have gone, free, without me.

I seemed to be specialising in holding more than one job at once, and nearly starving on the combined honoraria. At the noble J.A.B.C.O.S.A.I.C.P. I got about two dollars per letter per week. I was not only night agent, but by day I was an 'investigator'. Applicants for more extensive relief gave us the name of a former employer, and I went down there—usually it was a loft on West Broadway or Bayard Street or some other thoroughfare you never heard of—and asked about him. If the patient really had worked there and had never shot any pussy-cats or stolen the fixtures, we gave him enough relief so that he did not starve immediately, not for several more days.

The two jobs together brought me seventy-five dollars a month from the J.A.B. ETC., plus whatever I could knock down on the swindle sheet. I did fairly well at that. I never dreamed of taking anything so gaudy as a street-car; I charged up an entire ten cents of car fare, but actually I walked, even if it was over to Brooklyn. By such sheer embezzlement—for which I can probably still be indicted, and the memory of which still keeps me from being too superior towards what society considers 'bad people'—I managed on some days to add as much as thirty beautiful, beautiful cents to my income, and on those days I had lunch.

I shall now inform the J. ETC. that if I had not been on the philanthropic side of the charity desk, I might have been on the wrong side, begging the night agent not to send me to the MooniCIPal Lodging House.

I was rescued by two women writers, sisters and collaborators, Grace Macgowan Cook and Alice Macgowan, bless their souls, who wired me from Carmel, California, asking whether I would care to consider going out as their secretary.

Care? Consider? It must have taken me all of ten hours to resign from the charity-automat, pack my treasures—I now had *two* books and *two* extra pairs of trousers—and get on the train for California. Day-coach, naturally, and perhaps six nights to San Francisco, but you slept half of every hour, round the clock, and popped out at every station, to tramp the platform and explain to the emigrant farmers you had met on the train: "I'm from New York—I'm a newspaper reporter—but I like to run out to California every now and then."

Carmel-by-the-Sea, loafing beside its crescent bay, was then the nearest to a young writer's paradise that I have ever seen. It has now become jammed with movie theatres, garages, playwrights, glass brick, surrealists, and people so rich that they own original paintings—well, pretty original. But in 1908 it was a drift of redwood bungalows lost among the pines. We were all poor as well as poetic. There was only one automobile in town, and the old lady who owned it apologetically offered us rides, but mostly we walked—walked the four miles to Monterey and lugged back a hamburg steak and a gallon of muscatel, walked down the coast to a nest of rocks and picnicked with the breakers for orchestra. We wore corduroy and sweaters and sneakers and nothing much else. But we had one treasure that no Hollywood star, very few famous writers, can afford: we had leisure.

If you make three thousand dollars a week, naturally you can't afford to take a fortnight off, because it would cost you six thousand dollars. Outrageous! But among our hobohemians at Carmel, it would not have cost even the richest of us more than a hundred dollars for two weeks' freedom, and for a lot of our young geniuses the budget would have been nearer twenty. So we could afford to do exactly what we wanted to, which, among the eucalyptus, the poppies, the rafts of kelp agitated by the pale green-glass breakers, the still hollows in the pines, was usually doing nothing 'useful' whatever.

William Rose Benét came down from Benicia, California, where his great father was commandant of the Arsenal, and Bill and I shared a cottage for which we paid fifteen dollars a month, furnished. We washed our own clothes—that is, except when we just went in swimming in them, and sensibly called that enough—and we did our own cooking. As, between us, we knew how to make only boiled eggs, fried eggs, and something that for convenience we called coffee, we decided that it wasn't good for young poets to eat too much, and we depended on the almost daily picnics given by Grace and Alice, at which we filled up on a twenty-four-hour supply of abalone and Spanish beans.

My job as secretary left me adequate leisure and I kept on writing and, I may tell you, not without success. For in a little less than six months I produced a very fine joke, which was accepted by *Puck,* and paid for! in money! and I composed a wonderful story which . . . Well, it never did exactly get printed, ever, anywhere, but it had an excellent title: 'Citizen of the Mirage.'

And I was, for a time, a citizen in a Californian mirage. It was probably the most sensible time of my life. If I regret anything, it is that for only a couple of years was I a patently useless, irregular, undependable young man, wandering and getting fired, earning almost nothing and seeing almost everything. Then I became a fairly responsible young editor in New York and acquired grim habits of industry and punctuality, and what a mistake that was! If I had had a few more drops of the tramp in me, like Hemingway or Poe, I might have become a great writer instead of a careful chronicler of domestic rows.

The best night of my six months in Arcady was when in a carry-all—yes, with a fringed top—a dozen of us drove miles down the coast and, in the light of a vast bonfire shining out on tides that came straight from China, George Sterling, looking a little like Dante and a good deal like François Villon, challenged the ocean roar by singing Kipling's 'The Last Chantey', and then we all slept on the cliff, among the poppies.

The high literary point was watching Jack London read Henry James for the first time.

I hand this study on to the professors who deal with a mystery called Artistic Influences. Jack had quit being a galloping adventurer and had become a country gent, devoted to bridge-playing and pig-breeding. He used to stay with the Sterlings at Carmel, and though the great man was extremely friendly to the skinny, the red-headed, the practically anonymous secretary, it bothered that secretary to find that Jack seemed content now to play bridge all afternoon, all evening.

At a neighbouring cabin Jack picked up James's *The Wings of the Dove* and, standing there, short, burly, in soft shirt and black tie, the Master read aloud in a bewildered way while Henry James's sliding, slithering, glittering verbiage unwound itself on and on. Jack banged the book down and wailed: "Do any of you know what all this junk is about?"

It was the clash between Main Street and Beacon Street that is eternal in American culture.

With all the pines and tamales and mountain snow, I was not getting on with my newspaper career. Why, I hadn't been really fired for almost a year now, and while one joke in six months was a nice clean output, it lacked box-office promise. So I went to San Francisco to hunt a job, and I did get on with the newspaper career and I did get fired—twice—and so I was a normal and promising young reporter again.

As we shall see.

YOU GET AROUND SO MUCH

NOW, AS AN HONEST MASSACHUSETTS FARMER, I AM AMAZED TO see how much embezzlement, chicanery, incompetence, and general anti-social behaviour is revealed, as I study the career of Harry, the Demon Reporter. It makes me suspicious of all the standard biographies, which never admit such crimes.

Certainly George Sterling, the poet, was guilty at least of perjury and excessive imagination when he told Joe Noel, sports writer on the San Francisco *Evening Bulletin,* to let his city editor in on the secret that there was a wonderful young reporter and magazine writer named Mr. Lewis around those parts, that he seemed to like California almost as well as his native New York (Fifth Avenue), and might conceivably be persuaded to stay here. An interview between Mr. Lewis and that innocent city editor was arranged with the pomp of a royal wedding.

I had planned to Accept the Position at thirty a week— which was vastly higher than my value in the labour market had ever been—but as I walked into the editor's office, Joe mysteriously handed me a slip reading: 'Hit him for 35.'

Hit? Me, the international journalist? I did nothing so

vulgar as to hit. I permitted the editor to know that I was a Yale man and had had things published in these magazines, and I knew New York like the inside of my hat (about which current hat, which I had left outside, the less that was said, the better). But I liked his nice little city, and I would be willing to stay around a while at—should we say forty or fifty a week?—oh, what did it matter—make it thirty-five—expenses so much less in these smaller towns.

So I tilted back in my chair and looked casually down on Market Street.

Indeed it didn't matter at all, except that if I didn't get the thirty-five (and I would have listened happily to an offer of thirteen-fifty) I would have stopped eating, and sleeping under cover.

He was a hard-boiled city editor and as credulous as all hard-boiled people, who are too busy admiring their own hard-boiledness to study other people. I got the job.

If it were 1909 again and I were that editor, I would either fire this Lewis the first week, or create a special department for him in the Saturday Supplement, and let him write his fool imaginative head off, and raise him and raise him—perhaps to thirty-seven-fifty in ten or twelve years. Lewis was good at 'human-interest stories', but he never saw the news or heard the news or brought in the news, and if the governor had shot the mayor at the ferry house and Lewis had been the only reporter there, he would have come sunnily trotting into the office with a lovely piece about Sunset Over the Golden Gate. Again does his real career make me suspect all the published Lives, especially the autobiographies, and when I read the triumphant pomposities of prime ministers and bishops and department-store barons, I suspect that along with their youthful twenty-six hours a day of industry and probity, they must have had endearing times of being ornery and idiotic.

This Lewis discovered in San Francisco a den, plagiarised from Robert Louis Stevenson, where the hoboes drank only wine, all evening long, wine at five cents a can, and they were gently crazy, and in a room where shadows slid along the huge wooden tables they told one another stories from the South Seas or sang together as languidly as the Lotos Eaters. But that story the editor would not let our young wonder hero write. Instead the editor told him that there were murmurings of financial scandal about a large orphan asylum, and would he kindly hustle out and get the dirt?

I found that the asylum was surrounded by a brutally high red-brick wall. A real reporter would presumably have climbed the wall at midnight, wriggled across the courtyard, anæsthetised the night watchman, removed the ledgers from the safe, and have had a front-page story for next afternoon's papers. But it pains me to say that I walked twice clear round that uncommunicative wall and just could not get any spiritual urge to shin over it. Nor was I properly resolved to ring at the unfriendly gate and ask the watchman: "Is the head of this institution a crook, and have you any proofs handy?" I am not boasting of this, mind you; I am sore lamenting it; but I went home to my boarding-house (and I want to inform my landlord now, thirty-eight years later, that I *did* know he sneaked in and used my typewriter) and wrote a very nice poem about Helen's eyebrows or some equally newsy topic.

Oh, valiant and ingenious youth! Was it William Pitt who was prime minister at twenty-three—and was it twenty-three and was it prime minister or president of the University of Chicago?

Not all of my epoch-making career by the Pacific had to do with odes to eyebrows. We were an afternoon paper, and I was in the office by 8 a.m., writing headlines. I never did master the composition of headlines, an art even more deft and passionate than the old-time writing of epitaphs but highly resembling it, for are not headlines little tombstones for items of news that are now dead and frequently decayed? But still, I could manage a few curious masterpieces, such as:

English Sir Says S.F.
Be Biggest U.S. Burg

From ten to four, we were supposed to go out and ask embarrassing questions of people who much preferred to be let alone, and then, in the evening, we really got to work. An agitated election was coming, and every evening I had to report three or four oratorical debauches.

The chief figure in the election was a gentleman known to spellbinders as 'P. Haitch McCarthy, standard-bearer of th' City'n'County of San Francisco'. I ineffaceably remember his golden smile, his beautiful moustache, and the heartiness with which he greeted the reporters, "Well, boys, God bless you," and it is characteristic of American politics, in which we have always been so much more ardent about personalities than about real principles, that the only things I now forget about P. Haitch are what he stood for, and whether we were adoringly for him or belligerently against him, and whether he won or lost!

And that is how you write history. You collect the evidence of eye-witnesses who were right there when it happened and who remember exactly what kind of a fancy vest Dickens wore and forget only whether he liked Christmas and the little ones and benevolent fat gentlemen, or hated the whole lot of them and tried to get them abolished.

Such things as elections paled beside the Epic of the Vanishing Bell-boy and the Grateful Whaleback.

I was on the *Bulletin* hotel-beat at the time, engaged in persuading such distinguished visitors as English lecturers to state that, yes, San Francisco was larger than Los Angeles and more romantic than London. And on that beat I had an Adventure in Culture. We were told that a Chinese prince had just landed, and I skipped happily to his hotel to interview him. On the way I planned my story, which would obviously be very funny. He would be a fat and waddling prince, with comic moustachios and a long sabre, and he would say, "Me heapee biggee princee," and with the superiority of all the Sauk Centres and the New Havens to such ridiculous outlanders, I would tease him with clever questions.

I never did see that prince. At the door of his suite I was greeted by a slim Chinaman in morning coat, quite the suavest and coldest and best-spoken man I had ever met, with an Oxford accent and a Mayfair blankness, and he murmured: "It would be quite impossible for you to see His Highness, but I should be glad to answer any questions."

Questions? I don't think I had any, beyond the familiar "Huh?" It was a moment of revelation about the world, as swift and complete as Mr. Hendryx's explanation of why you don't write "a good time was reported by all".

But the bell-hop epic was more triumphant.

At a hotel which we shall call the Brown, there was an amiable assistant manager whom we might call Smith. Now I won't say that Mr. Smith ever tried to bribe me, but I did just happen to get around to the Brown very often at one o'clock, and Mr. Smith did just happen to think that the Brown would be honoured to entertain a distinguished literary man like me at lunch—no obligations. And if afterwards Mr. Smith introduced me to a charming man who was—he *said*—an explorer from Arabia or a renowned soil-chemist from Kansas, it would make an interesting essay for the readers of the *Bulletin*. Would it?

I enjoyed those lunches—three kinds of soup and four kinds

of dessert. At first, a salary of thirty-five a week had seemed magnificent, but I had now learned to eat regularly, and that devastating habit ruins more idealistic young men than love or liquor.

Breezed up to me in the refined Brown lobby, one fine day, this Smith, bountifully beaming, and said Smith: "I got a swell story for you—exclusive. Last winter we had an old lady from Connecticut staying here, terrible old crank, always complaining—what we call a Whaleback. But there was one bell-boy—he said she was so like his mother—he never got sore at her, he just used to laugh and do any errand she asked him, and evenings when he was off duty—and, mind you, she never tipped him one red cent—he'd sit and read to her, and all the other bell-hops laughed at him, he was such a sap. Well, she's just died, back East, and she's left this boy her entire fortune—seventy-five thousand dollars. How's that?"

"What's his name?"

"Who?"

"The bell-hop."

"Oh. His name? You mean you want to know the bell-hop's name? Can't you make . . . ? Well, they used to call him Robert."

"Last name?"

"Oh—uh—Johnson."

"Where is he? I want to ask him some questions."

"He's in the old lady's town in Connecticut, collecting the fortune. The eighty-five thousand."

"What town?"

"Medford."

"That's in Massachusetts."

"Oh, sure. I meant Massachusetts."

"Look. Make it twenty thousand and I'll run the story."

"Do you mean to say . . . ?"

"Twenty thousand!"

"Okay!"

Now the moral of this chronicle would be irretrievably bad, except that, as I wrote the story for the *Bulletin,* I made our Bobby Johnson so tender to his elders, so given to brushing his teeth and combing his hair and saving of electric lights and pieces of string, that he was a model for all future youth. Probably you can still see the influence of it, almost forty years later.

When the story was published—for once, uncut—the hotel-beat man on the *Chronicle* exclaimed, at the nearest bar: "Smith gave me that story before he did you and my city editor wouldn't let me use it. He said it sounded phony. Don't that show what dumb tyrants they put over us reporters?"

I had incautiously announced that Bobby Johnson was coming back this week, to go around with the twenty thousand and be oppressively kind to all the other bell-hops in town and teach them to save string and read to old ladies. Now the sob-squad lady on the *Bulletin* was no less a mistress of heart-throbs than Bessie Beattie, now famous for her hour on the radio. The city editor said: "I'll have Bessie interview the kid. We'll give him a big spread on Saturday, with photos."

"You better let me do it," I begged.

"You? You couldn't write a tender human story about a kid like that. Bessie will do it."

My brain-child! My own Little Lord Fauntleroy and string-saver and crusader against the life-sapping cigarette! I couldn't do his biography!

I did not explain why Bobby would not be coming home this week. I let Mr. Smith of the hotel do all his own lying. I turned to ways of nobility and exact truth which, as is well known, unlike many fiction-writers whom I could and in private do name, I have followed ever since.

Months later, when I was on the Associated Press—after I had been fired from the *Bulletin* and just before I was fired from the A.P., which was No. 4—Mr. Smith showed me a scrapbook full of press clippings about the Bell-hop and the Whaleback. I was again confused about the moral philosophy. This business simply did not go with the ethics I had learned from Spinoza and Horatio Alger, Junior. Many pure-minded vignettes had I written on suburban flower-shows, visiting swamis and the facts of wild-swan life which had never been read clear through even by the city editor, who tossed them into the waste-basket. But this atrocity, this betrayal, this maudlin waterworks about that blithering and non-existent young prig, Robert, had been read and fondly reprinted all over the world—all mentioning the hotel! The diabolic Mr. Smith let me see that it had appeared—sometimes with a favourable editorial—in every city in America, in Paris, London, Berlin, Rome, Pekin, Kandahar.

And I, the author of this revised and more pestilential Tiny Tim, had not only been fired but was ripe for being fired again. One happy Californian eve on the night desk of the A.P., my immediate boss—then a mild and scholarly indoor man given to the study of magic, but some time to be known as a galloping foreign correspondent, a peering man with thick glasses and the kindest heart, a man named Karl von Wiegand—muttered to me: "Do you know that the Coast Superintendent is planning to fire you tomorrow, because you just can't see a good news-story? You might beat him to it."

I walked languidly in on Charley Kloeber, the superintendent, next day, and drawled, in the grossest imitation of English novels: "My dear fellow, I do hope I shall not inconvenience your overworked little staff too much, but I really must sever my connection here. The literary standard is too shockingly low."

Charley was a Virginian, soft-voiced and soft-eyed and he

had played poker in Alaska and Lima and Helsinki. I had hoped that he would be furious at losing such a jewel, but he just looked mildly at me, and sighed: "Ah'd give a lot to know who told you ah was goin' to fire you!"

So I went back East to Occupy a Responsible Position, on a magazine called *The Volta Review*, a journal for teachers of the deaf, a subject of which I knew less than I did of radar, even though radar had not yet been invented. The salary was fifteen a week, but they could not hold me, could never hold the literary parent of the Edifying Bell-hop. In less than a year I was back in New York, as editor for a book-publishing house, and you may be sure I wasn't getting any miserable fifteen dollars a week—not at the age of twenty-five!

No, I was getting twelve-fifty a week.

So you can see how, without influence, solely by the exercise of my industry and genius, I had progressed not only socially but financially. In less than two years I had climbed from $35 a week on the *Bulletin* to $30 on the Associated Press to $15 on *The Volta Review* to $12.50 at the sedate and honourable firm of Frederick A. Stokes Company.

Ah, youth and glory!

I hope that you youngsters of the Mid-Century will have been moved by this chronicle of how masterful we all were in your fathers' day, to bustle out and emulate us. But humbly, boys, humbly!

EARLY PUBLISHING DAYS

¶ *Mr. Lewis understood better than most authors the intimate problems of publishing his books. Much of this knowledge derived from the fact of his having served a long stint in the profession, first with the Frederick A. Stokes Company and some years later with George H. Doran. Also, as noted elsewhere, he had worked on several magazines.*

This piece is included as a significant fragment of his early experience. It also provides a nostalgic portrait of all the young men who were winning their spurs in publishing nearly thirty years ago. So far as known, the complete article never appeared in print. A condensed version was published in the 'Doubleday Books News', a brochure, in 1947. It was written at Thorvale Farm, Williamstown, Massachusetts, and dated October 23, 1946.

This memoir will be of special interest to those who were part of the publishing scene of those early days, both for the names of those with whom publicity-man–editor Lewis associated and for its tribute to a group of indefatigable salesmen who have since become subject for legend. Too little tribute has been paid to that strange and temperamental genius, the publisher's book traveller. Lewis knew their prima-donna qualities and appreciated their position as indispensable envoys to The Trade.

OVER THIRTY YEARS AGO, BACK IN 1914 AND 1915, THERE WERE three young editors for publishers who used to meet at lunch at the aged Grand Hotel, and try to steal ideas from one another. There was the editor for Holt, who was going to stay with that firm for ever and become its president; the editor for Doubleday, whose liveliest interest was in magazine stories; the editor for George H. Doran—later a large, clear tributary of the rolling Mississippi flood of the new Doubleday —who had tried to be a writer of fiction and had given up that folly for ever and wistfully hoped some day to be George Doran's partner (in charge of author-lunching and London-trips).

The names of these three young men (well, along about thirty) were Alfred Harcourt, Harry Maule, and Sinclair Lewis, and all of us turned deftly from manuscript-reading to writing advertisements and jolly little publicity notes to the effect that Wratislaw Pallister-Wallow, the English detective-story manufacturer, was fond of cats and Brussels sprouts, which, in those days, was our notion of hysterical press-agentry.

There were no page-advertisements of single (and not very good) books; no book clubs; certainly no radio programmes on which authors disputed their rather doubtful right to live. In one quarter-page notice I would list twenty new books, each of them with no more descriptive text than: " 'Amusing story,' *N.Y. Herald.*" Sometimes I think that this was excellent; that the danger today is of too-much, too-commercial exploitation of books, to the end that they shall become almost as profitable and dreary as blue razor-blades and three-way cough cures. And I note that the 'historical novels' which we were so naïve as to produce then were certainly less offensive than the much touted treatises on immorals at the court of King Charles which today are solemnly published even by the worthiest firms.

But one thing in publishing today is vastly better: the hospitality to the young writer, even to him who as yet shows only unripened promise. In most firms, thirty years ago, such an aspirant would have been able to see only an eye-glassed iceberg who wanted to give him back to the office boy, but now, if he has completed so much as the dedication page and half the title, he is likely to be invited by the president of the firm himself to go out and enact a few scenes from *The Lost Week-End.*

In my day of publishing, a young author's suggestion that an advance would enable him to complete his half-finished novel would have been countered by dropping him out of the window—and some of our publishing houses were way, way up, three or four storeys up, in the twelve-storey skyscrapers of that era. Now, it is just as likely to be the publisher himself who suggests an advance—and how wrong he is, too, at times!

We were still, thirty years ago, letting ourselves be warmly mothered by Britain. A good author meant an English author, and there was something comic, to most publishers then, in the vanity of a youngster so bumptious as to think that a first-rate American author might be almost as good as a fifth-rate English author. Sound publishers then went twice a year to London, and came proudly back with the latest tea-and-lilacs romance of Mrs. Littleton Pagways (aunt of the vicar of Twit) and the new volume of Travels in Burma by General Sir Victor Llwellwyn, and never knew that in a college twenty miles away or a Greenwich Village flat a mile away or at a desk in his own office, thirty feet away, was an unknown boy or girl who was a neater and vastly more important writer than all save ten or fifteen of England's best.

If we lacked then some of these modernities, we did have in the pre-Anschluss Doran one thing that cannot be improved today: a selling staff that, without page ads or radio roars to back them, were a perfect Foreign Legion among the heathen. Billy Corrigan, who knew the numbers and ages of children of every store-buyer from Camden, Maine, to San Socratio, the swift and quiet and efficient Bob Hayes, Rotch Drake, who was equally good at selling our 'religious line' to pious buyers and at passing the latest Broadway anecdote on to provincial golf-clubs, and Eddie Ziegler, the baby of the lot, so youthfully enthusiastic that he not only loved selling books but did not mind reading them—I do not think that any new atomic-power methods can produce a greater corps.

Alas, I am getting over my publishing days. They are so far back now that I am beginning to be able to like some

authors—a few of them—provided I do not have to do business
with them!

A NOTE ON BOOK COLLECTING

From *Samples: A Book Containing Many Fine Pages from
the Books to be Published by The Limited Editions Club,
Seventh Series, in 1941*

¶ *Never a collector of anything (except that he accumulated
books as a magnet draws steel), Mr. Lewis here pays tribute
to the collector's pursuit and the rewards to be derived from
having good books appropriately printed and bound. In
doing so he gives us a glimpse of the Sauk Centre library of
his father, Dr. E. J. Lewis, and the ten-year-old boy stealing
in to make acquaintance with Dickens, Scott, Goethe, Milton,
Tennyson, not to mention the horrendous illustrations of his
father's medical books.*

*Mr. Lewis also wrote prefaces for several books issued by
The Limited Editions Club and was once a member of the
jury, along with Clifton Fadiman and Sterling North, which
awarded The Limited Editions Club Gold Medal to Ernest
Hemingway.*

LOOKING BACK FORTY YEARS, TO THE TIME WHEN I WAS TEN, I CAN
remember every volume among the three or four hundred
books that made up the library of my father, the country
doctor—three or four hundred, besides those portentous
leather-clad depositories of medical mystery filled with colour
plates depicting the awful intimacies of the innards; which,

when The Doctor was safely away on a Case, you sneaked the gang in to behold and shiver over. There were Christmas Gift novels, of course, in a false brightness of gilt-stamped bindings, and a dismal condensed cyclopædia with wiggly line drawings, and *Beacon Lights of History,* and a Bible Concordance—how that ever got there, into a household that accepted whatever the preacher in his black Prince Albert told us about Biblical history and let it go at that, without monkeying with the faith, I do not know.

But among these slightly drab shelf-backs I can see four exciting bits: a set of Dickens, a set of Scott, a Goethe, and a leather-bound edition of Milton; exciting not only because of the great people who inhabited them but because of the books themselves. Probably I would have loved Ivanhoe and Rebecca and Rowena anyway, but I know that after four decades I still see them in steel-engraved voluptuousness: the wan knight from the Crusades returning, the tower complete with ivy, the tresses of a maid forlorn. I am not certain whether, sociologically, these illustrations, these winsome type pages, were good for a small boy in a prairie village. Perhaps they merely veiled from him the realistic joys of tramping the stubble fields and of fishing for perch in the crick. But that they were infinitely dear and stirring to him, I do know.

And that I should have met Pickwick and Mrs. Nickleby and the Mysterious Stranger of *Great Expectations* in the drawings of Phiz and Cruikshank was important; and perhaps important that back in 1895, when almost all current 'trade books' were wretchedly designed and drably bound in penitential-looking brown cloth, the Milton should have been handsomely armoured in leather. It was the first book, aside from school-books, that my father ever bought, and he got it with painful savings from his diminutive salary as a rustic school-teacher in the Pennsylvania hills, long before he studied medicine. No ancestral sword could be a prouder memory.

As mysterious as the Concordance was his *Wilhelm Meister* in German. Heaven knows where he got it; he had never been nearer to Germany than Connecticut; and though his spoken German was fluent it was as innocent of grammar as a Hottentot, and consisted in such phrases as '*Nun, Emil, wie ist die bellyache seit Sie die pork-chops fressen geendet?*'! Yet there it was; the glow and scent of Europe in that embossed book with the Gothic type and the delicate pen-and-ink sketches. No contemporary travel film, with the impertinent guffaws of the commentator, no glaring 1941 'rotogravure sections', could have given the small boy so quivering a sense of the old, the alien, the strange yet inexplicably familiar, as that beautiful book. I am glad that my father had it instead of a marble 'Greek slave' or a surrey with chestnut horses. Here I learned how the garment may be fitted to the spirit of a book.

There are two sorts of book collecting: of books fine and memorable in themselves, and of 'items' that are merely rare—and generally monstrously expensive. Devotees of the second sort of collecting I suspect of being just such exhibitionists as are the dreary people who are renowned for having the largest house on Myrtle Avenue or the costliest limousine in Omaha or the longest string of honorary degrees in the university. To possess one of the three copies extant of a dingy little pamphlet written by Thomas Hardy before he knew better; to hunt down, and pay real book-money for, one of the second issue of the first edition of a Kipling novel (the issue in which, on page 7, Smith is spelled Smiht): this is less noble than stamp collecting, for stamps do at least have fairly pretty little pictures on them, and they do instruct avid youth that there really may be such places as Sokotra, Cyrenaica, and the Kingdom of Bhutan (capital, Punakha, a strong natural fortress; ruler, Maharajah Jik-me Wangchuk). No, the collection of books for their rarity ranks with the collection of walking-sticks, match-books, or the shirts of movie heroes.

But the collection of books that are distinguished in themselves, that are a delight to the hand as they are to the eye, that are masterful in paper, in binding, in the arrangement of the page, this is not so very different from the collection of superior paintings—and it is a hundred times or so more possible for purses that are none too fat.

Yet even such books, I hear from friends much richer than I, are too costly for them. Well, these lads will spend two or three thousand for a car; three or four hundred for a radio; four hundred a month for rent, and think nothing of it—and a heavenly collection of fine books can be made, and I know because I have done it, through The Limited Editions Club at not more than ten dollars apiece. I think that I would rather leave to my two boys, just as my father left me his leather Milton, a hundred or so books, each of which would be a delight that would last a hundred or so years, rather than the remains of a ten-year-old Rolls Royce, the cabinet of an obsolete radio, and a bunch of rent receipts!

THE DEATH OF ARROWSMITH

From *Coronet,* July, 1941

¶ *This self-composed obituary, done in 1941, was obviously a sardonic thrust at the great American pastime of stalking the literary lion. Reading it more than a decade later, however, one is struck by its poignancy, by the aura of sadness surrounding it.*

Instead of living out his days as a benign octogenarian, Lewis died in harness at the age of sixty-five, alone in a hospital in Rome. His son Wells had died six years earlier, having been killed in service on October 29, 1944.

Of the literary giants mentioned, Van Doren, Dreiser and Willa Cather have all passed from the ranks. Hemingway still lives. Michael, Lewis's younger son, is married and beginning a career in the theatre. Freeman Lewis, son of Sinclair Lewis's brother Claude, is Executive Vice-President of Pocket Books, Inc. Brother Claude himself, ten years older than Red, who always called his brother Sinclair, is still practising medicine in St. Cloud, Minnesota, not far from the town where Lewis was born. He accompanied Red on his last trip to Europe.

SINCLAIR LEWIS, WHO DIED PEACEFULLY IN HIS SLEEP YESTERDAY afternoon, at his small country place in North-Western Connecticut, has, at the age of eighty-six, been rather generally forgotten. For the past ten or fifteen years he has indulged in so secluded a life, devoting himself, apparently, only to his cats, his gardens, and brief essays on such little-read novelists as Mark Twain, that to many persons it may have been a surprise to find that he was still living. Yet at one time he was a figure of considerable notoriety, because of his jeering yet essentially kindly shafts at the pomposity and inefficiency of contemporary politicians and industrialists.

Although now they are almost unread, a few of his novels, particularly *Main Street, Arrowsmith, Babbitt, Elmer Gantry,* and the ponderous four-volume chronicle of an American family, *The Tintayres,* which Mr. Lewis began in 1944 and completed in 1950, are familiar to all sociologists and literary historians, for their picture of the priggish and naïve first half of this century. That this picture was well rounded or unprejudiced, no one will maintain. Mr. Lewis seems essentially to have been a cheerful pathologist, exposing the clichés and sentimentalities of his day—the hearty falseness of senators and what were once known as 'business boosters', the smirking attitudes toward women in his times, the personal ambitiousness of the clergy, the artists and the professional men, and the brazen mawkishness of patriotism.

To the discerning reader of later years, it is evident that Mr. Lewis smote—or tried to smite—sentimentality because he knew himself to be, at heart, a sentimentalist, a romanticist, to whom green hills and barricade-jumping soldiers and smiling girls and winter storms were as childishly exciting as they were to any popular female novelist, and that he mocked the cruder manifestations of Yankee Imperialism because he was, at heart, a fanatic American, who never really liked the condescensions of the English people among whom he often lived—including two solid years in Derbyshire in 1951–2.

The 'style' of Mr. Lewis's rather long-winded pictures of Americana seems, on recent study, to indicate a descent from extraordinarily discrepant literary ancestors. From a perusal of his books, together with his own admissions, one may find him astonishingly deriving from both Dickens and Swinburne, H. G. Wells and A. E. Housman, Thomas Hardy and H. L. Mencken and Hamlin Garland. On the other hand, he seems to have left no literary descendants. Unlike his celebrated contemporaries, Theodore Dreiser (1871–1952) and Colonel Ernest Hemingway, who was so dramatically killed while leading his mixed Filipino and Chinese troops in the storming of Tokyo in 1949, Mr. Lewis seems to have affected but little the work of younger writers of fiction. Whether this is a basic criticism of his pretensions to power and originality, or whether, like another contemporary, Miss Willa Cather, he was an inevitably lone and insulated figure, we have not as yet the perspective to see.

For a good many years, Mr. Lewis was an extensive and, it would almost seem, a foolishly experimental wanderer. He began his work with years on newspapers and in magazines and publishing offices; he travelled through every state in the Union; he knew most of Europe and, after the end of World War II, in 1944, most of Asia. He even—possibly in unconscious imitation of his idol, Dickens—dabbled with acting, over three or four years, appearing in various professional companies, with no especial credit or discredit either.

But on his return from England in 1952, he settled immovably in the rural Connecticut to which he had many ties. Though Mr. Lewis himself was born (in 1885) in a Minnesota prairie hamlet, where his father was a quite typical country physician, that father and his ancestors for eight or nine generations were born in Connecticut, along the Housatonic River, near which Mr. Lewis himself has lived these past twenty years. He attended Yale, and did his first newspaper work on the New Haven *Journal and Courier*. It was natural, then, that he should have settled in Connecticut, being weary of travel and of what he himself once called (in his brief travel book, *Tea for 1½*, Random House, 1945) "the chronic wanderer's discovery that he is everywhere such an Outsider that no one will listen to him even when he kicks about the taxes and the beer."

Lewis was tall, lean, awkward, with a rough complexion and, in his later years, a skull completely bald, save for a fringe of still rusty hair. Had he sported a tousled wig and a chin whisker, he would almost comically have been taken for an impersonation of Uncle Sam, and a large share of the yearly dwindling number of interviewers and librarians who made a pilgrimage to his home (a pilgrimage invariably ruined by the old man's derisive frivolity about all artistic poses) have noted that with advancing years he became more and more the Last Surviving Connecticut Yankee. Even his voice assumed a Yankee twang that is now forgotten except in bad plays.

His neighbours tell, as their liveliest recollection of him, that when Dr. Sir Wilfred Willoughby Westfrisket, Eisenbein Professor of American Literature at Oxford, waited for him at the home, one entire afternoon, Mr. Lewis was at a local garage, playing pinochle with the village constable-undertaker.

Although, as remarked, Lewis seems to have had no 'school' of imitators whatever, it is to be surmised that his influence on our literature has been healthful in his derision of dullness and formalism, his use of American lingo and humorous exaggeration intermingled with the more nearly scholastic manner that was an inheritance from his college days—and in a valid democracy whereby, in the world of Lewisian characters, a country editor or a Swedish farmhand is at least the equal in dignity, worth, and romantic charm of any prince, any labour-leader with 10,000,000 followers—or any novelist!

His only surviving near relatives are his elder son, Wells, who was, it will be remembered, a captain in the A.E.F. of 1942, and who is probably a more distinguished, certainly a far more subtle and fastidious, novelist than his father; his younger son, Michael, president of the Afro–China Airways; and his nephew Freeman Lewis, the publisher. The funeral, at the Millerton Cremation Sanctuary, was, by Mr. Lewis's dying request, attended only by the three servants (or, as he eccentrically called them, the 'helpers') on his estate, together with the venerable Dr. Carl Van Doren, president emeritus of Columbia University and formerly Ambassador to France. The only music was the playing of Beethoven's Seventh Symphony, on records, and the only oratory Dr. Van Doren's sole observation: "This was a good workman and a good friend, who could still laugh in days when the world had almost worried itself out of the power of laughter."

III

LITERARY VIEWS

THE AMERICAN SCENE IN FICTION

From the *New York Herald Tribune Books,* April 14, 1929

¶ *A typical comment on the literary landscape of 1929 by the author of* Main Street. *Although Mr. Lewis cites many authors who are no longer in the public eye, the principles which he sets forth reveal his general attitude towards books about his native land.*

I USED TO ARGUE WITH GEORGE SOULE IN THE BRAVE DAYS WHEN I was twenty-six, when I earned $15 a week by reading manuscripts and never could afford breakfast on Saturday—when, in fact, I knew so much that I could distinguish a metathesis from a cæsura—I used to argue about the importance of the scene in fiction. Both of us hoped then, perhaps both of us still hope, to be competent writers.

George insisted that the scene did not count; that, since human passion and hunger and fear are universal, it did not matter whether a fiction writer or the composer of an opera set his scene in Detroit in A.D. 1910, Athens in 1910 B.C., or in that No Man's Land which is common to Italian librettists and to musical comedies featuring Fred Stone. But he was, I think, in error. The scene of a story is the environment affecting the character, and that scene, the fact that it is chill or tropic, rustic or boilingly urban, voluptuous or ironed with poverty, brisk with State Street efficiency or creeping like a Wiltshire village, is as much a part of the protagonist's character and development as his heart.

And one can express adequately only a scene which one knows by the ten thousand unconscious experiences which come from living in it. One can 'get up' a scene by reading about it, by visiting it as a stranger, but he has just that much more given himself a handicap. One can also conceivably write in a foreign language, but it is probable that Conrad would have been greater in Polish or in his almost native French than in the alien English. The Flaubert who wrote of the provincial French of which he had a back-yard and side-street knowledge is greater than the Flaubert who mugged up history and produced the four-ringed failure of *Salammbo*— Edith Wharton of *Ethan Frome* is greater than the Edith Wharton of *The Valley of Decision*.

But there is the other extreme—the school largely of bustling amateurs, to whom the scene is everything; who feel that if they have moved the ancient story of man's lust and courage from Florence to Dade County, Fla., if they have renamed Juliet 'Liza Jane' and Romeo 'Robby', then they have done something altogether original, and incidentally so benefited Dade County that their novels should sell at least a hundred thousand there. It is they who discover the Golden Wheat-lands or Golden South-West and are by their professionally enthusiastic publishers proclaimed as pioneers comparable to Kipling. With two weeks of research they can do you a story of Harlem or Sicily, a searching study of bootleggers in Ontario or the very soul of a Russian priest. They rank with the hacks who follow magazine fashions and at the proper season obediently produce 'detective stories', 'dog stories' 'prize-fight stories', or 'stories of a pure love'.

Somewhere between the extremists who desire characters to float in chaos and those who try to adorn their conventional tales with a new setting, as a cigarette manufacturer adorns his undistinguishable wares with a new slogan, is the wise realm that recognises the value of the scene without trading on it.

And it is astonishing how many American scenes have yet been untouched, and quite as astonishing how many others have been not merely touched but mauled.

New York—arty parties in Greenwich Village, night clubs, the private woes of reporters, the rise of Jews from peddlers to clothing magnates with Riverside Drive apartments, the heroism of cops—these tales have been done to stupefaction. Yet there are ten thousand aspects of New York which have been untouched. There is the river front, which at night is straight out of Dickens. There are the clerks who live in the Bronx, a village life that yells to be chronicled by another Zona Gale. There are alimony hounds with their freakish society of bogus nobility and more bogus gin. There are, in this city of seven million people—almost twice the population of Ireland—countless scenes for such writers (if they may ever be found) as care, for a day a month, to escape from literary teas and the kind of parties that have to be thrown; who will actually walk ten blocks and use their eyes.

America—the literary map of it, apparently, shows three cities, New York, Chicago and New Orleans; then a stretch inhabited by industrious Swedes who invariably (after an edifying struggle) become college professors or rich farmers; then a noble waste still populated by cowpunchers speaking the purest 1870; finally, a vast domain called Hollywood. But actually there are portions of the United States not included in this favourite chart.

A tourists' motor camp, under the cottonwoods of Dakota or the Spanish oaks of Florida; twenty cars from as many states; fifty campers with five hundred tragedies and farces: the desperate family in the 1916 flivver, gambling their last cent in quest of that perfect job which is always to be found in the next state; the honeymoon couple wondering at vast cities of five thousand population; the old man, very quiet, who has to sleep sitting up in his car because of his heart.

Or a town in the new commercial Georgia, where ante-bellum tradition and the Fordian system are at war—a town with galleried houses on the outskirts but on Main Street a Movie Palace. Equally the towns in Vermont or Maine which are feeding that New South and feeding the farms of Iowa, the factories of Cleveland—ancient white towns whose mansions tomorrow will all of them be owned not by Hookers and Trowbridges and Twitchells, but by Italians and Germans and raceless summerites from New York. Gone or going are these traditions, Georgian and New England, and in their passing is tragedy and complicated wonder; yet for the most part the writers who condescend to those states seem not to have heard that anything important has happened since the last drums of 1865.

The universities! These preposterous factories with their ten or twenty thousands of conflicting spirits. Yet who, save Percy Marks and Robert Herrick and, so charmingly in *A Man of Learning,* Nelson Antrim Crawford, has written their Gargantuan modern tale?

And industrialism itself—more dramatic than the universities, more impressive and more terrible than any army with banners, a topic for a Shakespeare and a Zola combined, single organisations with 200,000 employees engaged in the most active and cunning war with half a dozen like armies—who of our young people longing for Greenwich Village or Paris so that they may "find something to write about" has been able to see, or has dared to attempt, this authentically epic theme? Is Waterloo a more gigantic spectacle than the Ford plant at River Rouge? Is the conquest of an Indian kingdom by an English proconsul more adventurous than the General Motors' invasion of the German motor world? He that hath eyes to see, let him see!

There is a common plaint that Americans are so much alike, divided into so few classes, that there is no chance for the portrayer of the American scene to find fresh aspects. "No! We must go to France, where people are individual, different."

It is true that the Babbitt of Boston, the Babbitt of Charleston and the Babbitt of Seattle are confusingly alike, but I do not know that they are much more alike than two English gentlemen from Manchester and Maidstone, two shopkeepers from Lyons and Amiens. And, however alike, it is the job of the writer of fiction to discover the differences beneath the similarities. (Though, mind you, no matter how you differentiate, unless you portray such obviously exceptional, such meretriciously 'quaint', characters as Yankee philosophers or bootleggers, if ever you deal accurately with real contemporaries in Hart, Schaffner & Marx clothes, the critics will accuse you of 'creating nothing but types'. It's a way critics have. It's like the journalists whose liveliest insult to a writer is to say that he is merely a journalist!)

How vastly Americans differ may, if you will, be found in Willa Cather. She saw, therefore she gave breath of life to the Bohemians of Nebraska. She saw and made living the professor of history whose history could not quite make up for his loss of living life. She saw, in *The Lost Lady,* the small-town good woman who was also a big-town bad woman, without conflict. Even in the arty circles of New York, as viewed in *Youth and the Bright Medusa,* she got so far away from the conventional magazine conception of Greenwich Village parties that her Village seems divided by the seven seas from the coy studios of magazine fiction.

Americans alike? Is there even in the multiform Balkans a difference greater than that between the Iowa farmers of Ruth Suckow and the Provincetown fishermen of Wilbur Daniel Steele? Simple people are their characters, equally; they drive, or seek to drive, the same Fords; they study the same movies and comic strips, yet where her farmers are all heavy simplicity, his fishermen are mystic as a Blake engraving.

You say, and rightly, that the difference is not between the actual fishermen and farmers, but between the minds of Miss Suckow and of Mr. Steele—that these are veritable artists, creating their own worlds. Of course. But it is important that she should, with apparent contentment, certainly without having to run off to Paris, find in her own back-yard material for many books, and that Wilbur—though he is as restless-footed as Bill Seabrook, though he can by no violence be kept from slipping off to St. Kitts and Africa—dredges as much colour, as much strangeness, out of the sands of Cape Cod as ever he has from Arab bazaars and Antilles cane-fields.

No one today—if one may venture to claim Toronto as part of the American scene—is more brilliantly finding the remarkable in the ordinary than Morley Callaghan. Here is magnificently the seeing eye. His publishers tell me that Callaghan has been in New York only once or twice, on the briefest of business trips—certainly he has not been instructed in vision by attendance on literary teas. His persons and places are of the most commonplace; his technique is so simple that it is apparently not a technique at all; and out of a street corner in a drab town, out of two lovers talking on a mean wooden bridge, out of a carpenter lying on a roof and eating an apple and thinking about a girl of whom he should not think, he makes pictures that one will remember for years after the most exotic and obviously dramatic chromo has faded.

I had a letter once from a woman somewhere in the Middle West. She wanted, she said, to be a writer. But she had never had any experiences about which to write. All that she had known had been her town and the farms about; all that she had experienced had been birth, childhood, marriage, giving birth to two children, widowhood, poverty, and longing to do something beyond Main Street. Did I, she queried, think it was absolutely necessary for her to come to New York, live in Greenwich Village, get a job in a publishing-house? (For all these things, of course, promising writers do, in a proper literary novel.) Or, by any miracle, could she write only of what she knew?

If, some miraculous day, there appeared a man or a woman who could adequately write of a Mid-Western woman who had been born, married, given birth to children and become a widow, if that genius could fully and passionately do only that one novel, he could sit down beside Flaubert forever content. But then that genius would not ask such a question as did the good lady in her letter, and he would not care a hang what anyone might write of the richness of the American scene. He would be too busy revealing it. For this is the law of instruction in writing, as it is in all other education—to him that hath shall be given, and he shall refuse it, because he needs it not; and to no one can you teach anything save to him who already knows it of himself and is bored by your instruction.

GENTLEMEN, THIS IS REVOLUTION

From *Esquire*, June, 1945

¶ *For some months in 1945 Mr. Lewis conducted the Books section of* Esquire *magazine, reviewing only those publications which interested him or which seemed to him significant. His novel* Kingsblood Royal, *about a young Minnesota banker who learned that he had an infinitesimal strain of negro blood in him and turned to negroes as his own people, was published in 1947. Yet those close to Lewis knew in 1945 that he was making a note-book and doing the research for a 'negro novel'. That is all his confidants knew, because in later years while Lewis was incubating a book, he never talked about it. (He*

*was eloquent on the subject of writers who 'talked their books
out' and never got around to writing them.) Of his earlier
books* Arrowsmith *and* Elmer Gantry *could be mentioned as
exceptions, because in the case of* Arrowsmith *Paul de Kruif
worked closely with him on technical research, and in the case
of* Gantry *he saw and consulted many preachers.*

*The fact remains that he was very close-mouthed about
Kingsblood. In the light of later events it is understandable
that he should have been interested in the current literature
by and about negroes. His last will carries bequests to the
National Association for the Advancement of Coloured
People and to the National Urban League.*

*In the following review he states some of his own beliefs on
the subject that was uppermost in his thought during that
period.*

Black Boy, THE STORY OF HIS OWN YOUTH IN THE SOUTH BY
Richard Wright, the enormously talented young negro who
also wrote *Native Son,* has been greeted by several placidly
busy white reviewers and by a couple of agitated negro reviewers as betraying too much 'emotion', too much 'bitterness'.

Now this is the story of a coloured boy who, just yesterday, found in his native community not merely that he was
penalised for having the same qualities that in a white boy
would have warmed his neighbours to universal praise—the
qualities of courage, energy, curiosity, refusal to be subservient,
the impulse to record life in words—but that he was in danger
of disapproval, then of beatings, then of being killed, for these
qualities, for being 'uppity'. Not bitterness but fear charges
the book, and how this young crusader can be expected to look
back only a few years to the quiet torture with anything except
hatred is beyond me.

When we have a successful comedy by an ex-prisoner about

the kindness and humour of the warders in a German concentration camp, then I shall expect Mr. Wright to mellow and to speak amiably of the teachers who flattered him, his coloured neighbours and relatives who denounced him, the merchants who cheated him, the white fellow-mechanics who threatened him for wanting to learn their skills, and the librarian who suspected him—quite rightly—of reading that militant and bewhiskered Bolshevik, that polluter of temples and Chambers of Commerce, Comrade H. L. Mencken.

There has recently appeared, at the same time as *Black Boy,* the skilled and important report by the secretary of the National Association for the Advancement of Coloured People, my friend Walter White, upon what has been happening to American negro soldiers in our camps at home and in England, and at the battle-front in Italy and Africa. There are in this report numerous exact incidents of Jim Crowism lugged into our Army of Democracy. The main impressions that come out of reading it are the continued segregation of negro soldiers from their white comrades in Red Cross clubs and even in adjacent villages, and the fact that, except for a few sectors in which negroes have brilliantly fought and flown, they have been restricted to labour units instead of being trusted as fighters.

Soldier workers, lugging supplies ashore during landings, or driving trucks or repairing roads under fire, get killed just as frequently—it may even be just as painfully—as the white fighters, but there is no credit in it. They are expected to live like dogs and not even to die as heroes.

The assertions of Mr. White are amply backed up by a woman, a white woman, a woman from a Navy family, in another just-issued book, *Jim Crow Grows Up,* by Ruth Danenhower Wilson.

If there had appeared only these three books, these three disturbing Border Incidents, they would still be enough to make the wise observer fear that a revolution in negro affairs is threatened. But one may go beyond them to a score of other related books published in the past three years, and if America can possibly take the time from its study of comic strips to discover even the titles of these books, it may realise that this is a revolution, and that it is not coming—it is here.

The unwritten manifesto of this revolution states that the negro, backed by a number of whites in every section of the land, is finished with being classed as not quite human; that he is no longer humble and patient—and unlettered; and that an astonishingly large group of negro scholars and journalists and artists are expressiong their resolution with courage and skill. They are no longer 'coloured people'. They are *people*.

Lillian Smith's novel, *Strange Fruit,* still a best seller and as such revealing new audiences, is not merely a small tragedy about two lovers separated by a colour line which bothered everybody except the lovers themselves. It is a condensation of the entire history of one-tenth of our population.

That amusing and amazingly informative book, *New World a-Coming,* by Roi Ottley, published in 1943, is not just a report of the new negro life in Harlem. It is a portent of an entire new life for all American negroes, and it was written by what is naïvely known as a 'coloured man'—that is, a man who has by nature the fine rich skin that the rest of us try to acquire by expensive winter trips to Florida.

And the 1943 biography of Dr. George Washington Carver by Rackham Holt—who, like Lillian Smith, is very much the White Lady—portrays, on the positive side of the question, what one negro could do, given any chance at all, even so small a chance that to a white man it would have seemed a balk. Dr. Carver, whose discovery that the food and the plastics to be found in the once disenfranchised peanut was salvation for large sections of the South, was the greatest agricultural chemist of our time. It is doubtful whether any flamboyant soldier or statesman or author has done more solid good for America than this negro, the child of slaves.

But in one thing the intellectual or just the plain reasoning negro today has broken away from the doctrines of Dr. Carver. This newcomer has progressed or seriously retrogressed, whichever you prefer. He is no longer, like Dr. Carver, ecstatic with gratitude to the white men who permit him the singular privilege of enabling them to make millions of dollars.

To such innocent readers as have not known that the negro doesn't really like things as they are, such as have been shocked by the 'bitterness' of Mr. Wright's *Black Boy,* there is to be recommended a book much more shocking. But here the shocks are communicated by graphs and columns of figures and grave chapters of sociology, which add up to exactly the same doctrines as Mr. Wright's.

This is *An American Dilemma,* a 1,483-page treatise by Professor Gunnar Myrdal of Sweden and a staff of American assistants. Mr. Myrdal was invited by the Carnegie Corporation to come to America precisely because he was a foreigner, and less subject to our own prejudices.

Anyone who reads through this vast work will really know something about the identity and the social position of the negro, and anyone who desires to 'argue the question' is invited to read it, whether he was born in Maine or Mississippi. Probably no other book has more exact information, more richness of negro lore. Here is his complex origin, whereby the yardman whom you think so clownish may have in him the blood of Arabian princes as well as of Bantu warriors; here are his economic status today, his religion and culture, his past and present share in politics, his social conflicts, his actual and possible jobs, his dollars-and-cents budget today. It is all as impersonal as penicillin, and as powerful.

To this sober pair of volumes should be added the enlightenment and stimulation and considerable entertainment in a book published a few months ago by that excellent Southern institution, the University of North Carolina Press, at Chapel Hill; a book called *What the Negro Wants*. In this, fourteen distinguished negro writers, such as Langston Hughes, A. Philip Randolph, Dr. W. E. B. Du Bois, Mary Bethune, Roy Wilkins, tell precisely what they think of it all.

They are all serious, honest, and informed, but among them I prefer George Schuyler of the Pittsburgh *Courier,* who, despite his wit and easy urbanity, is perhaps the most serious of the lot. How any person so cultured that he can add two and two and get as much as three out of it can read the deft pages of Mr. Schuyler and still accept any of the Comical Coon, the Dancing Dinge, the Grateful Bell-hop, the "Mah brethrens, Ah absquatulates tuh consider" theory of negro culture, I cannot understand.

His thesis, bland as dynamite soup, is that there is no Negro Problem at all, but there decidedly is a Caucasian Problem: that of the universal American-English-Belgian-Dutch-French-German-Portuguese exploiter who smugly talks about the 'white man's burden' while he squats on the shoulders of all the 'coloured men' in the world. Mr. Schuyler suggests that in Kenya and Burma and Jamaica and Java and Peking just as much as in America these coloured races are now effectively sick of it. He is, however, too polite to point up the facts that there are a lot more of them than there are of us, and that a machine-gun does not inquire into the complexion of the man who uses it.

Here all of these books begin to fit into a pattern. This suggestion of a universal revolt against the domination of white smugness is also the conclusion of *A Rising Wind,* even though the author is so gay and gentle a leader as Walter White. Quoting from Pearl Buck, another white woman who is not content to be nothing more than that, Mr. White indicates with what frightening care the entire 'coloured world'—including Japan—is watching and reporting upon our treatment of our own negroes in Army and Navy, in hotel and bus, in factory and pulpit and Congressional committee-room.

Gentlemen, my pukka English-Irish-Yank-Swede-Dutch brethren, it behoves us to find out what this larger part of the world is thinking and most articulately saying about us. A slight injection of knowledge may hurt our feelings, but it may save our lives.

I am delighted that in my first column for that stately household compendium, *Esquire,* I have been able to uphold the standards of refined and uncontaminated rhetoric and, here in my ivory tower in Duluth, to keep from taking sides and to conceal my personal views upon Messrs. White, Wright, Schuyler and Myrdal. Let us by all means avoid distasteful subjects and think only of the brightest and best.

FOOLS, LIARS AND MR. DeVOTO

¶ *Having been the storm centre of several memorable controversies, Mr. Lewis in his later years sedulously avoided personal publicity and rarely answered any attack upon himself or his books. His brush with Bernard DeVoto was a notable exception. The following article was published as a leader in* The Saturday Review of Literature *of April 15, 1944. The* Saturday Review *used the following editor's note explaining the background of the article: "In its preceding issue, The* Saturday Review *published as a preview of the book the last chapter of Bernard DeVoto's* The Literary Fallacy, *a series of lectures delivered by the author last year at the University of Indiana under the auspices of the Patten Foundation. Mr.*

DeVoto drew up a sweeping and incisive indictment of the leading writers of the 1920s. He wrote that: 'Never in any country or any age had writers so misrepresented their culture, never had they been so unanimously wrong. Never had writers been so completely separated from the experiences that alone give life and validity to literature. . . . The American people were not what their writers had believed them to be. Only persons so lost in logic, dreams, and theory that they were cut off from their heritage could have held those ideas. . . .' The following article was written in reply."

IN LITERARY TREATISES IT HAS NOT BEEN CUSTOMARY TO MAKE one's points by yelling "Fool" and "Liar", but perhaps we have all been wrong. In his new volume, *The Literary Fallacy*, my old friend Mr. Bernard DeVoto—large D and no space before the V, apparently—has this pronouncement:

"Writers must be content to hold their peace until they know what they are talking about. Readers must be willing to hold them to the job if they refuse to hold themselves. An uninstructed gentleness towards writers has been the mistake of readers in our time. Words like 'fool' and 'liar' might profitably come back to use. . . . If literature is to be serious, then it cannot be permitted folly and lying, and when they appear in it, then they must be labelled and denounced."

Very well. I denounce Mr. Bernard DeVoto as a fool and a tedious and egotistical fool, as a liar and a pompous and boresome liar.

He is a liar in his statement of the purposes of *The Literary Fallacy,* and a fool in his repetitious announcements that he is the one authority on the American frontier, psycho-analysis, family life, the literature of geology, the technic of biography, the treatment of burns, and on Mark Twain, and all New England writers whatsoever.

The intrepid Mr. DeVoto rather fondles the offensive words. He writes: "Mr. Brooks's ignorance was for years a public instrument of literature. With its aid many writers . . . *lied* flatly about the people they were presuming to interpret." And: "As a mind Martin (Arrowsmith) suffers from arrested development, as a scientist he is a *fool*."

Here is what, not very truthfully, Mr. DeVoto declares to be the thesis of his book. It is a four-barrelled or machine-gun thesis. (1) There was a mysterious age of literature known as the 'twenties, confined to exactly ten years. [Upon whose completion, at 12.01 a.m., January 1, 1930, God sighed: "I'll never try anything like that again!" S.L.]

Mr. DeVoto admits that a few of the writers who exhibited in the 'twenties may have been born several months before them and a still smaller squad may go on existing in the 1940s, but he implies that their publishing books in the 'twenties miraculously made all these zombies exactly alike—for instance, Eugene O'Neill, Dale Carnegie, and Edith Wharton, perhaps?

(2) All of these scoundrels have maintained that a culture may best be understood by its books, and (3) such a belief in their own profession, like that of a priest, a soldier, a judge, or a teacher, is very naughty of them, and (4) to quote from *The Literary Fallacy*: "Never in any country or any age had writers so misrepresented their culture."

Now, all of this makes up an obvious lie, but the double lie comes in the fact that none of this actually belongs to Mr. DeVoto's thesis. What he really says in this booklet is merely that Mr. DeVoto is an incalculably wiser and nobler man than Mr. Van Wyck Brooks.

This is the third or fourth book now in which DeVoto has led a frantic one-man revolution with the slogan: 'Brooks must go!' I do not believe that Mr. Brooks has ever answered or ever will answer. He is too gentle, too just, too scholarly—and perhaps too pitying.

My first encounter with DeVoto was on a train to Philadelphia, years ago. He timidly introduced himself as a teacher who was trying to write for *The Saturday Evening Post*. I had never heard of him, but I was interested in that frog-like face, those bright eyes, that boyish and febrile longing to be noticed. I was reasonably polite to him, and he was grateful. I saw him several times afterwards, but his screaming, his bumptiousness, his conviction that he was a combination of Walter Winchell and Erasmus, grew hard to take, and it is a long time now since I have seen him. And I note that in the same way a good many reviewers find the growing noisiness and cocksureness of his books increasingly irritating.

The man must be studied. Like his fellow ornaments of New England, Lydia Pinkham, William Dudley Pelley, and Phineas T. Barnum, he has by brashness and self-advertisement pushed himself into notoriety, and since no serious critic, like Mr. Brooks or Mr. Carl Van Doren or Mr. Fadiman or Mr. Edmund Wilson, has thought it worth while to deflate him, many innocent and youthful believers still listen to him.

When his *The Year of Decision* appeared last year and we found that if he would but gag his babbling ego he could still write remarkably sound and unhackneyed history, many of us believed, however, that he still had a soul to save, and that the salvation might require nothing beyond a couple of miracles and twenty years of patience.

The Literary Fallacy is, aside from a few rather anxious introductory pages, composed of lectures delivered to the fortunate students of the University of Indiana in 1942-3. A foreword issued by the Patten Foundation of the University explains: 'The purpose of this prescription [*sic*] is to provide an opportunity for members and friends of the University to enjoy the privilege and advantage of personal acquaintance with the Visiting Professor."

Let us not stray into speculation as to what the members and friends later thought about having had the privilege of personal acquaintance with the Visiting Professor.

This is a small, thin book, prosily dull, carelessly planned, presenting nothing but Mr. DeVoto's bellows about his own importance. Why then waste bombs on it?

I want to point the way to an adventure too beautiful for realisation. What would happen if men like O'Neill and Hemingway, who have been too busy with living and writing to take time out for self-defence, should some day turn on such talmudists as DeVoto, Howard Mumford Jones, Allen Tate, R. P. Blackmur, Yvor Winters, and Edmund Wilson—I wonder if it is an accident that Mr. Wilson's invariable nickname, 'Bunny', so resembles Mr. DeVoto's 'Benny'? Most of them are dryer and more fastidious and responsible critics than DeVoto and much less given to shouting "Notice me—notice me", but they all have a kinship and it is their influence that has caused every college instructor now living to write, very badly, another book about Henry Adams, Henry James, T. S. Eliot, and William Faulkner.

It might be impossible to persuade Ernest Hemingway to spend even one hour in reading the pomposities of Benny and Bunny, but if he should ever see how easy it is to crush them at their own game, then God help those mincing messiahs.

Mr. DeVoto often seems to be taking a pose and waiting for a camera, any camera. He does so in the first pages of *The Literary Fallacy,* where he worries:

"Since ways of thinking are fairly constant, the fallacy which this book examines is likely to appear in some of the reviews of the book in literary periodicals. Readers who may want to see the fallacy in actual operation are advised to look for it there. The book . . . does not try to describe American literature during the 1920s completely, to tell the whole truth about it, or to pass judgment on it as a whole, but some reviewers may report on it in an understanding that it tries to do all three."

With only a passing wonder as to why DeVoto repeats a statement three times and then calls it three statements, and as to whether it is his personal knowledge of reviewing that makes him so jumpily apprehensive about the intelligence and honesty of his fellow-reviewers, let us note that for once he does tell the truth about this book.

It certainly is not a complete account of the literary crimes of the 1920s. In fact, it is nothing at all but a long-winded confession of DeVoto's obsession about Van Wyck Brooks, plus a few envious references to other contemporaries, and two essays, one on the geologist John Wesley Powell and the other on the medical treatment of burns. These essays, which are as original and definitive as a high-school theme, are supposed to indicate how many things we others failed to know and write about in the 1920s and to show how our books would have been written if we had been so lucky as to have Mr. DeVoto write them for us.

How it must irritate him to have to sit around year after year waiting to find out what Van Wyck Brooks's next book will be, so that he may know what *his* new book will be. If Brooks ever tackles Proust or anything else east of Massachusetts or south of New Jersey, then DeVoto is sunk for life.

Let us check all this.

Out of the 169 actually printed pages of this small book (on sale for $2.50 at several book-stores, if you want to pay that much), one to four pages each are devoted to the sins of Dos

Passos, Hemingway, Lewis, Wilson, Eliot, and Pound, and to the virtues of Frost and Farrell. Other writers are disposed of more briefly. Mr. DeVoto finds twenty-one lines quite enough to deal with Willa Cather, E. A. Robinson, Sandburg, and Stephen Benét all put together, and from five to fifty words each, sufficient to finish up Mencken, Jeffers, Hecht, Dreiser, Dell, Tate, Fitzgerald, Frank, Mumford, Tom Wolfe, Carl and Mark Van Doren, MacLeish, Kazin, Beard, and Cabell. How right you are, Mr. DeVoto. Your treatise cannot be accused of completeness.

Indeed it is so far from that foible that, in an account of the 1920s, it does not even mention Booth Tarkington, eleven of whose books appeared in the 1920s, Thornton Wilder, whose *The Bridge of San Luis Rey* came out in 1927, Hergesheimer, Sherwood Anderson, Elinor Wylie, Edna Millay, Upton Sinclair, Ellen Glasgow, Edith Wharton, any dramatist whatever except O'Neill—whom DeVoto hates—Hervey Allen, Conrad Aiken, Glenway Wescott, E. E. Cummings, Ring Lardner, Evelyn Scott, Louis Bromfield, Hart Crane, Zona Gale, or the Will Beebe who did for biology all that Mr. DeVoto's Mr. Powell did for geology.

He may explain that he knows intimately and hates all of these figures, but that in his gay little sloop he simply hasn't room for them.

But he does have room for seventy pages, seventy out of the total 169, for his attack on Van Wyck Brooks!

And he has room for the twelve pages of his medical treatise, the purpose of which is to prove that he knows more about medicine than Dr. Jacques Loeb, Dr. Paul de Kruif, and Dr. Martin Arrowsmith put together. And he can take ten pages for an account of Powell, the actual purpose of which is revealed on page 133:

"For this man (Major Powell) wrote . . . books, one of which we must glance at, his 'Report on the Lands of the Arid Region of the United States.' Mr. Brooks has not heard about it, nor Mr. Mumford, Mr. Stearns, Mr. Lewisohn, Mr. Frank, Mr. Parrington, or Mr. Hicks, nor even Mr. Edmund Wilson or Mr. Kazin."

With all of his God-complex, Mr. DeVoto has never been so papal. Just how does he know what these men have heard of? I should think it likely that the late Vernon Parrington and the extremely learned Lewis Mumford, who have really inspired thought in America where DeVoto has merely done some inaccurate book-keeping on it, have heard a great deal about Major Powell. I doubt their ever having made a habit of running to Father DeVoto and reporting to him everything they have heard.

But suppose none of them had heard of Powell. So, as under any of his pen-names Mr. DeVoto would write, what? It is the job of all historians to revive forgotten men of importance. They do it daily and, because it *is* their job, none of them except DeVoto would ever wind up an historical report with: "Look at me! How much smarter I am than any of you! You never heard of that! Yah, yah, yah!"

That's how the yahoos got their name.

While we are on Powell, let us note Mr. DeVoto's acknowledgment to Wallace Stegner "for checking my account of Powell". Why he should need Mr. Stegner for that task, which any child with the extensive account of Powell in the *Dictionary of American Biography* before him could do in ten minutes, is a puzzle. For Wallace Stegner, author of *On a Darkling Plain, The Big Rock Candy Mountain, et al.,* is already one of the most important novelists in America, an incomparably better writer than DeVoto, and a number of us go daily to the cathedral and pray that he will get out of Harvard, get away from all the cultural quacks like Mr.

DeVoto, go back to Utah and Iowa, and put on the mantle of greatness that is awaiting him.

It's a dull pamphlet, this *The Literary Fallacy,* and stumble-footed in style. On page 63 appears this example:

" 'Literary climate' is a phrase of literary shorthand which stands for the moods and feelings and ideas of writers, the ways in which books are conceived and the daily excitements in which they are written, for literary associations, literary experience, the tones and shades and nuances and colorations of writers' minds in relation to their books and to literature in general—in short for the whole sum of literary affect and effect."

The publishers' blurb says: "Mr. DeVoto makes his point with thoroughness, humour and truly brilliant phraseology." You can see that humour above, and the brilliance of the following must have brought the Indiana students right up out of their seats, cheering:

"It is not my finding but that of criticism itself that in its new occupations also it still finds frustration, that in fact it is not merely frustrated but ignominiously routed."

Thus powerfully does he show that the writers of the 1920s —say Dorothy Canfield Fisher, George Kaufman, and James Branch Cabell—so lastingly corrupted our land as to have contaminated the entire 11,000,000 of our fighting forces today. Until he pointed it out, I didn't know we were that good.

Aside from its complaints about Mr. Brooks, the brochure contains two charges as specific and sensational as the remarks of a Senator who should reveal: "There are certain persons in a State which I shall not mention who have performed actions, or at least shown tendencies, that I can regard only as, if not sinister, then at least, beyond peradventure, pretty lousy." It is with this and no other courage and definiteness that Mr. DeVoto attacks his old literary buddies.

Says he on page 167—and don't forget the new rule is that Fool and Liar *must* be applied to writers who make dishonourable statements—"Never in any country or any age had writers so misrepresented their culture, never had they been so unanimously wrong (as in America in the 1920s). Never had writers been so completely separated from the experiences that alone give life and validity to literature."

Just whom do you mean, Mr. DeVoto? Do you mean Hart Crane or Dreiser or Miss Glasgow or Edgar Guest? Surely even you can't be such an undeviating fool as to hint that *all* of the hundred or two hundred writers, including a second-rate hack-writer of fiction named Bernard Augustine DeVoto, were so precisely alike as to be 'unanimous' about *all* great spiritual issues from 1920 to 1930? If you don't mean a hundred, or seventy-five, or fifty, whom do you mean? Just those whom you mention? You don't mean Tarkington, Wilder, Sherwood Anderson, Hergesheimer, Ring Lardner or Elinor Wylie, then? Or are you too important, too busy with pious thoughts of Van Wyck Brooks, to be interested in these last at all? For a Visiting Professor, who considers his lectures important enough to be preserved in a book, instead of just sighing and burning them up like the rest of us, you are rather unclear, Mr. DeVoto.

If the people you indict are those whom you have mentioned, let's hear more of them. Exactly what are the valid experiences that they have been so "completely separated from"?

From loving a red-headed girl, or being a grandmother, or serving in the navy, or committing a crime, or being converted to Episcopalianism, or reading Bernard DeVoto—which can be quite an experience, sometimes, I assure you. And just which writers lacked just which experiences?

You mean to say that you know all of this, Benny? You know what Waldo Frank thinks about war and God? You know the intimate family relationships, so revelatory of their philosophy, and the neighbourhood friendships of Mencken and Jeffers and Mumford and Dos Passos?

If you don't, then you are a nebulous liar. If you do, for Heaven's sake write out all that rich stuff instead of a piffling little pocket-book about how much smarter than Van Wyck Brooks you are.

It is astonishing that, though he was bouncingly with us in the lethal 'twenties, DeVoto never saw how bad we were. Oh, he was there. There is no reason why any reader should remember them or even be able to give their titles, but he did publish novels in 1924, 1926, and 1928. He didn't notice then that most of his colleagues were assassins. In fact, it has taken him fourteen years to notice it.

I wonder if he could have been aroused from his sinful ignorance by the evangelical Mr. Archibald MacLeish, who, for about ten minutes, took charge of the press of America and explained that he had to save our youth from the evil medicine we had brewed in the 'twenties.

MacLeish's doctrine was rather insulting to the millions of Americans whom he pictured as being so feeble-minded that we could utterly ruin them merely by saying that we considered service club luncheons and Americans on the Riviera dull. In other decades a like charge of infidelity has been attached to many others writers, to Dickens, Zola, Hawthorne, Tom Paine, and the Mark Twain who, unfortunately for his future reputation, has now been taken over by Mr. Bernard DeVoto as executor.

Just as fair—and just as unprovable—an assertion would be that the major writers of the 'twenties, men who so loved their country that they were willing to report its transient dangers and stupidities, have been as valuable an influence as America has ever known. DeVoto shouldn't have been so innocent as to take his doctrine from MacLeish, who, through a large part of the beleaguered 'twenties, was living in France and reading T. S. Eliot and Ezra Pound.

Mr. DeVoto feels a good deal of agony over the inconsistencies of Mr. Van Wyck Brooks, which appear to be very much like the inconsistencies of Mr. DeVoto, who, in 'Minority Report', published only four years ago, so warmly liked some of the writers he now finds vile or watery that he rebuked other critics for underrating them. He scolds Mr. Brooks for not writing about Francis Parkman as Mr. DeVoto would have written, and presents a sample of his own method, which sounds very much like what Mr. John Fiske actually did write on that subject long ago.

Constantly busy with Brooks though Benny is, lately he has also been busy with writing a novel of his own. It is called *The Woman in the Picture,* and it was published only about a month before *The Literary Fallacy,* and by the same firm.

Not that *The Woman in the Picture* is signed by Mr. DeVoto. Certainly not. It is signed with his pen-name, 'John August', and a damn silly pen-name it is, too. 'Sardanapalus September' would have been much more convincing.

Its scholarly and strictly non-commercial publishers say of *The Woman in the Picture*: "Sophisticated romance and fast-moving adventure make this as exciting a tale as the author's last novel, *Advance Agent.* No more need be said."

Oh yes, Messrs. Little, Brown, a lot more need be said.

In *The Woman in the Picture* Mr. Bernard DeAugust shows his belief in the people of these United States by depicting us as so dumb, soft-headed, and ill-governed, with such idiotic police and F.B.I. and army and navy intelligence, that in the summer of 1942 a villain out of the movies, one of these cold-eyed and non-alcoholic power-maniacs, was, with only half a dozen other plotters, going to take over and destroy our democracy.

The only thing that saved us was a liberal journalist, equally good at economic theorising and at eye-gouging, assisted by an intellectual comic relief, who shows his training in Pareto and Emerson by constantly speaking with such humour as this: "You better buy a four-leaf clover. Yeah, get an asking price on rabbit's feet, too. So now what?"

Serious literature, Mr. DeVoto.

The hero has to drive the heroine half-way across the country, spending most of his time peeping at her bare legs and bosom, as enthusiastically reported by Mr. DeAugust with a ten-year-old, behind-the-barn eroticism which has now been discarded by most of the pulps. There is also in the story the standard *B*-picture equipment of aeroplanes, automatic revolvers, telegraph codes, and gentlemen constantly getting themselves tied to logs, box-cars, telegraph-poles, automobiles, Rocky Mountains, fences, statues of Ole Bull, coincidences, and lapses in the plot. But no cord can hold these guys, not when a serious writer who knows all about the literature of geology is creating 'em!

I wonder how much Visiting Professor DeVoto told the students at the University of Indiana about John August and his ideals and methods of work and his blessed freedom from any influence by Van Wyck Brooks? I hope he wasn't ashamed of John August; I hope he didn't keep silent about his jolly yarn, *The Woman Who Will Be Sold to the Pictures*. Because in originality, in lucidity, in decent humanness it is much better fiction than *The Literary Fallacy*.

On pages 170–2 of *The Literary Fallacy* Mr. DeVoto promises the dawn:

"There is a haste of literary people to exalt democracy, to exult in the native grain. . . . The American writer . . . has undertaken to re-create his personality with the proper proportions of Daniel Boone and Walt Whitman. His eyes have seen the glory of the coming of the Lord. O beautiful for spacious skies, for amber waves of grain, he sings with a loving and compassionate heart. . . . Books will continue to be written by writers. [Extraordinary! S.L.] They will faithfully present the ideas and emotions of writers. When those ideas and emotions chance to be true or great, books will be true and great. When they chance to be childish or frivolous or silly, books will correspond."

And with that, Mr. DeVoto yanks off the priestly robe, puts on a Hollywood jacket, and finishes *The Woman in the Picture,* the most childish, frivolous, and silly dime-novel, the most lacking in any beautiful for spacious skies, the least perceptive of the coming of the Lord, the most re-created with the proportions of Tarzan and M.G.M., that I have read for years.

Is he a liar? Perhaps not unintentionally. And fool? It is he who writes himself down a fool. And I quote again his: "Literature cannot be permitted folly and lying, and when they appear in it they must be labelled and denounced."

Yet Mr. DeVoto is a fool of cleverness, not of malice. He really has done all the bumptious monkey-tricks I ascribe to him, yet at heart he loves books and streets and laboratories, he wants to be liked, and lets his glibness run away with him. Can't you be a good boy, Benny, and stop yelling "Liar!" at your little playmates? You see, they might answer you—more and more of them might answer you, Benny.

A PILGRIM'S PROGRESS

*¶ Only a small sprinkling of Mr. Lewis's published criticisms
of books have been included in this volume. Over a period of
twenty-five years or more he contributed book reviews or
critical essays sporadically to various literary magazines, and
there were times when he wrote regularly for such magazines
as* The Nation, Newsweek *and* Esquire. *The following review
of* A Story Teller's Story *by Sherwood Anderson, was published on November 9, 1924, in the* New York Herald Tribune
Books. *Aside from his comment on a significant writer, Mr.
Lewis here reveals several aspects of his own literary creed.*

NOW, OF ALL THE TOPICS IN THE WORLD, THE MOST INTERESTING
is humankind, people and what they are like, the tale of what
they have done and speculations upon their confused reasons
for doing it. That is why fiction—the recounting of human
customs—is the most popular form of writing; that is why, in
fiction, a garrulous account of human foibles is more stirring
than the trickiest melodrama or the sublimest philosophy.

Mr. Sherlock Holmes remains our favourite detective not
because he was engaged in more dangerous and complicated
matters than his imitators, not because his creator has a less
naïve theory of the causes of crime, but because we behold
him, smoking his pipe, morosely fiddling, loafing in his
dressing-gown.

That is why the successful religions have been focused not
upon ethics so much as upon a familiar human figure, why
successful political movements have been inspired not by great
economic principles but by a man—a Cromwell, a Lenin, a
Lincoln, a Napoleon—figures produced, it may be, by accumu-

lated submerged forces, yet necessary to those forces as outlets.

A book, then, which really discloses a human being becomes important, and such a disclosure we tremendously have in Mr. Sherwood Anderson's new volume, *A Story Teller's Story*.

Mr. Anderson begins with the gaiety and gallantry and thoroughgoing shiftlessness of his father, himself another story-teller, but born out of his own time and place, therefore a sign-painter and magic-lantern showman and tinker in Victorian Ohio, instead of honoured chronicler in New York or Paris or San Francisco. Tenderly Mr. Anderson recalls his boyhood. He does not whine about its poverty; does not, indeed, consider it in any degree impoverished, for were not his brothers and he Fenimore Cooper Indians, despising the softness of the city pale-faces?

From this ardent small-town boyhood Mr. Anderson moves to factory jobs, to advertisement writing, to stolen glorious weeks when, with a whole hundred dollars saved, he could afford a stuffy furnished room where, lying on a dingy red comforter on a shaky cot, he could read all night, could absorb *cinquecento* Italy, so that gonfalons filled the room, and it was little matter that behind them the walls were spotty with washing-water.

Then he lost himself in the writing of tales; timeless hours of creation of human souls, not of canny endeavours to Put 'Em Across in the popular magazines. When he was already acclaimed as a person of power he came to New York—he came, this sign-painter, this advertisement-scribbler, this bicycle-assembler, to the Great Ones, humbly to ask what secrets they had of artistry. Surely in universities or in the chattering studios of New York and Europe they must have discovered formulæ unrevealed to a frequenter of saloon back-rooms.

It must be, one would think, a matter of enduring pride to Margaret Anderson, Waldo Frank, Van Wyck Brooks, Paul Rosenfeld, Gertrude Stein, Alfred Stieglitz, Stark Young, Jane

Heap and some half a dozen others, the humility with which this vagrant and utterly original genius turned to them for wisdom, the gratitude with which he listened to their friendship. . . . And all the while he continued, and gladly continued, to be one who did not come as a Distinguished Author affably occupying hotel suites, but as a poor man outstretched on rooming-house cots with dingy red comforters, meditating upon what at his highest he might do.

There is the outline of the book: the pilgrim's progress of a man at once a genuine artist (in the rarely used exact sense of 'genuine') and a small-town, pool-playing, story-telling Mid-Westerner.

Sherwood Anderson is of importance in American letters—in all of modern letters. Whether by reason of admiration or sharp dislike, all of us who desire fiction to be something more than a Ford manufactory of smart anecdotes must consider his stories of American peasant life, so rigorously simple in expression, so forthright in thought. We have damned or adored him or uncomfortably done both. Either way, there are few of us who have not been guilty of stating that, of course, whatever his merits, Mr. Anderson "lacks a sense of humour" and "is obsessed by sex".

Aside from the pleasure of viewing a human soul, it will be for the beneficial increase in our humility to read *A Story Teller's Story* and to discover that Sherwood Anderson is not obsessed by sex and that he has a shining sense of humour.

When he portrays his father telling a farmer audience of Civil War heroisms, Mr. Anderson shows a humour equally free of the hysterical vulgarity of the Bill Nye school and the neat little jabs of contemporary New York wit. The father changes and enhances his tale to suit his auditors. He never exactly lies, but—wouldn't it be just as well, when in the story he returns to his old Southern home as a pro-Lincoln prisoner in the hands of stern Southern troops, to contrive to meet on the doorstep his non-existent but otherwise absolutely satisfactory former body-servant?

Another example of humour which the reviewer commends to the study of all anti-Andersonites is his explanation that there is reason for the frequent comparison of his stories to those of the Russians, since, like them, he was reared on cabbage soup. It is an admirable burlesque of the literary influence brand of criticism.

Humour—in plenty. And as to this matter of 'sex'—the intense terrifying vision which intimidated or revolted so great a share of us in Mr. Anderson's *Many Marriages*—he honestly shows us in this volume how bewildered he has been that the critics should call him 'unclean' for attributing to his characters the experiences and chaotic beautiful bewilderments which in real life do secretly besiege every man and woman.

Aside from the book's absolute worth and its special value as a revelation of an authentic craftsman, it has another value as an explanation of that emerging Middle West of whose recent literature so much has been written—so little understood.

Like Mr. Carl Sandburg, Mr. Anderson has the calmness to see that the most vulgar and seemingly inarticulate of his corn-belt villagers are not inarticulate or in any slightest way vulgar, but rich with all life—significant and beautiful as any Russian peasant, any naughty French countess, any English vicar, any tiresomely familiar dummy of standard fiction. A negro race-track follower, a nail factory truck-man, the daughter of a boarding-house keeper, a man who to the eye was but a small-town merchant forgetting his invalidism in a periodical drunk in Chicago, yet to the understanding a seer—such people come out, in *A Story Teller's Story,* in all their friendliness, their *importance.*

A HAMLET OF THE PLAINS

¶ *It was, of course, inevitable that Mr. Lewis would have a deep and abiding interest in the work of Willa Cather, who presented fictional portraits of the farmers and townspeople of Nebraska, living in communities not very far west of his native Minnesota. This review of* One of Ours, *which was published by Alfred A. Knopf in 1922, appeared in the Literary Review of* The New York Evening Post *on September 22nd of the same year.*

MOMENTS OF BEAUTY WHICH REVEAL NOT AN AMERICAN WEST of obvious heroisms, but the actual grain-brightened, wind-sharpened land of today; moments out of serene October afternoons and eager April mornings and cold-gasping winter nights; all of them as tenderly remembered as the hedges of *A Shropshire Lad*.

A portrait of a farm boy, whom the publisher in his rather vociferous jacket note has reasonably called "a young Hamlet of the prairies".

A decidedly interesting chronicle of the boy's marriage to a determined young female who loves the souls of the missionised Chinese, but who disdains to love the splendid flesh of the Nebraska farmer.

A question as to the value of modernising, of the motors, phonographs, cameras, farm machines for which the farmers trade their corn and wheat, their leisure and their contentment. A picture—scarce sketched before—of the new and mechanical type of farming which has been replacing the earlier isolated agriculture.

Half a dozen brilliant 'minor characters': Mahailey, the mountaineer woman; Mrs. Wheeler's shy beauty; Wheeler, the pioneer farmer, curious about everything, extravagantly fond of a jest, viewing a joy in learning as absurd; a German family which, in a diligent but dismal university town, retains the florid yet warm and comforting music love of its lost home.

The courage to be tender and perfectly simple, to let the reader suppose, if he so desire, that the author lacks all understanding of the hard, varnished, cosmopolitan cleverness which is the note of the hour.

These admirable discoveries are to be made in Miss Willa Cather's novel *One of Ours,* an addition to the ever-distinguished fiction list of Mr. Knopf. Miss Cather ranks with Mrs. Wharton, Mr. Tarkington, Mr. Hergesheimer, and a few others as one of the American talents which are not merely agreeable but worth the most exact study, and a new book by her is an event to be reported intently.

Yet her name is, even after such novels as *My Antonia* and *O Pioneers,* scarce known to the general public. Many a women's club which is fervent in its knowledge of all the novelists who seize attention by sneering, by describing frocks, or by fictionalising handbooks of psycho-analysis, has never heard of this quieter competence. Her style is so deftly a part of her theme that to the uncomprehending, to the seeker after verbal glass jewels, she is not perceivable as a 'stylist' at all. But to the more discerning Miss Cather is a phenomenon to be examined excitedly, both as a pure artist and as an interpreter. Particularly is that true at present, during the discussions of a so-called 'Middle-Western group', whose groupings lies in the fact that they happened to be born within a couple of thousand miles of one another. Of the somewhat fabulous Middle West not even Mr. Hamlin Garland has given a more valid and beautiful expression than has Miss Cather.

Because of these tokens of significance all sophisticated readers have prayed that the new novel, *One of Ours,* might be the book which would at last bring to her the public acclaim which she has never courted, yet without which, perhaps, she would never be quite content. Is *One of Ours* that book? Probably not. There is ground for fearing that, despite many excellences, it is inferior to others of her novels. It is indeed a book which, had it come from an experimenting youngster, would stir the most stimulating hope. And in any case it is one of the books of the year which one must recommend, which must be read. Yet from Miss Cather it is disappointing. The penalty of her talent is that she must be judged not by the tenderly paternal standards which one grants to clever children, but by the stern and demanding code befitting her caste.

The most important defect is that, having set the Enid problem, she evades it. Here is young Claude Wheeler, for all his undecisiveness a person of fine perceptions, valiant desires, and a thoroughly normal body, married to a bloodless, evangelical prig who very much knows what she doesn't want. The scene of Enid's casual cruelty on the wedding night is dramatic without affectation—a rare thing in domestic chronicles. And here are two possible and natural sources of complication: the young woman whom Claude should have chosen and the itinerant minister who fawns on Enid. In all of this, even without the conceivable external complications, there is infinitude of possible interest. But Miss Cather throws it away. With Claude's relations to Enid left all unresolved, the author sends Claude off to war. She might as well have pushed him down a well. Such things do happen; people with problems fairly explosive with vexatious interest do go off to war—and do fall down wells—but the error is to believe that they thereby become more dramatic.

The whole introduction of the great war is doubtful; it is a matter to be debated. It is fairly good journalism. Where she makes the collapse of a pig-pen important she makes the great war casual. In the war Claude is so heroic, so pure, so clever,

F*

so noble, that no one can believe in him. Except for the arousing scenes on the army transport, with influenza stalking,
her whole view of the war seems second-hand and—for her—
second-rate.

It is a common belief that when the mountain portentously
gives birth to a mouse the affair is ridiculous. In the arts the
opposite is clearly true. It would be absurd for an active mouse
to take time to produce a lumpish mountain. In Flaubert his
provincial housewife is more significant than Salammbo. The
Dutch pictures of old women and cheeses are not less but more
heroic and enduring than the eighteenth-century canvases
massing a dozen gods, a hundred generals, and a plainful of
bleeding soldiers.

In the world of the artist it is the little, immediate, com-
prehensible things—jack-knives or kisses, bath sponges or
children's wails—which illuminate and fix the human
spectacle; and for the would-be painter of our Western world
a Sears-Roebuck catalogue is (to one who knows how to
choose and who has his imagination from living life) a more
valuable reference book than a library of economics, poetry,
and the lives of the saints. This axiom Miss Cather knows;
she has lived by it not only in her prairie novels, but in the
sketches of that golden book, *Youth and the Bright Medusa,*
in which the artist's gas-stove and the cabman's hat are paths
to everlasting beauty. In *One of Ours* that truth does guide
the first part of the book, but she disastrously loses it in a
romance of violinists gallantly turned soldier, of self-sacrificing
sergeants, sallies at midnight, and all the commonplaces of
ordinary war novels. . . . Lieut. Claude Wheeler could not
have been purer if he had been depicted by that sweet singer
of lice and mud, Mr. Coningsby Dawson.

It may well be that Claude was suggested by some actual,
some very fine, person who was tragically lost in the war. It
may be that because in this book Miss Cather's own emotion

is the greater she rouses less emotion in the reader. Certainly there is no intentional cheapening of her work to tickle the banal reader. But it is the hard duty of the artist to slay his own desire for his eternally selfish characters; to be most cool when his own emotion is most fiery; and in the death of Claude Wheeler there is far less beauty than in the small-town burial of the sculptor in *Youth and the Bright Medusa*.

As to the story of *One of Ours,* it is excellently natural. It concerns the unfolding of a youngster who, more by his own inability to explain himself to his father's coarse incomprehension than by any tricky complication of fate, is torn from his career and a chance to discover what he wants to do with life and sent back to farm work, which is—for him if not for his mates—a prison. The war gives him an escape which is closed by his death.

Miss Cather does not seem to be quite certain what does happen to him. At times she is as undecisive as her own hero. There might be, in his losing all in what seemed to be the freedom of the war, a noble irony like the irony of the brooding Hardy. Perhaps there is meant to be. But it does not come through to the reader.

One of Ours is a book which must be read. It is a book to which it would be an insult to give facile and unbalanced praise. It is a book for discussion. And one reviewer, at least, will rejoice if he be convinced by more competent discriminations that *One of Ours* is not only as good as he thinks but incomparably better. There are books which it is a joy to attack; lying books, mawkish books, pretentious dull books, the books which stir a regrettable but natural spirit of deviltry, a desire to torture the authors, and a desire to keep the people from reading them. *One of Ours* is quite the opposite. It makes the reader, for a moment of modesty, hope more for its success than for the authority of his own judgment.

PREFACE TO *FATHERS AND SONS*

¶ *Mr. Lewis did not often write about books of foreign origin, but those who read the following preface to a special edition of* Fathers and Sons *by Ivan Turgenev will see why this work had a great appeal for the man from Sauk Centre. This edition was published for members of The Readers Club in 1943. It was done in the translation of Constance Garnett and, in addition to Mr. Lewis's preface, contained wood engravings by Fritz Eichenberg.*

DURING THE PRESENT VOGUE IN AMERICA OF THE CLASSIC RUSSIAN authors, which has come partly from our admiration of the war achievement of the U.S.S.R. and partly from an uneasy notion that our own fiction is, most of it, rather glib and shallow, the penitential gigantism of Tolstoy and Dostoevsky and the humorous sadness of Chekhov's plays have tended to screen a figure as great, if not so ponderous, as these—that of Turgenev. He has been a little forgotten, but he will return, as Trollope has. His tenderness is too rare a thing to lose.

Tolstoy and Dostoevsky have tenderness, too, but it is the savage love of a peasant mother for a sick child. One of their mottoes, printed larger than life, is *We are not amused*; they feel simultaneously that MANKIND must be saved and that it is not worth saving; and they never display Turgenev's ruling quality: gentleness. That civilised quality gives to his version of the celebrated Russian Character a delicate and tolerable grey, to relieve the lowering black and aching white of the other Russian masters. It is possible for us American extroverts to understand his characters, to smile at them, to love them.

It is hoped that this handsome new edition [of *Fathers and Sons*] will give to new readers a glimpse of a Russia that is more kindly and pastoral than the cellars of Gorki, but no less real and urgent.

The leading character, Bazarov, the medical student who believes more in test tubes than in faith and banners, stands for ever as the type of all young radicals and innovators in all ages, with his harsh honesty, his youthful disgust with all institutions founded on profit and honorifics, his bad manners, his generous friendships, and his final betrayal by just the sentimentality to which he thought he was most superior. Mr. Winterich, in describing how this book came to be, suggests that it dates; but to me it dates no more than an O'Neill play or a Hemingway novel. In 1943 the story of Bazarov illuminates, just as it did in 1862, when it was published, a human puzzle that has always been fascinating and difficult.

Bazarov called himself a 'nihilist'. Call him a Communist, or a surrealist, or a bio-physicist; give him cigarettes instead of cigars and a fast car instead of the post-chaises in which he galloped to see his brooding and elegant lady-love, Anna Sergyevna; and there will seem nothing outdated or naïve about the ardour of his heart and the rebellion of his brain. His name is one of the few in fiction that lives on, like Quixote and Micawber and Sherlock Holmes, more immortal than all but a few actual personages. Yet from time to time there are new readers to whom that name must be re-introduced.

And there is nothing outdated in the desperate affection of Bazarov's father and mother for him, when he has been educated out of the snugness of their little house. Parental tyranny to the young has been adequately chronicled, but there is more drama and pity in the less-often recounted case of the parents' longing to keep their children's friendship and affection. And how much drama and pity there is in it is shown by Turgenev here.

To a Mid-Western American reader, there is the charm of recognition in Turgenev's Russian landscapes: rolling fields with sparse woodlands, small streams, birch groves, skies quickened in early summer with larks; wheat and barley and plodding teams. . . . And serfs where once we had slaves and then changed them for share-croppers, in the South, with the Northern Liberals talking about emancipation just as do Turgenev's enlightened landowners.

Fathers and Sons is a profound tale, a gentle tale, starred with two simple-hearted but imaginative love stories, and in it the Russian Gloom is lightened by a friendliness that is better than any conscious parade of humour. The book is about as long as a full-dress chapter in Thomas Wolfe, that Russian from North Carolina, or in Tolstoy, that Carolina planter from Russia; and, with most readers, that will be all right.

OUR FRIEND, H.G.

From *New York Herald Tribune Books,* October 20, 1946

¶ *Like so many of his generation, Mr. Lewis was deeply influenced by the work of H. G. Wells. Indeed, Lewis rated Wells very high among the intellectual leaders of the times, and as the prophet of a sweeter, more reasonable world to come. Along with this admiration was great personal affection. The instant he arrived in England, as a successful author, he visited Wells. They warmed to each other immediately. It is significant that Lewis's first son was named Wells, after the author of* Tono-Bungay.

The following tribute, written shortly after Wells's death, extols H.G. both as a writer and as a man. The circumstances of their lives prevented the two authors seeing each other very much or very often, but when they did meet, they could pick up exactly where they had left off, as if there had never been an interruption.

THE DEATH OF H. G. WELLS HAS BEEN MOURNED IN ESSAYS THAT have amply recorded him as a prophet of world-government, a critic of human sloppiness in all its surprising variety, a competent biologist and historian, a magic story-teller. We who are over sixty have remembered all that he meant to us from 1910 to 1930, in Greenwich Village or Pekin or Sauk Centre or Twitterton-on-Twit. For here was a man who, more than any other of this century, more even than Shaw or a whole tribe of Huxleys, suggested to our young minds the gaudy fancy (which conceivaby might also be sober fact) that mankind can, by taking thought, by real education, acquire such strange, crimson-shot, altogether enchanted qualities as cheerfulness, kindness, honesty, plain decency, refusal to make ourselves miserable and guilty just to please some institution that for a century has been a walking and talking corpse.

But that real education, bubbled Wells, shouted Wells, had to be based on imagination combined with respect for known facts and zest in disclosing undiscovered facts, not on the sanctity of academic degrees as nice little introductions to business careers, or the jealousies of competitive schoolmasters, or athletic records and the design of new desks for schoolrooms.

We, say in Greenwich Village in 1910, were as stimulated by the drug of Wells's zeal and ingenuity and wit as these children today are by the new drugs of Stalinism and benzedrine. We caught from him not only the faith that education

159

can be as exciting as other forms of exploration and danger, but that marriage can be free of hate and competitiveness, that politicians could be as honest and as well trained in their profession as carpenters and printers in theirs, and that daily life might use the science which has been so revered and so strictly left out in a hermit's cell—that houses might become beautiful and easy of maintenance, clothing be elegant and somewhat less ridiculous than bowler hats, food be a delight without drudgery thrice a day, ships cease to be floating coal-sheds and take on something of a fish's ease and swiftness.

As book after book by Wells came out, we were as delighted by Mahatma Wells as the followers of Father Divine by his bounties. Particularly were we excited by *Tono-Bungay,* that liveliest of novels. I have just re-read it, this September. It seems to date only in the unimportant aspect of aviation-engineering; it is as fresh and surprising as when it first appeared, in 1909. And it is, fortunately, still in print; in the Modern Library series, if not elsewhere.

In *Tono-Bungay* that basic Anglo-American phenomenon, the quick acquisition of great wealth and the general obsequiousness that follows it, were treated in a new way, with derision yet without Marxian bitterness, with the nerve and the swindling and the accidents that made up the luck of Ponderevo, the titan of commerce, and explained with exact details that were sometimes dramatic and sometimes extremely funny.

The love affairs which were no minor occupation of Ponderevo's aide and nephew were related with a fresh, frank, quite new treatment of love stories, honest and human and just a bit absurd, and behind all of the several stories that intermingled in *Tono-Bungay* there was a sound social knowledge of what this whole business adventure meant, of how silly it was and how dangerous it could be.

This whole treatment of wealth was different from the

romantic awe and anger of the earlier novelists, except perhaps, the Mr. Merdle of Dickens, in *Little Dorrit*. To them, the bagging of a fortune, the ruin of a few hundred thousand trusting speculators, had been either the strategy (and edifying industry) of a genius, or the dirty tricks of a devil in human form. They did not know that there were economic accidents, as Wells did, and all their moral indignation was childish compared with his amused fury that sometimes a little man, a stupid little man, might have handed to him as playthings, to fondle or tear apart, the bank accounts of ten thousand people.

If Marx and Darwin came to their eras with surprising shocks of enlightenment, I doubt if those shocks were so emotional and moving as Wells's revelations of human motives were to us in the days of 'red-ink joints' and studios remarkable with batik hangings and arty ladies ditto, and the Lafayette and the basement of the Brevoort. For all the authenticity of its message—that mankind does not, as a matter of virtue and good form, *have* to be stupid—there was in the early Wells, especially in *Mr. Polly,* such a sensational gaiety. 'Fun', 'jolly', 'active'—such words were favourites of Wells, and he elevated their playground flavour to maturity.

Here was a new and livelier Plato—not necessarily a vastly inferior one—and of course the world knew nothing and did nothing about that phenomenon. The wealth of the Indies that had made Great Britain a power was nothing compared with the solider wealth which that nation might have built on the fantastic yet sound imagination of H. G. Wells, if they had known how to use him.

They have, of late, perceived the value of a Winston Churchill and, still later, his danger, but in an H. G. Wells they saw nothing but an amusing spinner of yarns. When he stood for Parliament, he was defeated—of course. That may have been as well for the happiness of the House of Commons. It is easy to conceive that if he had ever stood on that not too shining floor and said what he thought, about almost anything, the whole House might have blown up—"Whoosh!" as Uncle Ponderevo put it—and Britain might have found itself either back under King Arthur, with H.G. conducting the Round Table and Chivalry Ministry, or else in a collectivist commonwealth that would have made the mild arrangements of Comrade Stalin look like a college co-op.

Yes, there was truly a great man, and the citizens saw him walk among them and heard him talk, and knew nothing of what was there.

Now these various qualities of Wells as a great man have, as I said, been well studied since his death, particularly his premonitions of all the attitudes that produce an atomic bomb. What I have not seen, though it may have been well considered in some of the 150,000 magazines that, thank Heaven, I do not feel it my duty to read, is the great man as a man—a great man, a little man, a very funny man, a talkative man, a generous man, a recklessly romantic man, a round little bouncing ball of a man—a *man!*

If his appearance was their only guide, it is no particular wonder that the universities' constituency did not, when he campaigned, elect H.G. to Parliament. The son of a shop-keeper-cricketer, himself a shop-assistant in youth, he looked just that. You could, in his most spacious days, still see him at the counter, unimpressive, busy and serious about the brand of thread you wanted, cheery and chatty and commonplace, zealous to please though never at all humble.

He was round, dumpy, his moustache was ratty, and his voice a thin reed. He simply did not know how to be an exhibitionist; he never could have said to himself: "Gracious, how excited this waiter would be if he knew he was waiting on H. G. Wells!" I know of two cases, one in London and one in a suburb of New York, in which, at a 'party', a woman galloped up to the hostess to demand: "Who *is* that plump little man who talks so amusingly and so wisely?" One of the lady discoverers was the wife of a publisher and the other a professional journalist, but to neither did it occur that this casual man was the tremendous H.G.; merely that he was singularly charming and sensible.

Perhaps that casual humanness, more even than his fancy, his indignation at cruelty, or his sense of order—which is science—made him so great a novelist: teller of tales, discoverer of importance in the pettiest and drabbest 'character'. Perhaps it was his placid willingness to be a plain man—and nothing so ruggedly heroic as the plain man of the hills or the prairies, but merely the plain man of the side-streets, the dismal pubs, the workers' debating-hall—that kept him free of spuriousness even in his days of greatest glamour, and made his characters real even when, poor devils, they had to walk not through proper stories, but through labyrinths of social problemising.

H.G. was free, on one hand, of all the high-collared pomposity of the successful gent at his club, at committee meetings, on the lecture platform, and of the querulous self-importance and conniving of the Left Wing Gauleiter to whom Radicalism has become a career and a salve, and of the touchy dignity of the academic scientist. He was alien to all praying-mantis posing. On the other hand, he saw, knew, loved the genuine dignity of the little man of the streets and factories and upland farms, and was well content to be taken for one of them.

Nobody ever called him or could imagine ever calling him Dr. Wells or Professor Wells or Sir Herbert or Lord Bromley. He did pretty well when he got called Mister Wells and not the usual H.G.

Most Englishmen in his case would have been complimented

on having 'lived down the Cockney'. But H.G. lived *up* the Cockney, to glory.

It was part of this virtue that he could, at seventy, be as active as a small boy without feeling guilty of the crime of *lèse majesté* against himself. He could go into any grand society without feeling that he was being particularly honoured, into any humble circle, any drab village or hotel, without feeling that he was slumming.

I dined once with H.G., Arnold Bennett and Lord Beaverbrook—oh, innocent days of pre-World War II!—at the Chinese Restaurant on Oxford Circus, and not one of the four of us—the housekeeper's son, the pottery-town lawyer's clerk, the Canadian Scotch minister's son, the country doctor's son— felt that we were being ever so cute and adventurous. We just liked eggs foo yung and chicken chow mein and conversation —and low prices!

The three more-or-less British journalists tried to prove to the naïve American that they knew something about politics. But he had got about; he cannily refused to believe any of their stories that began: "I was saying to the Prince of Wales," or "to Baldwin", even though, probably, they were all exactly true.

I watched H.G. once at a party where Frank Harris elected himself guest of honour and Socrates. Frank brilliantly explained how he had come to be so intimate with people he had never met in his life; he revealed scandalous secrets about poets and statesmen that had only the minor defect of being entirely untrue; he laid down rules that were still just as true as when Aristotle had laid them down first. Through it all, H.G. looked about beadily, neither offended nor listening, till he decided which was the prettiest girl in the room, whereon he moved into a corner with her. I doubt if she ever knew that this was the great H.G. Wells. I doubt if H.G. ever knew that, either.

I saw him rather more grandly at his country place, north of London—a comfortable Georgian house, not impressive, but don't make any mistake: you were on a corner of the estate of the Countess of Warwick and you dressed for dinner and no hobohemian monkey-business. She was the lady bountiful of the newly forming Labour Party, but she was a countess, and don't forget it—the Labour leaders didn't.

There H.G. had an earnest tennis-court and you got dragged out to it on a Sunday early-afternoon, just when you wanted a nap—and you came, screaming or not. I was nearly twenty years younger than H.G., thinner, and six or seven inches taller, but the aggressive little fiend had me lying exhausted on the court within a quarter of an hour. He bounced so that, even with his ruddy face, in his white flannels you could not tell him from the tennis-balls, which led to mistakes in serving.

He had, too, a famous game of handball all over his ancient barn. You had to know every angle of the beams to play it well, and he knew them all, with a diplomat's cunning, and his energy was ferocious.

There, one afternoon twenty-odd years ago, we played with an unknown friend of H.G. who was, said everybody, a man with some future if there should ever be a successful Labour Party. He was some kind of a free-lance journalist, and though he had some importance in Labour circles, the visiting American fireman had never heard of him. He was rather tall, handsome in a sort of 1890 travelling-man-heartbreaker way, and very bad at handball. He pounded around the floor, flat-footed and awkward, with his big sneakers smacking the ancient boards like paddles. Nor, during halts, did he have anything of interest to say, and I firmly refused to take H.G.'s prediction of his coming glory.

His name was Ramsay MacDonald.

That evening, we had charades, ingenious, diabolic, and

H.G. acted better than any novelist that ever lived, except his not-too-dissimilar colleague, Charles Dickens. I wonder if that was accident?

It is a banality to compare lively novelists to Dickens. "Mr. Vernon Schmidt, author of the ever-popular Bronco Brown stories, is the Dickens of western South Dakota." But with Wells there is a link that is the clearer the more one thinks of it.

Though it may be that Wells never read it, though it certainly cannot be said that he was 'influenced' by it, David Copperfield's tale of his first year in London is so close to the beginning of *Tono-Bungay* that the reader becomes confused, remembering them. Humour—passion—devotion to dull but well-loved people—hatred of cruelty—joy in a story for the story's sake and in a phrase for its innocent-seeming kick—Dickens and Wells had them all. If Dickens had the greater inexplicable magic, Wells had the greater knowledge of hidden motives, the deeper comprehension of the world's peril of self-destruction, and infinitely more freedom from sentimentality. It may be that for us, now, he is the more important of the two novelists—which might leave only Tolstoy and Dostoevsky on higher thrones.

I wish I could have talked to you once more, H.G.!

IV

PROBLEMS OF THE CRAFT

No Flight to Olympus

A Letter on Style

My Maiden Effort

Rambling Thoughts on Literature as a Business

How I Wrote a Novel on Trains and beside the Kitchen Sink

Obscenity and Obscurity

Introduction to *Main Street*

The Art of Dramatisation

Novelist Bites Art

NO FLIGHT TO OLYMPUS

¶ The following essay was published in the American People's
Encyclopedia *in 1948. When the editors of this reference work
asked Mr. Lewis to contribute an article on the subject of
fiction-writing, they perhaps did not anticipate the sort of
thing he sent them. He refers to his lines as 'surly remarks'.
Several times when college professors invited Mr. Lewis to
address their classes in creative writing, they were surprised
to hear him speak in the same tenor. His comments should
offer a healthy and astringent antidote to the widespread idea
that writing can be taught—or learned—from text-books.*

THERE IS NO COUNTRY OTHER THAN THE UNITED STATES IN WHICH,
in so permanent a work as an encyclopædia, it is desirable to
treat the writing of fiction with the following surly remarks.

In a democracy like this, while we stimulate a young man
with belief that he may some day be president—at least of a
motor agency—we also fail to inform him that in his competi-
tion with other equally fortunate free men it will be well for
him to have more talent and industry than the others. This is
especially the case with writing fiction. Thanks to sentimental
school-teachers and the advertisements of firms which are not
without guile in screaming that they can teach you to write,
there is a general belief that anybody, man or woman, who
has failed at plumbing, farming or housewifery has only to
take a couple of easy lessons—dealing with such trade secrets
as: should you write with pen or typewriter; and are blonde
aeroplane stewardesses or red-haired girls from Iceland the
snappier heroines just now—to be able to compose a novel

which will win the Pulitzer Prize and be sold to the movies for a million dollars.

The art of fiction is expected to pay off the widow's mortgage, to enable young people to get even with their relatives, and to bring fame and innumerable love letters to the bored bachelor. These are all worthy purposes, but the professional writer must keep warning the simple-hearted amateurs that he doubts their being able to learn in twenty hours what has taken him twenty years.

The attitude of the bogus craftsman is often betrayed by his use of such phrases as 'the writing game' and 'the fiction racket', which are supposed to convey that the speaker is a modest fellow, but which, to a serious worker, are as offensive as 'the religious racket' would be to a sincere Churchman.

If the amateur writer has pleasure out of trying to set down his opinions of people and places, that is excellent, a worthy hobby; but if he expects some magic to select him from among the myriad other aspirants who are just as competent as he is—well, gambling on the horse-races would be a better investment. Nor is it dangerous to discourage him, because if he is really good he will pay no attention to me or any other policeman.

Almost all rules about 'how to write' are nonsense. They are based upon what some writer did in the past, upon something which may have been very useful for him but may not suit anybody else in history. Writing is not so easy as all that; a man cannot borrow a way of work from others; upon him is the responsibility of finding his own way. One man works best in a desert and the next in a jazz rehearsal-room; one before breakfast and one after midnight; one makes a 50,000-word plan and one, like Dickens, lists a couple of names and goes to work. There is only one fixed rule for writing, and that is hard and unpopular; the story that you have not set down in words will never win glory, no matter how many evenings you have spent in delighting yourself and annoying your relatives by relating its plot. Which is an elaborate way of saying: Work!

There are a few footnotes: don't ask professional writers for their advice—they have a hard enough time doing their own work without doing yours; the most suitable 'setting' for a story is one that interests you, and only you can decide that; and if you feel that you have a 'message for the world', make some wistful effort to discover whether it is yours or something you heard in a sermon, an editorial, or a funny story on the radio last week.

There is a belief that the first concept of a story is either a 'plot', or the portrait of a person, or the impression of a place. Actually, these three are from the beginning mixed in your mind; you want to do a story about a person who, as he becomes real to you, dwells in a very definite house, street, city, class of society. You cannot tuck your imagination into compartments. The fancies of a child, who in a clump of weeds so vividly sees a dragon that he is frightened, are nearer to true greatness of creation than any technique invented by the editor of a magazine whose real artistic purpose is to sell space to advertisers.

The rules are nonsense because writing of any distinction is a mental process, not an air-conditioned shop under union rules. Most of the work of writing a novel is done in the author's mind before he makes a mark on paper—though after that he must have the patience to make such marks, eight hours a day for a year or so. Without regarding any of the rules, if you have a story that you passionately want to tell, if you can think about it by yourself, no matter what your hands and feet are doing, if you can keep from draining out all your interest by talking about it to other people, then you may have something—maybe.

Even commercially, to compose as most 'teachers of creative

writing' advise is a good way to starve, because there will be a million other unfortunates trying to obey that same teaching, producing that same banal tale. The most correct sparrows are rarely purchased for the better aviaries.

If I knew a novice who really wanted to write, I would urge him to spend ten years (1) in looking at and listening to everything about him and asking himself: "What is this actually like, not what have I always heard about it?" and (2) in reading such novelists as Tolstoy, Dostoevsky, Chekhov, Hawthorne, Herman Melville, Hemingway, Cather, Thomas Wolfe, Dos Passos, Henry James, Mark Twain, Wharton, Faulkner, Richard Wright, Maritta Wolff, Caldwell, Farrell, Steinbeck, Dickens, Hardy, Thackeray, Evelyn Waugh, Scott, the Brontë sisters, Samuel Butler, H. G. Wells, Arnold Bennett, E. M. Forster, Kipling, Maugham, George Moore, Balzac, and Proust.

I would not guarantee that at the end of this probation he would be able to write one good paragraph, but certainly he would be less likely to write a bad one, and he would have had a golden decade. And if he did write at all then, *and if he had talent,* his work might faintly belong with that of the masters, and not be standardised junk turned out on an assembly line—ill-made and selling cheap.

A LETTER ON STYLE

From *Types and Times in the Essay* selected and arranged by Warner Taylor, Harper and Brothers, 1932

¶ *This letter was written at the solicitation of Professor Taylor for that section of his book entitled* Essays and Letters on the Art of Writing. *Again Mr. Lewis takes a position typically contradictory to what one supposes to be the general belief.* *"He [the author] writes as God lets him," says Mr. Lewis.*

I SUSPECT THAT NO COMPETENT AND ADEQUATELY TRAINED WRITER ever, after his apprenticeship, used the word 'style' in regard to his own work. If he did, he would become so self-conscious that he would be quite unable to write. He may—if I myself am normal he certainly does—consider specific problems of 'style'. He may say: "That sentence hasn't the right swing," or "That speech is too highfalutin for a plain chap like this character," or "That sentence is banal—got it from that idiotic editorial I was reading yesterday." The generic concept of 'style', as something apart from, distinguishable from, the matter, the thought, the story, does not come to his mind.

He writes as God lets him. He writes—if he is good enough! —as Tilden plays tennis or as Dempsey fights, which is to say, he throws himself into it with never a moment of the dilettante's sitting back and watching himself perform.

This whole question of style *v.* matter, of elegant style *v.* vulgar, of simplicity *v.* embroidering, is as metaphysical and vain as the outmoded (and I suspect the word 'outmoded' is a signal of 'bad style') discussions of Body and Soul and Mind. Of such metaphysics we have had enough. Today, east and north of Kansas City, Kansas, we do not writhe in such fantasies. We cannot see that there is any distinction between Soul and Mind. And we believe that we know that, with a sick Soul-Mind, we shall have a sick Body; and that, with a sick Body, the Mind-Soul cannot be sane. And, still more, we are weary of even such a clarification of that metaphysics. We do not, mostly, talk of Body generically, but say, prosaically: "My liver's bad and so I feel cross."

So is it with that outworn conception called 'style'.

'Style' is the manner in which a person expresses what he feels. It is dependent on two things: his ability to feel, and his possession, through reading or conversation, of a vocabulary adequate to express his feeling. Without adequate feeling, which is a quality not to be learned in schools, and without vocabulary, which is a treasure less to be derived from exterior instruction than from the inexplicable qualities of memory and good taste, he will have no style.

There is probably more nonsense written regarding the anatomy of 'style' than even the anatomies of virtue, sound government, and love. Instruction in 'style', like instruction in every other aspect of education, cannot be given to anyone who does not instinctively know it at the beginning.

This is good style:

John Smith meets James Brown on Main Street, Sauk Centre, Minnesota, and remarks: "Mornin'! Nice day!" It is not merely good style; it is perfect. Were he to say "Hey, youse", or were he to say "My dear neighbour, it refreshes the soul to encounter you this daedal morn, when from yon hill the early sun its beams displays", he would equally have bad style.

And this is good style: In *The Principles and Practice of Medicine,* by Osler and McCrae, it stands:

"Apart from dysentery of the Shiga type, the amoebic and terminal forms, there is a variety of ulcerative colitis, some-

174

times of great severity, not uncommon in England and the United States."

And this to come is also good style, no better than the preceding and no worse, since each of them completely expresses its thought:

> A savage place! as holy and enchanted
> As e'er beneath a waning moon was haunted
> By woman wailing for her demon-lover!

That I should write ever as absolutely as Coleridge, as Osler and McCrae, or as Jack Smith at ease with Jim Brown, seems to me improbable. But at least I hope that, like them, I shall ever be so absorbed in what I have to say that I shall, like them, write without for one moment stopping to say: "Is this good style?"

MY MAIDEN EFFORT

¶ *In 1921 Doubleday, Page and Company published for the Authors League of America, with an introduction by Gellett Burgess, a symposium entitled 'My Maiden Effort, Being the Personal Confessions of Well-Known American Authors as to Their Literary Beginnings'. In this piece Mr. Lewis describes what is inferentially his first writing to see print. It was an article in which he told how he had discovered what he thought was a plagiarism. The piece was published in the magazine called* The Critic. *He was a sophomore at the time, so it probably appeared in the year 1904–5. He refers to himself as "a heeler of the Yale Lit. exulting in tenth-rate Tennysonian verses about Launcelot". It is a fact that a poem entitled*

'Launcelot' appeared in the Yale Lit. *and was dated March, 1904. It becomes a nice problem to determine what was really Mr. Lewis's first published work. The writer of these lines is inclined to believe that Lewis simply forgot or ignored what he had written for the* Yale Literary Magazine. *Scholars who delight in tracing such literary problems may start figuring this one. Harvey Taylor, whose bibliography of Lewis's writings was published by Doubleday, Doran & Company in 1933, lists the items as "the earliest known published writing by Sinclair Lewis", and notes that a limited edition of one hundred copies was privately printed for him (Harvey Taylor) in 1932 by the Harvard Press. A collector's item indeed!*

A YALE SOPHOMORE, WITH NEITHER THE PICTURESQUENESS OF THE lads who work their way through and study Greek in the box-offices of burlesque theatres, nor the wealth and good-fellowship of the men who are admitted to the sanctity of junior societies. A heeler of the *Yale Lit.*, exulting in tenth-rate Tennysonian verses about Launcelot, troubadours, and young females reading poetry by firelight. All the while an imagination as full of puerile make-believe as that of a ten-year-old boy.

Katherine Cecil Thurston's *The Masquerader* appeared, and the romantic read it at one sitting, in Phil Morrison's room—a rich room, with etchings! Thereafter he was in his make-believe a masquerader; now a disguised nobody thrilling the House of Commons; now a ruined Cabinet Minister.

In the old Brothers and Linonia Library he found a novel written by Israel Zangwill in his first days and signed with a pen name. The title of the novel was *The Premier and the Painter,* and in plot and characters it was a prototype of *The Masquerader.*

The sophomore was thrilled; he was a Discoverer; he had found a Plagiarism; he could Collate, now, like Billy Phelps or Tinker. He wrote an aged-sounding article about the similarity of the two books, and it was typed by a class-mate, Allan Updegraff, later to be a novelist and an innovator in poetry. The two discussed the name to be signed. The author had three names, whereof the first was Harry. Now, Harry, they agreed, was quite all right for the Commons and the Chat Noir lunch counter, but not for the 1904 literary world where one could meet geniuses who had seen Richard Le Gallienne and James Huneker, where bearded men sat up late nights to discuss George Meredith, where one could, if a whopping success, make five thousand dollars a year!

The 'Harry' was buried—and the article was accepted by *The Critic, selig.*

To the sophomore's flustered delight it was taken seriously. The *New York Times Book Review* gave a mildly cynical editorial to it, and Mrs. Thurston made answer—effectively.

The sophomore was altogether certain that he had arrived. He "dashed off a little thing"—it was an era when one still said that, and spoke of one's "brain children". The little thing was a child verse, and as the author had, at the time, never had anything to do with children, it was realistic and optimistic. Not only was it taken by a woman's magazine, but three dollars was, or were, paid for it!

The sophomore began to spout verse, short stories, Whimsical Essays; he kept a dozen of them on the road at once; and for the next five years he was a commercial success. True, his contributions were artistically worthless, but he must have made, by working every evening and every Sunday, an average of nearly forty dollars a year.

But since then he has suspected that commercialism, even thus rewarded, is not enough—no, not enough!

RAMBLING THOUGHTS ON LITERATURE
AS A BUSINESS

From the *Yale Literary Magazine,* Centennial Number, 1936

¶ *No one was better equipped than Mr. Lewis to speak on the subject of literature as a business. The pieces in this book show clearly that in his early career, before the publication of* Main Street, *the energetic Hal Lewis knew as much about writing and selling magazine articles as anyone on the scene. This essay, written in 1936, is of course based on conditions in the literary market-place of that day; nevertheless the author of* Main Street *and* Babbitt *sets forth some of the cardinal principles which governed his working life up to that time.*

IF I WERE A TEACHER OF LITERATURE IN YALE OR ANY OTHER university today, or if I were an editor of the *Lit.,* I would discourse less to my disciples upon Joyce or proletarianism in the arts than upon the problem of helping such of them as have the itch and the ability to write to make a living.

We of an older generation have done well. Indeed, in a great many cases we have received, both in money and in praise, so much more than we have ever deserved that if we were to run into Poe in the club, and he were to scoff "I hear you're doing very well, my lad!" we would blush distressingly, in memory of his struggles. And those of a somewhat younger generation cannot complain. Among Yalensians, there are Harrison Smith and John Farrar, who are as important as any publishers in America; there are Stephen Benét, and the John Chamberlain who has managed to make the sedate *New York Times* swallow liberalism and gaiety, and like it.

But I am afraid that there is under way a change which is

somewhat menacing to the youngsters under twenty-five who believe that they, too, will, by their typewriters, acquire Rolls-Royces, the unabridged *Oxford Dictionary,* the right to talk to Scott Fitzgerald at Mentone, Jermyn Street shoes, and all the other precious sweets which older writers have coveted and gained.

That books "simply do not sell any more" is almost true. There are plenty of novels which have sold only ten thousand copies this past year of 1935 which fifteen years ago would have sold fifty thousand. I know of a really indispensable biography which certainly deserved a sale of five thousand and of which now, in two years, a whole six hundred copies have been taken by our celebrated culture-hungry nation. The author spent a solid year of work on it, and made a hundred and eighty dollars.

All this is by no means the fault of the Depression only. The movie, the automobile, the road-house, bridge, and, most of all, the radio are the enemies of magazine-reading, book-reading, and homicidally the enemies of book-buying, because they absorb both the leisure and the share in the family budget which our poor, wretched ancestors devoted to books. And, with the rise in the wages of servants, we build smaller houses, rent smaller flats, today, and have no room for books. . . . Oh, of course we have room enough for one or two cars, for one or two coffin-sized radios, for the electric refrigerator and (if you live in a suburb, as I do) for a 'game-room' decorated in the style of a rathskeller, but certainly no room for a couple of hundred books . . . Besides. Who would read Sir Thomas Browne, or William Faulkner, if you prefer it that way, when he could be listening to Eddie Cantor or Ray Knight's Cockoos or, with the little ones, to the Itty Bitty Kiddy Hour? (Cross my heart! This last item was listed for 9 p.m., Sunday, December 22, 1935, on station WHN.)

I suspect that in the future a writer will be able to make a respectable living (say a thousand a year or so) only by toiling for the radio or Hollywood, and while there may arise geniuses who will be able to create century-enduring beauty and strength in those media . . . yes? and I suppose some day there will be photographers as great as Rembrandt? . . . yet from what I know of those nimble arts, and from what I know of writers of the last five hundred years, it is about as probable as to suppose that bran will presently become a tastier dish than grouse. Even in such magnificent films as 'Mutiny on the Bounty' and 'The Informer', I suspect that the actors, the camera-men, and the director were much more important than any writer connected with the job; and as to the picture from *David Copperfield,* I am glad that Mr. Dickens wrote it in an innocent supposition that books were books and not, at their highest, raw material for the Film Industry.

And there are 'good programmes' on the radio. Woollcott and Van Loon have the dramatic gift which, in general, most writers lack in speech. Practically all 'good programmes' are music and nothing else, and for writers in general I should say that deep-sea diving or manicuring has considerably livelier promise than the microphone, and that in general, if they will persist in writing, they may expect considerably less bread than stones—the latter not necessarily handed to them.

Now of course this prospect will not stop, will scarcely halt, any writer who is authentic. You can't keep him from writing! A Bunyan or a Raleigh or an O. Henry, even, is rapturous about the leisure and seclusion for writing that he finds in prison. A man who will not write as zealously for the *Yale Lit.* as for the *Yale Review*—or *The Saturday Evening Post*— is a bad craftsman, and all Nature rejoices when a bad craftsman passes to his bad forefathers.

What the young writer of today should contemplate is a dual profession—and incidentally it would be the best thing in the world for his tortured creativeness to be forced to touch some non-literary world, forced to remember what saner folk are daily up to. Let the young Balzac or Byron not only wear his elbows shiny at his desk, but let him with equal assiduity learn another and slightly more lucrative calling. But I would like him to keep out of advertising, journalism, and the teaching of literature, if possible, because they are too much akin to his writing. No, let him become a doctor or a grocer, a mail-flying aviator or a carpenter, a farmer or a bacteriologist, a priest or a Communist agitator, and with the two professions together he may make a living . . . provided any of us will be 'making a living' a couple of decades from now.

I do not jest. I really know a poet, a good poet, who keeps alive by conducting a grocery store, with a gasoline pump in front of it, in northern Vermont. He has time not only to write, but to edit and, himself, by hand, to print a small magazine. I know of no chromium-plated, streamlined writer of magazine serials who has half his leisure or a tenth of his dignity.

Were we all to do this, perhaps we might advance backwards to the nobility of Emerson, the preacher and lecturer, Hawthorne, the customs-house clerk and foreign consul, Whittier, the farmer and editor, Longfellow, the teacher, Lowell, the teacher and diplomat, Holmes, the doctor, Whitman, the government clerk, and Thoreau, the pencil-maker. Not one 'professional writer' in the lot!

I warn you, though, that if you become like any of these, you will not win the approval of Mr. Ernest Hemingway. In *Men Without Women, Farewell* and *Sun Also Rises* it was indicated that Tom Wolfe and he are far the best among the fictioneers now under forty, but in his new book, *Green Hills of Africa,* a volume in which he tells how extremely amusing it is to shoot lots and lots of wild animals, to hear their quite-human moaning, and see them lurch off with their guts dragging, Mr. Hemingway notes:

"Emerson, Hawthorne, Whittier, and Company . . . All these men were gentlemen, or wished to be. They were all very respectable. They did not use the words that people always have used in speech, the words that survive in language. Nor would you gather that they had bodies. They had minds, yes. Nice, dry, clean minds. This is all very dull." (Check!)

I told you this essay would be rambling. As always, Mr. Hemingway has inspired me; this time to the following 'Lines to a College Professor':

> Mister Ernest Hemingway
> Halts his slaughter of the kudu
> To remind you that you may
> Risk his sacerdotal hoodoo
> If you go on, day by day,
> Talking priggishly as you do.
> Speak up, man! Be bravely heard
> Bawling the four-letter word!
> And wear your mind décolleté
> Like Mr. Ernest Hemingway.

No, if you take my advice and combine the delights of selling coffee and pickles and figs with the delights of writing about them, you will never be allowed to throw the bull with Mr. Hemingway. But I wonder if you will care much.

And about my taking my own advice? Too late; about twenty years too late. But I would give a lot if, between spells of the enchanted dreariness of writing, I could go to work in a biological laboratory, or possess an inn of my own to fuss over (in the kitchen rather than in the elegance of the 'front office'), or be able to build a chicken-house instead of forever sitting reading. Be off to your grocing, young man!

HOW I WROTE A NOVEL ON TRAINS AND BESIDE THE KITCHEN SINK

¶ *In 1917 Hal Lewis, as he was then known to his friends, lived in Port Washington, Long Island, with his first wife, Grace Hegger Lewis, and commuted to an editorial and publicity job in New York with the old George H. Doran Company. A lot of us knew he was working on a novel. Of course, he was always writing; indeed, had published two books and had been a regular contributor to* The Saturday Evening Post *and other magazines for several years. But this novel, we sensed, was different, although he never told us anything about it.*

The following article in The American Magazine *for April, 1921, tells how he squeezed out the time. The book was* The Trail of the Hawk, *published in 1915 by Harper & Brothers.*

His first book, Hike and the Aeroplane, *was published by Frederick A. Stokes Company under the pseudonym of Tom Graham. It was written for boys and the author's own copy was inscribed 'To Sinclair Lewis from the author, Tom Graham, his altered ego.' His first novel,* Our Mr. Wrenn, *signed by himself, was published by Harper & Brothers in 1914.*

It will be noted that this article appeared in 1921, approximately a year after the publication of Main Street *and six years after the publication of* The Trail of the Hawk.

I HAVE A PHILOSOPHICAL PRINCIPLE, A HANDY AND PORTABLE KEY to achievement, for the twenty or thirty million young Americans who at the present second are wondering how they can attain it. It applies to shoemakers as much as to authors. It is: Six times one equals six. It sounds simple and rather foolish, and it is harder to carry out than an altitude flight.

Being a professional writer, not a good one but quite a hard-working one, I hear at least once a week: "What's the trick? How can I break into the magazine game? I want to write. I've been reading your stuff, and I think I could do something like it. What must I do?"

My first answer is: "Well, you can save a great deal of time by not reading my stuff. Read Thomas Hardy, Conrad, Anatole France. Or, if you want the younger men, look at Joseph Hergesheimer, James Branch Cabell, Henry Mencken; and all of these astonishing young Englishmen—Walpole, Maugham, Cannan, Lawrence, and the rest."

The achievement hunter ferrets an ancient envelope out of his pocket and solemnly notes down the names, as though they were magic formulas, and I have a private fit of despair in the most convenient corner, because young men who solemnly note down things rarely put their notes into life. And, to defend my own sex, let me say that frequently the young man in question is a young woman. One out of every three women of any leisure will, without much pressing, confide that she "wants to write"—not to write anything in particular, but just write.

After restoring the annotated envelope to a pocket where it will be lost for keeps, he, or she, confides that he—confound those pronouns—they confide that they are peculiar, quite different from all other humans, because, by the most extraordinary circumstances, they "haven't much time".

The young newspaperman boasts that after a night at the grind he is tired. And he says it with a haughty air of being the only person on the entire earth and suburban planets who works hard enough to get tired. And a young married woman tranquilly asserts that after a conference with cook, a bridge-tea, labouring at eating dinner, and watching the nurse put baby to bed, she is so exhausted that she cannot possibly carry out her acute ambition to write.

I want to add to recorded history the fact that there is no patent on being tired and no monopoly in it. Several people have been tired since the days of Assyria. It is not so novel a state that it is worth much publicity. When I hear of a marvellous new case of it on the part of a yearner, I sigh:

"But do you really want to write?"

"Oh, yessssss!"

"Why?"

"Oh, it must be such a fascinating life."

"Huh!" the boorish professional grunts, "I don't see anything very fascinating about sitting before a typewriter six or seven hours a day."

"Oh, yes, but the—the joy of self-expression, and the fame."

"Fame! Huh! I'll lay you nine to one that if Rudyard Kipling and Jack Dempsey arrived on the same train, Kipling wouldn't even be able to hire a taxi."

"I don't *care,*" the yearner insists. "I think my present life is intolerably dull, and I do want to write."

"Very well, then. I'll tell you the trick. You have to do only one thing: Make black marks on white paper. That little detail of writing is one that is neglected by almost all the aspirants I meet."

He—and especially she—is horribly disappointed by my cynicism. He—and often she—finds nothing interesting in making marks on paper. What he, she, it, they, and sometimes W and Y, want to do is to sit dreaming purple visions, and have them automatically appear: (1) on a manuscript; (2) on a cheque from the editor. So he, and the rest of the pronouns, usually finds the same clever excuse:

"But I simply can't seem to find the time. Oh, I just lonnnnnnnnnng to write, but when I sit down to it, someone always comes and disturbs me, and I'm so tired, and—Well, I always tell Adolphus that some day I'll have six months free, and I'll devote them to writing, and then I just know

I'll succeed. I always say to Dolph, I know I can write better stuff than I read in all these magazines."

"Look here. Could you get an hour free every day?"

After a certain amount of bullying, they usually admit the hour. The newspaper reporter who desires to follow Irv Cobb confesses that he could make use of an hour while he is waiting for an assignment. The young housewife who wishes to produce a volume of fairy-stories for children—and 96.3 per cent of all young housewives do so wish—grants that if she hustled a little with her sewing and marketing and telephoning to other housewives, she could have an hour free.

"All right!" the discouraging philosopher concludes, "an hour a day for six days is six hours a week, twenty-five or so hours a month. Anybody who is not deaf, blind, and addicted to *dementia præcox,* can write between a hundred and a thousand words an hour. Making it a minimum of a hundred, you can do five thousand words in two months—and that is a fair-sized short story. At the maximum of a thousand, you could do a short story in a week.

"Very few writers produce more than one short story a month, in the long average, though they can use as much as they wish of twenty-four hours a day. That is because they become wearied of invention, of planning new stories; must spur themselves by the refreshment and recreation of real life. But that real life you are getting all day. You have, as far as time goes, just as much chance as they. If you concentrate an hour a day you can produce somewhere between half as much as, and four times as much as, a professional writer.

"Providing always—providing you can write. And providing you have enough will-power to use your ability. And providing you stop deceiving yourself about not having the time!"

Six times one is six, in hours as much as in the potatoes which William is always selling to John in the arithmetic. But you can vary the multiplication. Of those few people who cannot control an hour a day, there are probably none above the mental grade of *moron* who cannot get in a quarter of an hour daily. If the aspirant actually is too tired at night, he can get up a quarter of an hour earlier in the morning.

If a man wrote only twenty-five words a day, but kept that up for twelve years, he would have a full-length novel. Twelve years for one novel will seem slow to the get-literary-quick yearners. Yet most good writers toil through fifteen or twenty years of apprenticeship before they succeed, and a scholar thinks nothing of twenty years spent on a work of research which does well if it sells a thousand copies.

If you have it in you to produce one thundering good novel, one really big novel, just one, your place in American literature will be safe for the next hundred years. For very few even of the well-known novelists ever produce as much as one thoroughly good novel in all their lives, and still fewer produce more than one. You can rival or excel them with twenty-five words a day—if you have the ability—and *if you really want to*. If you haven't the ability, and if you don't violently want to, then you couldn't do it with twenty-four hours free every day.

But once you understand this principle, you must also grasp another thing: the need of concentration. Each daily hour must instantly hook on the hour of the day before. Concentration can be learned—and without any trick exercises. It is largely habit. The taxi-driver, calm and concentrated in traffic that would shatter an amateur, the policeman attending strictly to the crowd and ignoring the King driving by, the button-maker serene on the job all day long—none of them are heroic exceptions, but all of them are practising excellent concentration. It can be learned—if you want to. But for Heaven's sake, if you don't sufficiently want to, stop yearning for the almost entirely imaginary glories of the literary career.

Now, if all of this applied only to writing, it would scarce be worth recording. But it happens to apply equally to the ambition of almost every young man or woman, whether that ambition is the study of law, the designing of new types of aeroplanes—or of hats—the mastery of business detail, or gaining promotion and greater knowledge in your present work, your present office or shop.

A large percentage of people go on vaguely believing that they would like to be lawyers or executives, vaguely desiring to do something about it, vaguely talking about it, vaguely excusing themselves. And the years slip on, treacherous and swift and cruel; and by and by they are seventy, and the chance has gone—for want of understanding that six times one daily hour is six hours every week.

But let me tremulously endeavour to remove myself from the category of chest-pounding, imitate-me-and-you-will-be-successful inspiration-mongers by hastening to admit that I have had many years of laziness. I have beat the job in about all the known ways. Jack Dunnigan fired me from the San Francisco *Bulletin* because I was a rotten reporter; and with amazing unanimity Charley Kloeber fired me from the Associated Press. But there did come a time when I desperately saw that if I was ever going to be free to write, I must—write!

I, too, 'had no time for it'. I was, by now, a rather busy editor for a publishing firm. I read manuscripts, saw authors and artists, answered telephone calls from the printer, wrote advertising, devised devilish ways of getting publicity, from nine-fifteen to five or six or seven, with forty miles a day of commuting besides. And, like the complainants of whom I complain, I was dead tired every evening—too tired to think of anything but the Krazy Kat pictures and the inviting genius of the man who invented sleeping.

So I decided that I would not have time for being tired, instead of not having time for writing.

I wrote practically all of a novel on trains, and the rest of it I wrote at times when I didn't have time to write!

About one morning a week—not oftener, I confess—I had courage enough to get up an hour earlier than usual. Our Long Island bungalow took an hour to heat after the furnace had been fed; but the kitchen was warm, and before the cook arrived from her palatial mansion I got in most of an hour of writing—with the drain-board in the kitchen as my desk!

Between adjectives I made a cup of coffee on the gas range. By request, my wife did not get up to make it for me. I wanted to concentrate on the job. And I may say that no studio—I believe there are writers who have things called studios—and no Hepplewhite chairs and Spanish tapestries and Sheraton desks ever made a better environment for writing than a drain-board, with a cup of coffee steaming beside me in the sink.

There was an hour a week, at least; and that was fifty hours a year.

Commuting into New York took from thirty-five to fifty minutes. I finished the morning paper in seven or eight minutes, and after that I did not, as invariably I wanted to, gossip about golf, the water-rates, and Tammany with my fellow commuters. I looked around, got ready to be queer, hauled out a plain manila filing folder, and began to write in pencil, with the folder on my knee as a desk. I got from fifty to five hundred words done almost every morning.

There are many paragraphs in *The Trail of the Hawk*—probably the only arousing ones in that not very interesting novel—which were composed in order to give a good bewildered time to some shoe merchant or broker sitting beside me in the train. At first their ponderously cautious curiosity bothered me, but as I gradually got the habit of concentration, it amused me.

Returning on the train at night, I was usually too tired to

write again, but sometimes I did manage five minutes. And when I lunched alone I found that I could plan two or three days' work without having to 'find time'. I don't know that thinking about story plots took any longer than meditating on the impossibility of finding time to think about plots.

In the evening, after dinner and playing and loafing and perhaps reading a manuscript not finished in office hours, I could usually capture another hour or two. Oh, I didn't want to work. I was tired. I longed to go to bed. But I didn't let myself do it till midnight.

Nor did Saturday afternoon have to be devoted entirely to tramping or tennis or a swim. I compromised. I was home by one; wrote for two hours; then enjoyed ten times more the beautiful freedom of a hike across the Long Island hills.

A lot of you, my dear young friends, whose candid face I see here before me tonight—and let me say that I am always glad to get back to your beautiful little city, the loveliest spot on my entire Lyceum circuit—many of you will endeavour to avoid my prosaic principle of six times one is six by turning virtuous; by quoting some of my predecessors on this platform, and stating in pure and ringing accents that you can't write, or read law, or design frocks, or study for promotion in the office, at 6.30 a.m., on the drain-board, because that would be unfair to your present job.

I have yet to learn why excited, future-reaching, adventurous work at your real ambition should be more injurious to your job than sitting up half the night to play poker, or gossiping in a smoke-filled room till you are a pulp of aimlessness, or painstakingly cooking fudge, or yawning at a sentimental movie full of domestic virtues and kitties, or industriously reading the social column in a newspaper.

Oh, I've been guilty. I've dawdled through the movies, sat talking about things that did not interest me with people who bored me—because it was too much trouble to shake them off and go home. The last time I committed these two faults in one evening was something less than twenty-four hours before striking out these majestic chords on the typewriter.

But at least I have learned this: When I have not done the things I thought I wanted to do; if, in the future, I shall not do the things I now think I want to do, the one excuse I may *not* use is: "I can't find the time." I have, and you have, twenty-four hours a day. And that is, so far as I can find out, approximately the same amount of daily time that was granted to Michelangelo, Pasteur, Shakespeare, or Ty Cobb.

"I want to write." Well then, hang it—write!

If you decide that the one way to do the job is to do it, kindly get through it without the use of any of the following words: Pep, punch, jazz, hustle, snap, virile, and, most of all, red-blooded.

These words are the symbols of what may well be the worst fault in American philosophy—a belief that a shallow appearance of energy actually is energy. In begging people to use the selvages and scraps of their time, I wish them to understand that I am not advocating the Pep creed: that religion of making a lot of noise about what you're going to do as soon as you can take time off from making a lot of noise.

There is no Pep, there is no phonographic bellowing of the cant phrases of the market-place, in a quiet, resolute desire for daily concentration. In fact, the man who pounds his desk, and scatters papers all over the floor, and yells at the telephone operator, and bursts into flights of optimism, has no time to settle down to the job.

To the man with a sense of humour, this clamorous insistence on violently hustling nowhere in particular, and standing on one's hind legs to advocate that form of activity as contributing to the welfare of the nation, is simply impossible.

To the man with a passionate desire for beauty, with a longing to build—whether it is to build novels or stone walls or shoes—there is only shrinking disgust at the yapping of the man whose entire creed is: "What you guys want to do is to jazz up the business and keep the iron men doing quick turnovers."

The real disciple of success is diligent about the Lord's affairs, yet he is curiously gentle. He uses his reason. And he does something more subtle than merely spending his spare quarter-hours in working for advancement. He thinks. Most people do not actively think about anything beyond the immediate details of food and the job. For it is not easy to detach one's self from pleased self-approbation and to see clearly one's relation to the round of life.

The builder, and he may be a builder in business as much as in any art, concentrates on his building, yet sees all of life expanding, as circle beyond circle of possible achievement is disclosed. He will neither whine "I can't find time," nor, at the other extreme, will he pound his own back and bellow "Oh, I'm one grand little worker." His idol is neither the young man sighing over a listless pipe, nor the human calliope. He works, persistently, swiftly, without jar.

OBSCENITY AND OBSCURITY

From *Esquire*, July, 1945

¶ *Mr. Lewis here pays his respects to two trends which have been matters of controversy and puzzlement to authors, readers, publishers, critics, purity societies, voluntary censors and the public guardians of our morals, for a generation. (We needn't go into the trends from Chaucer, to Jane Austen, to*

Henry James.) Some people may be surprised at Lewis's position on the Anglo-Saxon four-letter words; yet if they reflect on his books, they will find here a principle that guided his whole writing career.

SO, MOST RESPECTED SIR, YOU'RE SHOCKED BY SEEING THAT MOST disgusting of words printed right out in a book? You've never used it but once, and you felt so soiled afterwards that you washed out your mouth, did you? And you simply won't have in the house a book that contains it, eh? No doubt you say: "Can they really print that now and not get arrested? Why, just a few years ago, every decent person was shocked if he saw *damn* in print, but now authors corrupt the morals of all virgins, smash up the home, and offend against the standards of Good Taste and the Bishop by printing that word. . . ."

Which word do I mean, most respected Sir? I haven't said it, but you know exactly which one I mean—and you did *not* "just see it written on a fence one time". How can you continue to be shocked by anything so familiar to you? No, your real feeling is not moral at all but social. You regard it as you would regard the wearing of a red tie with evening clothes, or drinking cocktails after dinner.

Hypocrisy is never pretty, but this one of yours is also a symptom of retarded juvenility, and a sign of futility, because once youngsters start using That Word, you can't stop them.

So, having depicted your provincial childishness, I shall now turn right around and join you.

I don't like That Word any better than you do, m.r.S. I don't like the use, either in a book or in the parlour, the use of any of those Nine Saxon Monosyllables which the sly and the roughneck use to describe natural functions, just to be spicy. Yes, m.r.S., there is actually one worse imbecile than you, with your queasy reticences, and that is the literary botcher who is so limited in his vocabulary and in his understanding of human society that he can express reality or indignation only by those illiterate, privy-wall, yahoo animal sounds.

I was shocked not by the immorality but by the clumsiness of two current authors who, trying to make clear the woes of Southern negroes, could show their squalor only by having the characters use That Word or its kinsmen. They do not know their business as missionaries. They slap the very ears that they are trying to cajole. Mr. Shaw and Mr. Karl Marx knew their job better.

It is not merely that the dirty words—what do I mean by 'dirty words'?—you know what I mean!—it is not merely that they are childish and shock all the *gefüllte* goldfish, but that they have no great value as 'realism'. The pious manurists insist: "That's the way people do talk," but if an author really wanted to transcribe completely the conversation of the low-lifes, he could not do it just by using two or three dirty words to a page; he would have to use two or three or four to every sentence, until he was as sick of them as his readers.

In a novel like *Ward 20,* by James Warner Bellah, a picture of the humanness and agony of mutilated soldiers in a hospital, the democratic purpose is obviously to show the nobility in these slangy youngsters, but by unsparingly repeating the same dull, dirty words Mr. Bellah makes it as dull as a clinical report. Far better is *The Brick Foxhole,* by a really important new writer, Richard Brooks, now a Marine. He courageously faces every seaminess in a soldier's holiday, sexual or social, but as he is too competent merely to remouth the four-letter words, his characters become friends, not examples of the Priggishness of Conscientious Dirtiness.

A book goes into the living-room of strangers and the author with it, generously welcomed at first. Until he is certain that his hosts like to have their sociological revelations worded in the language of a vomiting coal-heaver, he would do well to be at least as diplomatic as a policeman.

Oh, my good friends Mr. Hemingway and Mr. Farrell, and you, Mr. D. H. Lawrence, *selig,* with the bleached sub-cellar smut of your *Lady Chatterley's Lover*—you boys started something when you began to undress in the drawing-room. When such of your followers as do not bathe or shave start imitating you, it doesn't look so romantic. They took your precept, "Be clever and dirty," but they were so dumb that they could follow only the last part of it.

But whether it is more dreary to over-use That Word or to try to censor people who do use it, the Supreme Court must decide.

Allied to the feeble violence of obscenity is the coy snootiness of obscurity, of taking a weak little newborn thought and dressing it up like a mikado. It is particularly to be noted in the poets whose attitude is: "If you're such an illiterate that you do not immediately see, when I speak of 'Dora', that I am really referring to *doryphora,* which is, as I have just this minute learned from the dictionary, the Latin scientific word for the potato bug, why, then I can't be bothered by your silly, senile, and probably Fascist opinion."

These are the boys and girls who simultaneously boast that their works are so subtle that only sixty-two living persons can appreciate them, and rage because their books do not have a sale of 62,000.

But not all of the obscurators are such warts. Unfortunately, among them are some of the most shining minds of our younger poets. Consider Marguerite Young, a scholar and a seer, who must be indicted for surrounding her real garden of beauty with a fence of fog through which no reader can peer. There seems to be no reason for having anything published—that is, given to the public—if none of that public can understand it. If one truly refuses to communicate, then he should keep his manuscripts in the mother-of-pearl desk at home.

Miss Young has a new prose volume, *Angel in the Forest* (Reynal & Hitchcock). It is the history of the Utopian colonies at New Harmony, Indiana, whose benevolent insanity suggests that the chronicle of America is not merely a financial chart prepared for Mr. Babbitt, but an intricate tapestry of many colours.

Over-mannered though this lively book may be, it is not unduly hard reading. But in her poetry Miss Young displays obscurity at its most irritating. Last year was published her volume of verse, *Moderate Fable,* with such riddles as this:

> By null of him unproved, pale unicorn
> And non-existent, each unearthly entity
> Like the hind which breeds only at the rising
> of Arcturus. . . .

Is that poetry, or is it the smoke of an ill-trimmed lamp in a handsome but unventilated room woven into a web whose most precious quality is that no one can guess its origin or its purpose?

The triple purposes of Symbolism, of the new Metaphysical poets, whose gods are T. S. Eliot and John Donne, are to perceive the complex strangeness beneath the commonplace surfaces of persons and circumstances, to recognise the unity of dissimilar functions of life, and to express these inexpressibles in pictorial symbols which may have a richer emotional power than rheumatic words.

Now to accomplish any of this incantation is difficult, and the sound writer slaves to make his visions clear to others. When the exhibitionist deliberately makes his rites as confusing as possible, he is permitted to go on only because so many people are afraid to blurt out: "I don't know what it means." For the same reason, Gertrude Stein, the Mother Superior of all that shoddy magic, is still extensively admired even though she is also extensively unread.

Here is a quotation from another obscurator, R. Y. Zachary, appearing in the last number of that fascinating annual of Modernism, *New Directions,* published by James Laughlin at Norfolk, Connecticut, and to be recommended to all persons who want to know what the more ardent youngsters are up to. In Mr. Zachary's case, it is this:

> The gardenia, with its plush-white modesty,
> Pre-empts a place for its red odour,
> Scent of Tlaelscuani, the goddess of mediocre beds,
> Her branchless turbary oozes
> In pallid minds . . .

What?

Now William Blake and Emily Dickinson were also symbolists, and no poets have ever been less stereotyped, timid, or commercial. Yet their thoughts became crystal. Listen to Emily, in an extremely important book of her hitherto unpublished poetry, *Bolts of Melody* (Harper's), just issued this spring:

> Tell all the truth but let it slant,
> Success in circuit lies,
> Too bright for our infirm delight
> The truth's superb surprise.

I cannot complain if the poets wish to commit suicide by convincing the world that all poetry has become so stylised and dreary that no sensible person will read any of it. But I do object when they begin to drag the veils of egotism over the hard clarity of prose.

Here is a young novelist, Naomi Gilpatrick, whose first novel, *The Broken Pitcher*, is under the spell of Faulkner, Tom Wolfe and, perhaps, the shaggier manuals of psychoanalysis. She is evidently a sensitive and really talented girl, but in her next book she must fight to be lucid as in this one she has fought to be allusive, illusive, and deep.

Here, with many omissions, is a conversation between her heroine's mother and stepfather, who is supposed to be a good scientific researcher.

Mother: "Isn't it funny how those old refusals-to-serve come back in new and more deceptive guises? Goethe said the devil is he-who-denies."

Father: "A scientist when he puts down the clean verities of fact wants the nuclear phrase. . . . We need what this poem gives—intimation."

"You mean," Mother said thoughtfully, "the same ineluctable we have found in W. H. Auden, Rosamond Haas, Francis Thompson, Rilke."

I guess that's what Miss Gilpatrick's hard-boiled old researcher did mean, and a hell of a house it must have been for the heroine to live in, if the Old Folks talked in that educated way very often.

There is one young woman who is accepted as 'different' and 'authentic' even by the best celebrants of the black mass in Taos and Carmel and Greenwich Village and Norfolk: the Eudora Welty who, with her two recent volumes of short stories, *A Curtain of Green* (Doubleday, Doran) and *The Wide Net* (Harcourt, Brace), has become possibly the most distinguished of the new story-tellers. Oh yes, she had heard of Symbolism, but her writing is as clear—and as free of obscenity—as the Gettysburg Address. Poor girl, she can't be either an Artist or a Modernist.

That's a pity, isn't it, most respected Sir, and don't forget that even the Sphinx could never decide whether it is more idiotic to use That Word or to try to censor the people who do use it! And stop repeating it to yourself now! Not nice at all!

INTRODUCTION TO *MAIN STREET*

¶ *The following introduction to* Main Street *was published in a handsome edition issued by The Limited Editions Club in 1937 with illustrations by Grant Wood. This was seventeen years after it was first published by Harcourt, Brace & Company.*

In this piece the author reveals that in 1905 he started a novel, out of which Main Street *grew, while he was at home in Sauk Centre for his summer vacation from Yale. Only then the title was* The Village Virus, *and the chief character was Guy Pollock. The final draft, he says, was made in 1919 in Washington, D.C. What Lewis tells here of the writing of* Main Street *is probably as much as ever will be known. A few people know some details; others know a few more. Obviously his first wife, Grace Hegger Lewis Casanova, knows most of all. But, as stated elsewhere in these notes, Lewis did not like to rob a work in progress of its freshness by talking it out.*

I MUST, SAYS THE PUBLISHER OF THIS EDITION OF *Main Street,* write an introduction; and what, he suggests, with the blandness characteristic of all publishers urging slothful writers to their task, would I like to say about the opus? What would I like to say? Nothing whatever! To me (and I think to most writers) there is no conceivable subject so uninteresting as one's own book, after you have finished the year of ditch-digging and bricklaying, read the proofs with the incessant irritation of realising how much better you might have said this or that if you had had another year, then fretted over the reviews—equally over those in which you are hoisted to the elevation of world master, and those in which you are disclosed as a hypocritical illiterate.

And years later, when a couple of million people have read your two-hundred-thousand-word essay on what you think of small towns, your laurels, weekly renewed, will be this letter:

"Our teacher in literature [*sic*] has set us a task we should each write to his favourite author please send me a signed photograph and write me by hand What do you think about small towns?"

II

Back in 1905, in America, it was almost universally known that though cities were evil and even in the farmland there were occasional men of wrath, our villages were approximately paradise. They were always made up of small white houses under large green trees; there was no poverty and no toil worth mentioning; every Sunday, sweet-tempered, silvery pastors poured forth comfort and learning; and while the banker might be a pretty doubtful dealer, he was inevitably worsted in the end by the honest yeomanry. But it was Neighbourliness that was the glory of the small town. In the cities nobody knew or cared; but back home the Neighbours were one great big jolly family. They lent you money, without questioning, to send Ed to business college; they soothed your brow in sickness—dozens of them, twenty-four hours a day, kept charging in and soothing your brow without a moment's cessation; and when you had nevertheless passed beyond, they sat up with your corpse and your widow. Invariably they encouraged youth to go to bigger and nobler things.

And in 1905 I returned to my own Minnesota village for vacation after my Sophomore year in Yale, and after two months of it, after two months of overhearing the villagers none too softly wonder "Why don't Doc Lewis make Harry get a job on a farm instead of letting him sit around readin' and readin' a lot of fool histories and God knows what all?" I was converted to the faith that a good deal of this Neighbourliness was a fake; that villages could be as inquisitorial as an army barracks. So in the third month of vacation, fifteen years before it was published, I began to write *Main Street*.

But the title then was *The Village Virus,* and the chief character was not Carol Kennicott but Guy Pollock, the lawyer, whom I depicted as a learned, amiable, and ambitious young man (altogether, you see, in the image of Doc Lewis's youngest boy, Harry) who started practice in a prairie village and spiritually starved. I must have written about twenty thousand words of that script, but I remember nothing whatever about the details, and the script is as clean gone and vanished away as the script of my first play, which was the libretto for a musical comedy called *President Poodle,* composed in 1911 with a zealous joy and an ignorance of the stage which I suppose rarely to have been equalled.*

Then, perhaps two or three years before 1919, when the final *Main Street* was started, I made another effort to tackle the book, now under the final title. I must have endured about thirty thousand words, this time, and, preserving that script, I was later to use about ten thousand in the final book. I felt that I wasn't up to it yet. (Whether I was up to it in

---

* The Yale Collection of American Literature, Yale University, includes a manuscript by Mr. Lewis of a musical comedy libretto which he composed in 1911, intending it as a vehicle for George M. Cohan: "*President Pip*: typewritten MS. of Act III only of Mr. Lewis's first play-comedy, composed while working for Frederick A. Stokes Publishing Company, 33 pages numbered '82' to '114'." This may be the *President Poodle* he refers to. But there is no copy of the first draft of the novel later to be entitled *Main Street*.

1919, either, I must leave to critics less prejudiced.) But that this was to be the book I was determined during the four years when, after quitting the publishing-house grind in New York, I wandered all over the United States (New York to Florida to Minnesota to Seattle to California to New Orleans to New York) making my living by writing short stories, mostly for *The Saturday Evening Post*. I spent a good deal of time in Mid-Western villages and, though I was now free of the inquisition, having a trade that was considered nearly as choice as medicine, law, the ministry, or even manufacturing, I still felt that the ghetto-like confinement of small towns could be—not always was, but so easily could be—a respectable form of hell.

The sudden sale of a *Post* serial called *Free Air* to the movies gave me the chance to take a year of freedom and write *Main Street*. I hastened to that ampler and pleasanter village, Washington, D.C., and in the autumn of 1919 I began the thing in a furnished room, somewhere or other near the present Mayflower Hotel. I took the room as an office because my three-storey residence up on Sixteenth Street was rather less stately and commodious than the description sounds. There were only six rooms in the three storeys, and they were considerably too small for free, joyous, uninhibited cat-swinging.

I finished the 200,000 (maybe it was 180,000) words of *Main Street* on a particularly hot afternoon in early summer of 1920, and that night took the script up to Alfred Harcourt. But I had managed to do so only by working eight hours a day, seven days in most weeks, though a normal number of daily hours of creative writing is supposed to be about four. . . . I never worked so hard, and never shall work so hard again. . . . That is, I mean, unless Comes the Revolution and I am driven from writing to real work, like bricklaying or soldiering or being a nurse-maid.

III

I suppose the book has sold a lot. I haven't the slightest notion how much, and not for years have I asked. But I do know that it is in the class of *Anthony Adverse, Fannie Farmer's Cook Book,* and the lesser-selling of the contract-bridge manuals. What more could an author ask? Even when my publishers of that day first had the MS, Harcourt agreed with me that, with luck, it had a very good chance of selling 15,000 copies. The sales manager, A. H. Gehrs, went mad and believed he could palm off 25,000—given a couple of years— but Alf and I smiled and let him rave.

IV

When the sale started and my first fan letters came—letters denouncing me for having sinned against the Holy Ghost; letters thanking me for having shown up the signator's neighbours—there appeared one on the stationery of a Salt Lake City hotel. That meant, of course, a travelling salesman, a little bored and killing time by correspondence. Opened, the manner of the letter seemed singularly distinguished, full of praise that was as discerning as it was cordial; and, looking back for the signature, I found that of a man whom I had never seen, never dreamed of seeing—John Galsworthy.

V

I have read, here and there, satisfying proof that *Main Street* was cribbed completely from *The Spoon River Anthology.* I have seen even more satisfying proof that it is a transcript of *Madame Bovary.* I am no critic. I wouldn't know. I also re-call happily an article—in *The Saturday Evening Post,* if I remember—which informed my ignorance that small towns in Europe are quite as narrow-minded as in America. True, I had myself said precisely the same thing in *Main Street,* years before, but it is always comforting to be corrected. Even more helpfully I remember an article—I think it was by Mr. Struthers Burt—which confided to the world that it was a tremendous joke on me that Carol wasn't of as good stuff as her husband. As I had most painstakingly planned that she shouldn't be—that she should be just bright enough to sniff a little but not bright enough to do anything about it—I was delighted to have Mr. Burt compliment me by indicating that he must have read my book before giving judgment on it.

It is gratifying still to be put in one's place. How unhappy I shall be when, sitting under my Vermont fig tree, no Mr. Struthers Burt takes the trouble to put me in my place. Perhaps in that barren time, twenty years from now, I shall become so desperate that I may even be willing to write about an ancient book called *Main Street*.

THE ART OF DRAMATISATION

From the Harcourt, Brace and Company edition of the play *Dodsworth,* as dramatised by Sidney Howard, with comments by Sinclair Lewis and Sidney Howard. Published in 1933

¶ *Again Mr. Lewis takes the unexpected position. Instead of the usual plaint of the author that the dramatist has ruined his book, he analyses with craftsman-like objectivity the problems of play-writing and points out the artistic and technical differences between a novel and a play. In so doing, he enunciates, with documentation, his own theories on the making of a play from a novel.*

A COUPLE OF YEARS AGO, WHEN THE FILM MADE FROM MY NOVEL *Arrowsmith* appeared, and I was quoted—correctly—in the press as hugely approving its manner of presentation, I had from an earnest Intellectual in Chicago a letter vigorously damning me for having 'sold out'. It was as though I had dined with Mussolini, campaigned for Hoover, or paid my debts. My epistolary friend could not believe that I had praised the film because I really liked it. There are two popular tenets regarding the dramatisation of fiction for the stage or the screen: The original author, if he be an honest fellow and not bribed by the producer, will loathe, abominate, and be sickened by the result, all in the most public manner possible, no matter how the dramatisation is done; and, second, such a dramatisation is valid only as it follows the smallest details of the original fiction.

This may be known as the 'trot theory' of dramatisation, since it is just as reasonable as it would be to assert that a translation from a foreign language is admirable in proportion as it is literal; to maintain that *"Sehe mal, ich bin ins Haus gegangen"* should be rendered as "See a time, I am into the house gone", as it would be rendered in one of those class-room necessities, a trot.

Actually, portions, and sometimes all, of a dramatisation are valuable precisely as they *depart* from the detail of the original fiction. An example is in Act II, Scene 4—beginning on page 92—of Mr. Howard's dramatisation of *Dodsworth* in this book. This scene, in which Sam is testy with Tub, Matey, Emily and everybody else, does not come from any specific scene in the original novel, and I never saw it nor knew anything about it till I heard it played at a dress rehearsal, yet it is my favourite scene in the whole play, and I feel that nothing more veraciously presents the theme and the characters of the original novel. That, that alone, a novelist may demand from the dramatist—that he preserve, and in the different *milieu* of the stage sincerely present, the real theme and characters of the story.

In this scene, taking but ten minutes or so to play, the characters and inter-relationships of Sam, Tubby, Matey, Emily, and Harry are immensely clarified. Especially do we see that the Sam who has been somewhat too meek and eager with Fran can also fight, and that it is not by accident that he has become head of his motor corporation. The story is carried on—and, most of all, the scene is amusing in itself, with the agreeably idiotic conversation about the picture puzzle.

But why could Mr. Howard not have done all this by dramatising some actual incident of the book? Well, it has not as yet been said more than a million times, so it is probably necessary to say a million more times that a play which an audience will enjoy for a period of never more than three hours and a half (and one hour and a half is more nearly the desirable length), which must be performed in a fixed and decidedly restricted space, in the presence of an audience of mixed and highly contradictory tastes, must have an utterly different set of incidents from a novel—incidents moving more swiftly and visually. A novelist can run on and on (and, alas, does!). He can perversely take twenty words to describe the Apocalypse and fifty pages to chronicle the hero's shaving, and still be endurable, because the reader can always slap the book shut and continue it only when he is in the mood. It is not quite so easy to see a play in instalments—to walk out after two scenes, catch the train back to Yonkers, and come in another night for another scene or two. I agree with Mr. Howard in his introduction—that in all the fifty pages chronicling Sam's return to America there is no one incident which could so well tell the tale as the scene he has invented for the play.

Novices who desire to dramatise novels—and they, I take it from my mail, make up 99.2% of all literary aspirants—should profit by the manner in which Mr. Howard has thus rendered the spirit of the novel by forgetting the letter. If they are to be perfectly successful in following his method, however, it might be well for them to have something of Mr. Howard's talent, and for the acquisition of that, unfortunately, I have not discovered a formula.

II

To show definitely just what Mr. Howard has done, I want to compare the end result with the original. The following lengthy quotation* is from pages 315-53 of the standard American edition of the novel *Dodsworth*: the section which recounts Sam's bewildered and lonely wandering through Europe between leaving Fran in Berlin, where she is supposed to get her divorce from him, and becoming sufficiently acquainted with Edith Cortright to see in her a possible companion for a new life.

In the play these thirty-eight pages of the novel are adequately represented in Act III, Scene 2, beginning on page 129 of the book of the play in this volume—thirty-eight pages reduced to nine. (Though in defence of the novelist it must be asserted that the dramatist does have the scenery, the lights, the actors and their costumes to fatten out his brevity, while the novelist must, as well as their arbitrary narrowness permits, do all of this with words—such a soul-grinding endlessness of words!)

III

Candidates for the head-aching job of dramatisation must not suppose that even Mr. Howard was immediately able to condense the preceding thirty-eight pages of the novel into the brevity of Act III, Scene 2. In preliminary versions of the dramatisation, there were a score of pages of play script which vanished before the final version, as acted and as presented in this volume, was evolved.

* Omitted.

In place of the dozen lines at the end of Act III, Scene 1—pages 128-9 in this volume—in which it is so briefly yet definitely foreshadowed that Fran will try to get her divorce, that Sam will be generous, and that he will be lonely, there was another entire scene in Berlin, laid on the morning after Sam's discovery of Fran's intentions towards Kurt. Sam is drinking a hasty cup of coffee, preparatory to taking the train in retreat from Fran, who, as the curtain rises, is off stage, dressing. The scene, condensed, is as follows:

FRAN [off stage]: I'm putting your dress collars and ties in with your dress shirts and your toilet kit in the other bag.

DODSWORTH: Thanks.

FRAN: Which did you decide on? Flying or the train?

DODSWORTH: I'm taking too much with me to fly.

FRAN: Got your *wagon-lit*?

DODSWORTH: The porter's got it. Don't you want some coffee?

FRAN: Pour it out for me. I'll be right in.

[He starts to pour. His face contracts.]

FRAN: There!

[She enters, wearing dressing-gown.]

It did shut.

DODSWORTH: It was nice of you to pack for me.

FRAN: I always have packed for you.

[She sits at the table.]

You didn't pour my coffee.

DODSWORTH: No.

[Their eyes meet for the first time. Hers fall. She pours coffee and hot milk into her cup.]

FRAN: Well, that's that.

Then, after a discussion of the probable divorce and of money which, compared with the final acted version, seems quite as wordy as the original novel, Fran has a lovely Frannish suggestion: she has telephoned Kurt to come round, because "try to remember that I'm in an anomalous position here in Berlin. It would be better for my reputation if you'd let Kurt and me see you off, so we'll look like just three friends together."

This invitation to Sam to save her face, and to exhibit before her and her lover his agony at parting, given with all of her characteristic thoughtfulness—about herself, Sam has the courage to refuse, though in real life he probably would accept. And the omitted scene ends as follows:

FRAN: Don't look so forlorn, Sam, darling! It *is* going to be a little hard to realise. But you and I just can't get on together. And I do love Kurt. I stand by that!

[*A step towards him.*]

Just the same, we've had many happy times, you and I! I won't forget them! Will you remember them?

[*She falters.*]

And . . . and will you try not to be too dreadfully lonely now?

DODSWORTH [*He has stood looking down. Now he looks up and smiles*]: Dear, did I remember to tell you today that I adore you?

[*His breath catches in a single sob. He goes out quickly, closing the door after him.*]

[*Black-out. End scene.*]

IV

The dramatist, then, has revised himself quite as sharply as he has revised the novelist. He has made, between novel and final stage versions, a dozen versions, and deleted anything from an occasional 'very' or 'dear' or 'of course' to whole scenes.

For in transporting the chapters of the book just given into the single American Express Office scene, Mr. Howard on the way not only finally omitted the above lengthy parting in

Berlin, but an entire scene in which, as in the book, Sam sought comfort in the arms of Nande Azeredo.

And it was an excellent scene—carefully worked out, quite complete, then calmly chucked by Mr. Howard into the waste-basket. In it we saw Sam, intolerably lonely, intolerably bored by the joys of travel, humped in a chair before the Café du Dôme. Near him sit three or four Nebraska James Joyces, who ridicule this bourgeois, this intruder on their practically native Olympus, but feel that it would be only just and right to give him the privilege of buying them drinks. The girl Intellectual of the lot goes to Sam's table, picks him up, prettily begs him for drinks in the manner which, among young females other than Intellectuals, is technically known as 'gold-digging', and is about to extend her favours to her boy friends when the brisk Nande pounces on her, chases off the infuri-ated gold-digger, and makes Sam welcome.

I hoped that Mr. Howard would retain this scene, but he was as ruthless with his own work as, when we first talked over the dramatisation, I was with the literal wording of my novel.

With several other scenes, also, he was wholesomely brutal. Where in the final version Sam gives his impression of Notre-Dame in six lines—at the bottom of page 59—there was origin-ally a whole scene (and to me a wholly desirable one) in which we beheld Sam sitting in Notre-Dame, silent, unmov-ing, absorbed in the rose window, while about him Parisian worshippers chattered as they entered and made exit, and a succession of tourists came in to listen, one party after another, to the inspiring and almost lyric revelation of the guides: "The cathedral is remarkable for its unity of design and measures four hundred and twenty-six feet long, one hundred and fifty-seven feet wide, and one hundred and fifteen feet high in the centre. The vaulting is supported by seventy-five large columns and one hundred and eight small columns.

The great organ has six thousand pipes, one hundred and ten stops, and five manuals. Here Napoleon was crowned Emperor of the French. Now if the ladies and gentlemen will return to the omnibus, we will visit the Latin Quarter, haunt of celebrated artists, and then Napoleon's tomb."

It was a scene at once amusing and impressive—Sam himself as solid and functional as one of the cathedral columns, silent amidst this mumbling. It would have played. But it was not necessary—and out it came. Yet probably it was necessary to have written it, and completely, before one could be sure whether it should be retained or not.

Mr. Howard also wrote, and then omitted, the bachelor dinner in London at which A. B. Hurd introduced Sam to the American business-men living in London; a scene, for whose life I pled, vainly, in which on their first night in London Sam sat at the telephone, typically an American husband, trying to get hold of someone else so that his wife would not have the agony of merely dining alone with her husband; and a scene at an English country house where Sam and Fran first meet Mrs. Cortright.

v

Anyone who sees the lovely Nan Sunderland impersonating Mrs. Cortright would have no notion of the difficulty of getting that Cortright devil into the play early enough so that she might be 'built up' for the final scenes. In the novel she does not appear till page 222, when Sam and Fran send a letter of introduction to her flat in Venice (a flat of which Mr. Howard has entirely robbed her, apparently). For the novelist that was all very well, because when he did reach her he could devote as much space to her as he desired. But in the play we must be conscious of her early, however briefly.

The reader, or the spectator at the spoken play, who finds her entrance, as I do, natural and easy, can have but little notion how the incidents and the characters had to be moved around to give her place. And that is again a departure from the detail of the novel—and that again is valid and honest dramatisation.

There are in the play several losses comparable to the stealing of Mrs. Cortright's flat. Sam and Fran lose an entire son—his personality absorbed by Emily, the daughter. And Mme. de Pénable seems to have lost an acute accent. And, by Heaven knows what accident, Kurt has been demoted from Count to Baron. I rather fancy that happened in the last days of dress rehearsals in Philadelphia, before the opening there, when between rewriting whole scenes of the play after midnight in Philadelphia, and contriving simultaneously to be in New York at the rehearsals of his *Yellow Jack* all the same week, Mr. Howard gave me an impression of being busy. One son, one earldom, and one acute accent—these seem like vital losses, yet somehow I, their parent, have never missed them.

VI

Just as it was more compact and less confusing to have, in the play, just the one daughter instead of a son and a daughter, so does the play character, Henry Hazzard, Sam's successor, represent the many friends of Sam mentioned in the book who, when he is exiled to Europe, forget him without losing fondness for him. There was no such character in the novel, and the name Henry Hazzard was given in the book to a doctor who has no relationship to Sam's business. And, as a more dramatic adventure, an interest in aviation replaces the interest in caravans and in suburban developments which are credited to Sam in the book.

The one thing a dramatisation should not be is a mere dramatisation. It is quite as much an act of creation as any play based entirely upon the dramatist's own design, and an acute study of the tale to be dramatised is less important than the process of imaginative reflection which re-casts the original elements for the stage. I listened once to the script of a play portraying the romance of a famous philosopher. To prepare for it, the dramatist had for months sedulously studied every word of the philosopher that was extant—letters as well as stories and essays—and it was her boast that, for the first time, here was an accurate portrait of the philosopher. For, as she correctly announced, every word of the dialogue attributed to him—except for an occasional "yes" or "no" or "good evening, fair me lord"—actually came from his own works

So, naturally, in the play he was deader than Moses.

For it is a fortunate fact of this otherwise intolerable life that in private conversation even the most elegant writers do not continually talk in balanced beauty. Even a Henry James when he burns his fingers does not say: "The, though inherently vulgar yet also inherently, in these industrialised days, necessary coffee-pot seems to me to possess a degree of heat which, in contact, is one of its lesser virtues." He just says: "Oh, damn!"

It is not as a mirror but as a new creation that one of the greatest dramatisations is still read, is even still acted, by a good many people—the dramatisation of a portion of Belleforest's 'Histoires Tragiques' made by one Shakespeare, and called *Hamlet*.

NOVELIST BITES ART

¶ *In this piece, written for the theatre section of the* The New York Times *of October 19, 1941, appears the only reference in this book to Mr. Lewis's days of barnstorming and directing. Perhaps readers will find it as interesting autobiographic-*

ally as for the deeper principles which he proclaims in regard to propaganda and/or art.

In any event, while acting and directing, Lewis took his job seriously and worked at it with all the sincerity and intensity which he brought to any other form of endeavour. The theatre may have been a passing phase in his life, but while he was in it, he worked at the job with characteristic humility.

REAL PROPAGANDA PLAYS, LIKE REAL PROPAGANDA NOVELS, ARE neither good literature nor good philosophy. They are advertisements and, like all competent advertisements, often catch the attention illicitly. Who is so little emotional that his heart does not flutter over a thumbnail biography of Erasmus, which turns out to be an ad for whisky, or the portrait of a lovely woman, which reveals not the joys of romance but the speed of washing machines?

But it is to be doubted whether the most purple ads have proved to be enduring literature. And the same doubt applies to all propaganda. In the Rollo books, so justly admired for presenting Victorian tightness, and in plays communicating the latest party-line from the Kremlin, there may be useful information, but no one has ever gone mad over a Rollo book.

I have never yet been altogether guilty of writing propaganda, not even in *It Can't Happen Here,* which is propaganda against the propaganda of the Fascists and of the mass-meeting addressers. I am consistent in finding pleasure over association with young Jack Levin's new play, *Good Neighbour,* of which I seem to be the director.

Good Neighbour is going to called propaganda. Inevitably it will be, since it portrays an old orthodox Jewish couple, a negro lady of the night and a German–American housewife and her timid son as being all of them the victims of the social majority, of the passionate mob. Yet his story is not 'propaganda', for that label should be used only on economic and religious patent medicines.

Mr. Levin does not make his characters shriek that if we could just create new Congressional districts in Oklahoma, or join the Swiss in teaching the Stanislavsky method to the Choctaws, or if we could make spinach-eating compulsory, then the world would turn perfect, and the Players' Club would lie down with the Lambs.

His most hortatory moment in *Good Neighbour* is when Hannah, the heroic Jewish matron, a true mother in Israel, muses to her friend the policeman: "A white Gentile American you are. To you liberty is a word you found in a book—something you got for nothing. When you ain't got it, then you know what it is."

That is the voice of freedom that is founded not on committee meetings and little red books illuminated with graphs, but on the respect of every sort of human being for every other sort. It is not propaganda; it is an expression of a human nobility eternal and pervasive, which is just as likely to be found in a share-cropper as in a professional orator, and which rises above all the busy viewers-with-alarm.

It has been something more than interesting to direct *Good Neighbour,* with a working day which, extending from 6 a.m. to midnight, has kept me out of the more vigorous forms of dissipation. It has been a professional job, not at all an 'advisory' one; and I have liked it not only because I admire the humanness of the play, but because directing is in itself the most exciting of activities, much more exciting than sitting in cafés, ski-ing or growing potatoes in Vermont, which are the three standard pleasures normally recommended to novelists by their bankers and their psycho-analysts.

To a venerable and somewhat rusty novelist, directing is much more comforting than acting. Of this latter form of exhibitionism I have done a good deal in the past four years, but I have grown steadily more apprehensive at the sneering moment when, shivering behind a blank-faced flat, you realise that in just a second now you will be galloping out there on the perilously bright stage, to carry on a lot of monkey-shines in the leering presence of several strangers—in the Summer theatre, several dozen.

A novelist is not merely permitted but encouraged to knock off and read a detective story the moment he feels tired. It is considered rather picturesque of him to be found doing something quite new every evening at 9.37. But in the theatre there is the most stubborn superstition about the need of an actor's being right there and coming on with exactly the same words at 9.37 every evening, and no picturesqueness wanted, please.

But a director, like a novelist, may drive his characters pretty much as he wants to. During rehearsals, if he has eaten too many egg noodles at lunch, it is not considered vicious of him to sneak off to the dark rear of the theatre auditorium for ten minutes of contemplation. And in action he can make pretty ingenues speak up and old troupers shut up and even tell radiant stars to scratch their noses—not that, of course, they will even think of going on scratching them after the run has started and the director has been sent back to the warehouse.

Then the director can either retire to his estate in Sauk Centre or hang around the theatre and play pinochle with those other unconsidered heroes, the stage-hands, while the toil of the poor actors out there on the stage is just beginning.

Whether or not *Good Neighbour* converts the world to neighbourliness—and it really might do a bit of that task— certainly it has done a striking job of corrupting a once-cloistered novelist by betraying to him the joys of directing.

There is no job beyond it—except being a traffic cop.

V

PLACES ON THE JOURNEY

The Long Arm of the Small Town

Minnesota, the Norse State

Back to Vermont

Americans in Italy

   1. Mr. Eglantine

   2. Ann Kullmer

THE LONG ARM OF THE SMALL TOWN

¶ *"It was a good time, a good place, and a good preparation for life,"* wrote Sinclair Lewis of his home town, Sauk Centre, Minnesota, twenty-nine years after he had left it to go to college. One of the least sentimental of men, Mr. Lewis accepted the invitation of his high-school annual, the 'O-Sa-Ge', to write a piece for its fiftieth anniversary issue. Thus did he pay homage to his old school and to the town where he was born.

'The Long Arm of the Small Town,' published in 1931, gave pleasure alike to old school-mates and the current crop of students. Thereafter it was forgotten until the Lewis memorial services held in Sauk Centre on January 28, 1951. At that simple, moving ceremony the article was read by Dr. J. F. DuBois, a school-mate. Those who attended the services will never forget the effect of those words, delivered before the boyhood friends and neighbours of a man who had travelled far from Sauk Centre and had become the first American winner of the Nobel Prize for literature.

IT IS EXTRAORDINARY HOW DEEP IS THE IMPRESSION MADE BY THE place of one's birth and rearing, and how lasting are its memories. It is twenty-nine years now since I left Sauk Centre to go East to college. In this more than a quarter of a century I have been back two or three times for a couple of months, several times for a couple of weeks, but otherwise I have been utterly out of touch with the town. Yet it is as vivid to my mind as though I had left there yesterday.

I find myself thinking of its streets and its people and the familiar, friendly faces when I am on the great avenues of New York, or Paris, or Berlin, or Stockholm; when I am in little stone hilly villages of Italy, or sun-basking villas in Spain, or the yellow ancient temples of Athens. To me, for ever, *ten miles* will not be a distance in the mathematical tables, but slightly more than the distance from Sauk Centre to Melrose. To me, for ever, though I should live to be ninety, the direction *west* will have nothing in particular to do with California or the Rockies; it will be that direction which is to the left—towards Hoboken Hill—if you face the house of Dr. E. J. Lewis.

So primitive and inherent are the impressions of boyhood. And I, who am writing this in Connecticut and shall go in mid-May to the farm which I have bought in Vermont, haven't the slightest regret that I was born and reared in a prairie village instead of in New England or New York, or old England or the Continent of Europe, for the matter of that.

If I seem to have criticised prairie villages, I have certainly criticised them no more than I have New York, or Paris, or the great universities. I am quite certain that I could have been born and reared in no place in the world where I would have had more friendliness. Indeed, as I look at these sons of rich men in New England with their motor-cars and their travel, it seems to me that they are not having one-tenth the fun which I had as a kid, swimming and fishing in Sauk Lake, or cruising its perilous depths on a raft (probably made of stolen logs), tramping out to Fairy Lake for a picnic, tramping ten miles on end, with a shot-gun, in October; sliding on Hoboken Hill, stealing melons, or listetning to the wonders of an elocutionist at the G.A.R. Hall. It was a good time, a good place, and a good preparation for life.

MINNESOTA, THE NORSE STATE

From *The Nation,* May 30, 1923. Reprinted in *These United States, A Symposium,* edited by Ernest Gruening, Second Series, Boni & Liveright, 1924

¶ *With typical force and gusto Mr. Lewis sets forth the social and political conditions of his native state which make it different from all others. In this precisely factual piece one will find not only the background of many of his novels, the milieu of Gopher Prairie, Zenith, Grand Republic, but also the actual living basis for most of his characters.*

ON MAY 9, 1922, MR. HENRY LORENZ OF PLEASANTDALE, Saskatchewan, milked the cows and fed the horses and received the calls of his next farm neighbours. Obviously he was still young and lively, though it did happen that on May 9 he was one hundred and seventeen years old. When St. Paul, Mendota, and Marine, the first towns in Minnesota, were established, Henry was a man in his mid-thirties—yes, and President Eliot was seven and Uncle Joe Cannon was five. As for Minneapolis, now a city of four hundred thousand people, seventy-five years ago it consisted of one cabin. Before 1837 there were less than three hundred whites and mixed breeds in all this Minnesotan domain of eighty thousand square miles—the size of England and Scotland put together.

It is so incredibly new; it has grown so dizzyingly. Here is a village which during the Civil War was merely a stockade with two or three log stores and a company of infantry, a refuge for the settlers when the Sioux came raiding. During a raid in 1863 a settler was scalped within sight of the stockade. Now on the spot where the settler was scalped is a bungalow farmhouse, with leaded casement windows, with radio and phonograph, and electric lights in house and garage and barns. A hundred blooded cows are milked there by machinery. The farmer goes into town for Kiwanis Club meetings, and last year he drove his Buick to Los Angeles. He is, or was, too prosperous to belong to the Non-Partisan League or to vote the Farmer–Labour ticket.

Minnesota is unknown to the Average Easterner, say to a Hartford insurance man or to a New York garment-worker, not so much because it is new as because it is neither Western and violent, nor Eastern and crystallised. Factories and shore hotels are inevitably associated with New Jersey, cowpunchers and buttes with Montana; California is apparent, and Florida and Maine. But Minnesota is unplaced. I have heard a Yale junior speculate: "Now you take those Minnesota cities—say, take Milwaukee, for instance. Why, it must have a couple of hundred thousand population, hasn't it?" (Nor is this fiction. He really said it.)

This would be a composite Eastern impression of Minnesota: a vastness of wind-beaten prairie, flat as a parade-ground, wholly given up to wheat-growing save for a fringe of pines at the north and a few market-towns at the south; these steppes inhabited by a few splendid Yankees—one's own sort of people—and by Swedes who always begin sentences with "Vell, Aye tank," who are farmhands, kitchen-maids, and ice-men, and who are invariably humorous.

This popular outline bears examination as well as most popular beliefs; quite as well as the concept that negroes born in Chicago are less courteous than those born in Alabama. Minnesota is not flat. It is far less flat than the province of Quebec. Most of it is prairie, but the prairie rolls and dips and curves; it lures the motorist like the English roads of Broad Highway fiction. Along the skyline the cumulus clouds for ever belly and, with our dry air, nothing is more spectacular than the crimson chaos of our sunsets. But our most obvious beauty is the lakes. There are thousands of them—nine or ten thousand—brilliant among suave grain-fields or masked by cool birch and maples. On the dozen mile-wide lakes of the north are summer cottages of the prosperous from Missouri, Illinois, even Texas.

Leagues of the prairie are utterly treeless, except for artificial wind-breaks of willows and cottonwoods encircling the farm-houses. Here the German Catholic spire can be seen a dozen miles off, and the smoke of the Soo Line freight two stations away. But from this plains country you come into a northern pine wilderness, 'the Big Woods', a land of lumber camps and reservation Indians and lonely tote-roads, kingdom of Paul Bunyan, the mythical hero of the lumberjacks.

The second error is to suppose that Minnesota is entirely a wheat State. It was, at one time, and the Minneapolis flour-mills are still the largest in the world. Not even Castoria is hymned by more billboards than is Minneapolis flour. But to-day it is Montana and Saskatchewan and the Dakotas which produce most of the wheat for our mills, while the Minnesota farmers, building tall red silos which adorn their barns like the turrets of Picardy, turn increasingly to dairying. We ship beef to London, butter to Philadelphia. The iron from our Mesaba mines is in Alaskan rails and South African bridges, and as to manufacturing, our refrigerators and heat-regulators comfort Park Avenue apartment-houses, while our chief underwear factory would satisfy a Massachusetts Brahmin or even a Chicago advertising man.

Greatest error of all is to believe that Minnesota is entirely Yankee and Scandinavian, and that the Swedes are helots and somehow ludicrous.

A school principal in New Duluth, analysed his three hundred and thirty children as Slovene, 49; Italian, 47; Serbian, 39; American, 37; Polish, 30; Austrian and Swedish, 22 each; Croatian, 20; coloured, 9 (it is instructive to note that he did

not include them among the 'Americans'); Finnish, 7;
Scotch, 6; Slav unspecified, 5; German, French, Bohemian,
and Jewish, 4 each; Rumanian, Norwegian, and Canadian,
3 each; Scandinavian unspecified, 8; Lithuanian, Irish,
Ukrainian, and Greek, 2 each; Russian and English, 1 each—
60% of them from Southern and Eastern Europe!

Such a Slavification would, of course, be true only of an
industrial or mining community, but it does indicate that the
whole Mid-Western population may alter as much as has the
East. In most of the State there is a predomination of Yankees,
Germans, Irish, and all branches of Scandinavians, Icelanders
and Danes as well as Swedes and Norwegians. And among
all racial misconceptions none is more vigorously absurd than
the belief that the Minnesota Scandinavians are, no matter
how long they remain here, like the characters of that
estimable old stock-company play *Yon Yonson*—a tribe
humorous, inferior, and unassimilable. To generalise, any
popular generalisation about Scandinavians in America is
completely and ingeniously and always wrong.

In Minnesota itself one does not hear (from the superior
Yankees whom one questions about that sort of thing) that
the Scandinavians are a comic people, but rather that they are
surly, that they are Socialistic, that they 'won't Americanise'.
Manufacturers and employing lumber-men speak of their
Swedish employees precisely as wealthy Seattleites speak of
the Japs, Bostonians of the Irish, South-Westerners of the
Mexicans, New Yorkers of the Jews, marine officers of the
Haitians, and Mr. Rudyard Kipling of nationalist Hindus—
or nationalist Americans. Unconsciously, all of them give
away the Inferior Race Theory, which is this: An inferior race
is one whose members work for me. They are treacherous,
ungrateful, ignorant, lazy, and agitator-ridden, because they
ask for higher wages and thus seek to rob me of the dollars
which I desire for my wife's frocks and for the charities which

glorify me. This inferiority is inherent. Never can they become Good Americans (or English Gentlemen, or High-wellborn Prussians). I know that this is so, because all my university class-mates and bridge-partners agree with me.

The truth is that the Scandinavians Americanise only too quickly. They Americanise much more quickly than Americans. For generation after generation there is a remnant of stubborn American abolitionist stock which either supports forlorn causes and in jail sings low ballads in a Harvard accent, or else upholds, like Lodge, an Adams tradition which is as poisonous as Communism to a joy in brotherly boosting. So thorough are the Scandinavians about it that in 1963 we shall be hearing Norwegian Trygavasons and Icelandic Gislasons saying of the Montenegrins and Letts: "They're reg'lar hogs about wages, but the worst is, they simply won't Americanise. They won't vote either the Rotary or the Ku Klux ticket. They keep hollering about wanting some kind of a doggone Third Party."

Scandinavians take to American commerce and schooling and journalism as do Scotsmen or Cockneys. Particularly they take to American politics, the good old politics of Harrison and McKinley and Charley Murphy. Usually, they bring nothing new from their own experimental countries. They permit their traditions to be snatched away. True, many of them have laboured for the Non-Partisan League, for woman suffrage, for co-operative societies. The late Governor John Johnson of Minnesota seems to have been a man of destiny; had he lived he would probably have been President, and possibly a President of power and originality. But again— there was Senator Knute Nelson, who made McCumber look like a Left Wing syndicalist and Judge Gary like François Villon. There is Congressman Steenerson of Minnesota, chairman of the House Postal Committee. Mr. Steenerson once produced, out of a rich talent matured by a quarter of a century in the House, an immortal sentence. He had been complaining at lunch that the Non-Partisan League had introduced the obscene writings of "this Russian woman, Ellen Key," into the innocent public schools. Someone hinted to the Scandinavian Mr. Steenerson: "But I thought she was a Swede."

He answered: *"No, the Key woman comes from Finland and the rest of Red Russia, where they nationalise the women."*

Naturally it is the two new Senators, Hendrik Shipstead and Magnus Johnson, who now represent to the world the Scandinavian element in Minnesota. How much they may bring to the cautious respectability of the Senate cannot be predicted, but certainly, like John Johnson, they vigorously represent everything that is pioneer, democratic, realistic, *American* in our history.

Good and bad, the Scandinavians monopolise Minnesota politics. Of the last nine governors of the State, including Senatorial-Candidate Preus, six have been Scandinavians. So is Harold Knutson, Republican Whip of the House. Scandinavians make up a large proportion of the Minnesota State Legislature, and while in Santa Fé the Mexican legislators speak Spanish, while in Quebec the representatives still debate in French, though for generations they have been citizens of a British dominion, in Minnesota the politicians who were born abroad are zealous to speak nothing but Americanese. Thus it is in business and the home. Though a man may not have left Scandinavia till he was twenty, his sons will use the same English, good and bad, as the sons of settlers from Maine, and his daughters will go into music clubs or into cocktail sets, into college or into factories, with the same prejudices and ideals and intonations as girls named Smith and Brewster.

The curious newness of Minnesota has been suggested, but the really astonishing thing is not the newness—it is the oldness, the solid, traditionalised, cotton-wrapped oldness. A study of it would be damaging to the Free and Fluid Young

America theory. While parts of the State are still so raw that the villages among the furrows or the dusty pines are but frontier camps, in the cities and in a few of the towns there is as firm a financial oligarchy and almost as definite a social system as London, and this power is behind all Sound Politics, in direct or indirect control of all business. It has its Old Families, who tend to marry only within their set. Anywhere in the world, an Old Family is one which has had wealth for at least thirty years longer than average families of the same neighbourhood. In England it takes (at most) five generations to absorb 'parvenus' and 'profiteers' into the gentry, whether they were steel profiteers in the Great War or yet untitled land profiteers under William the Conqueror. In New York it takes three generations—often. In the Middle West it takes one and a half.

No fable is more bracing, or more absurd, than that all the sons and grandsons of the pioneers, in Minnesota or in California, in Arizona or Nebraska, are racy and breezy, unmannerly but intoxicatingly free. The grandchildren of men who in 1862 fought the Minnesota Indians, who dog-trotted a hundred miles over swamp-blurred trails to bear the alarm to the nearest troops—some of them are still clearing the land, but some of them are complaining of the un-English quality of the Orange Pekoe in dainty painty city tea-rooms which stand where three generations ago the Red River fur-carts rested; their chauffeurs await them in Pierce-Arrow limousines (special bodies by Kimball, silver fittings from Tiffany); they present Schnitzler and St. John Ervine at their Little Theatres; between rehearsals they chatter of meeting James Joyce in Paris; and always in high-pitched Mayfair laughter they ridicule the Scandinavians and Finns who are trying to shoulder into their sacred, ancient Yankee caste. A good many of their names are German.

Naturally, beneath this Junker class there is a useful,

sophisticated, and growing company of doctors, teachers, newspapermen, liberal lawyers, musicians who have given up Munich and Milan for the interest of developing orchestras in the new land. There is a scientific body of farmers. The agricultural school of the huge University of Minnesota is sound and creative. And still more naturally, between Labour and Aristocracy there is an army of the peppy, poker-playing, sales-hustling He-men who are our most characteristic Americans. But even the He-men are not so obvious as they seem. What their future is, no man knows—and no woman dares believe. It is conceivable that, instead of being a menace in their naïve boosting and their fear of the unusual, they may pass only too soon; it is possible that their standardised bathrooms and Overlands will change to an equally standardised and formula-bound culture—yearning Culture, arty Art. We have been hurled from tobacco-chewing to tea-drinking with gasping speed; we may as quickly dash from boosting to a beautiful and languorous death. If it is necessary to be Fabian in politics, to keep the reformers (left wing or rigid right) from making us perfect too rapidly, it is yet more necessary to be a little doubtful about the ardent souls who would sell Culture; and if the Tired Business Man is unlovely and a little dull, at least he is real, and we shall build only on reality.

Small is the ducal set which controls these other classes. It need be but small. In our rapid accumulation of wealth we have been able to create an oligarchy with ease and efficiency, with none of the vulgar risks which sword-girt Norfolks and Percys encountered. This is one of the jests which we have perpetrated. The nimbler among our pioneering grandfathers appropriated to their private uses some thousands of square miles in northern Minnesota, and cut off—or cheerfully lost by forest fire—certain billions of feet of such lumber as will never be seen again. When the lumber was gone, the land seemed worthless. It was good for nothing but agriculture, which is an unromantic occupation, incapable of making millionaires in one generation. The owners had few of them acquired more than a million dollars, and now they could scarcely give their holdings away. Suddenly, on parts of this scraggly land, iron was discovered, iron in preposterous quantities, to be mined in the open pit, as easily as hauling out gravel. Here is the chief supply of the Gary and South Chicago mills. The owners of the land do not mine the ore. They have gracefully leased it—though we are but Westerners, we have our subsidiary of the United States Steel Company. The landowner himself has only to go abroad and sit in beauty like a flower, and every time a steam shovel dips into the ore, a quarter drops into his pocket.

So at last our iron-lumber-flour railroad aristocracy has begun to rival the beef barons of Chicago, the coal lords of Pennsylvania, and the bond princes of New York.

This article is intended to be a secret but flagrant boost. It is meant to increase civic pride and the value of Minnesota real estate. Yet the writer wonders if he will completely satisfy his chambers of commerce. There is a chance that they would prefer a statement of the value of our dairy products, the number of our admirable new school buildings, the number of motor tourists visiting our lakes, and an account of James J. Hill's encouraging progress from poverty to magnificence. But a skilled press agent knows that this would not be a boost; it would be an admission of commerce-ruled barrenness. The interesting thing in Minnesota is the swift evolution of a complex social system, and, since in two generations we have changed from wilderness to country clubs, the question is what the next two generations will produce. It defies certain answer; it demands a scrupulous speculation free equally from the bland certitudes of chambers of commerce and the sardonic impatience of professional radicals. To a realistic philosopher, the existence of an aristocracy is not (since it does exist) a thing to be bewailed, but to be examined as a fact.

There is one merit not of Minnesota alone but of all the Middle West which must be considered. The rulers of our new land may to the eye seem altogether like the rulers of the East—of New England, New York, Pennsylvania. Both groups are chiefly reverent towards banking, sound Republicanism, the playing of golf and bridge, and the possession of large motors. But whereas the Easterner is content with these symbols and smugly desires nothing else, the Westerner, however golfocentric he may be, is not altogether satisfied; and raucously though he may snortle at his wife's "fool suffrage ideas" and "all this highbrow junk the lecture-hounds spring on you", yet secretly, wistfully, he desires a beauty that he does not understand.

As a pendant, to hint that our society has become somewhat involved in the few years since Mr. Henry Lorenz of Saskatchewan was seventy, let me illogically lump a few personal observations of Minnesota:

Here is an ex-professor of history in the State University, an excellent scholar who, retiring after many years of service, cheerfully grows potatoes in a backwoods farm among the northern Minnesota pines, and builds up co-operative selling for all the farmers of his district.

Here is the head of a Minneapolis school for kindergartners, a woman who is summoned all over the country to address teachers' associations. She will not admit candidates for matriculation until she is sure that they have a gift for teaching. She does something of the work of a Montessori, with none of the trumpeting and anguish of the dottoressa.

Here is the greatest, or certainly the largest, medical clinic in the world—the Mayo Clinic, with over a hundred medical specialists besides the clerks and nurses. It is the supreme court of diagnosis. Though it is situated in a small town, off the through rail routes, it is besieged by patients from Utah and Ontario and New York as much as by Minnesotans. When the famous European doctors come to America, they may look at the Rockefeller Institute, they may stop at Harvard and Rush and Johns Hopkins and the headquarters of the American Medical Association, but certainly they will go on to Rochester. The names of 'Charley' and 'Will' have something of the familiarity of 'R.L.S.' and 'T.R.'

Here is a Chippewa as silent and swart as his grandfather, an active person whom the cavalry used to hunt every open season. The grandson conducts a garage, and he actually understands ignition. His farm among the lowering Norway pines he ploughs with a tractor.

Here is a new bookshop which is publishing the first English translation of the letters of Abélard. The translator, Henry Bellows, is a Ph.D., an editor, and a colonel of militia.

Here are really glorious buildings: the Minneapolis Art Institute, the State Capitol, the St. Paul Public Library, and Ralph Adams Cram's loveliest church. Here, on the shore of Lake of the Isles, is an Italian palace built by a wheat speculator. Here where five years ago were muddy ruts are perfect cement roads.

Here is a small town, a 'typical prairie town', which has just constructed a competent golf-course. From this town came a Minister to Siam and a professor of history in Columbia.

And here are certain Minnesota authors. You know what Mid-Western authors are—rough fellows but vigorous, ignorant of the classics and of Burgundy, yet close to the heart of humanity. They write about farmyards and wear flannel shirts. Let us confirm this portrait by a sketch of eleven Minnesota authors, most of them born in the State:

Charles Flandrau, author of *Harvard Episodes* and *Viva Mexico,* one-time Harvard instructor, now wandering in Spain (Agnes Repplier has called him the swiftest blade among

American essayists); Scott Fitzgerald, very much a Minnesotan, yet the father of the Long Island flapper, the prophet of the Ritz, the idol of every Junior League; Alice Ames Winter, recently president of the General Federation of Women's Clubs; Claude Washburn, author of *The Lonely Warrior* and several other novels which, though they are laid in America, imply a European background (he has lived for years now in France and Italy); Margaret Banning, author of *Spellbinders*; Thomas Boyd, author of that valiant impression of youth in battle, *Through the Wheat*; Grace Flandrau, of *Being Respectable* and other authentically sophisticated novels; Woodward Boyd, whose first novel, *The Love Legend*, is a raid on the domestic sentimentalists; Carlton Miles, a dramatic critic who gives his Minnesota readers the latest news of the Continental stage (he is just back from a European year spent with such men as Shaw, Drinkwater, and the director of La Scala); Brenda Ueland, who lives in Greenwich Village and writes for the *Atlantic Monthly;* Sinclair Lewis, known publicly as a scolding corn-belt realist, but actually (as betrayed by the samite-yclad, Tennyson-and-water verse which he wrote when he was in college) a yearner over what in private life he probably calls 'quaint ivied cottages'.

Seventy-five years ago—a Chippewa-haunted wilderness. To-day—a complex civilisation with a future which, stirring or dismaying or both, is altogether unknowable. To understand America, it is merely necessary to understand Minnesota. But to understand Minnesota you must be an historian, an ethnologist, a poet, a cynic, and a graduate prophet all in one.

BACK TO VERMONT

From *The Forum*, April, 1936

¶ They used to say of him that "Red is always buying places". Certainly that was true of the last dozen years of his life. He bought and furnished no less than five homes, including a house in Bronxville, N.Y., Twin Farms at South Pomfret, Vermont, a big duplex apartment in New York, a Tudor castle in Duluth, and Thorvale Farm, near Williamstown, Massachusetts, where he lived the last few years before his final trip to Italy. In that period he went abroad several times and stopped at innumerable New York hotels. This was, of course, a manifestation of his restlessness, his growing discontent with any one environment.

Here Mr. Lewis tells why he settled in Vermont "for good".

THIS REASONABLE AND WHOLESOME PLAN FOR FINDING A PLACE IN which one could be content to dwell does, I admit, start with rather a lot of Ifs, but then so do all plans for World Peace, Happy Marriage, and the Perfect Diet. *If* I could afford it—*if* self and family could instantly be transported from one country to another without the tedium of journeying—*if* one could be rid of the headache of packing and unpacking—and *if* there weren't quite so many different interesting kinds of income taxes—then it would all be simple.

From October 15 to January 1 I would live in New York, and for two reasons: it is the most exciting, idea-jammed, high-coloured city in the world, except perhaps Moscow, and I speak its language, at least some of its languages, better than I do the Muscovite. Second, on the blessed annual New Year's Day when I escaped from its bibulous hysteria, any place in the world, any place at all, even Addis Ababa, would seem enchantingly restful.

Bermuda, then, till the middle of February, and a pink cottage and golden sands and quiet driving on white roads and even—if not too large a proportion of New York has also simultaneously escaped to Bermuda—a fair amount of work. Till April, in California, but not near Los Angeles, no; rather in the Monterey Peninsula, with its memories of Robert Louis Stevenson, Herbert Hoover, Jack London, Aimée McPherson, and such-like romantics; where the witch cypresses breathe to the open Pacific and the polo-players breathe to the Del Monte bar-tender.

The stratospheric transfer is most needed now; from California to catch April in Venice, the one city that, despite motor-boats, tables d'hôte, and American papers in the kiosks, is as magic in daily experience as ever it was on canvas. All sound travel writers remark of the Grand Canyon and Venice: "Who could ever find words to describe their wonders?"— after which they find a lot of words, and often very good ones, to describe the same. I'm not sure whether I prefer sitting on Point Lobos, Carmel, looking out to Japan across the bewitched and mocking rocks, or sitting in Venice's Piazza San Marco, looking up to the cathedral across a mixed vermouth.

England, then, for May—half the time in London and half in any of twenty skylark-lilting counties: Devon or Kent or Sussex or Norfolk, where I have just been ambling along the Broads in a buxom wherry so well trained that without a touch of the tiller it stops at every river-side pub.

Oh, I am willing to be broad-minded; I am willing to change the schedule so that it shall be Venice or England in any month of the year except from mid-November to mid-March. And I can be tempted to Paris, Stockholm, Capri, Florence, the Good Hope Ranch in Jamaica, or Trinidad, in place of the amiable spots listed; and I'd like again to have an autumn in Minnesota, when the prairie chickens, what few are left, are out in the pale-gold stubble.

But, with all this flightiness, this conceivable change, I must—and as a matter of fact mostly do—have from the first of June to the middle of October on my farm in Vermont.

II

Some seven years ago my wife and I went there, without prejudice. We had lived a good deal abroad; we came back to America with only the unrigid notion that we should like a farm somewhere not too far from the New York where, by chance, lived most of our friends. We knew practically no one in Vermont; had no past ties to it—not till we had seen those friendly, shy-coloured, serene hills, when instantly we seemed to have ties past, present, and future. Here was a place of peace, yet not the cloying peace of an Italian vale, but the peace of clear, cool air and an easy vigour without nerves. Since then, without permission, we have added New Hampshire and the Berkshire Hills, on the New York side of the border as well as in Massachusetts, to that kingdom of the hills where sheep still graze on little trails among scrub maple and lichen-patterned rocks and people still have time to sit on the porches of country stores and milk comes out of cows, not out of cans. . . . Usually!

We had found on our quest for land—that so-ancient quest which America forgot for a generation, but has taken up again hungrily these last ten years—other contemplative valleys and hill-sides in Connecticut and Massachusetts, but the prices were too high then, in 1928. (They have dropped incredibly since.)

I refer you to Mrs. Fisher and Kit Morley and old Rowland E. Robinson for more detailed raving about the charms of our

Vermont. . . . Of secret streams, clear and tiny, slipping under an old stone wall, through an old upland pasture gone to seed, and in August a lovely tawniness, through a birch grove—the Grecian shrines must have been like that when they were new and really inhabited by the divinity that has died with the dying stone—and at last, among the needles in a solemn wood of spruce and hemlock, whispering in a tiny waterfall. . . . Of the mountains (not, like the Rockies, so vast as to terrify) when at twilight they begin to grow. I want, rather, to give details in a thoroughly realtor fashion. (No, I have no land to sell and, thank Heaven, I don't need to buy any, either!)

For most people who come from west of Buffalo or south of Washington, Vermont is doubtless too far away for a vacation home. Even for a New Yorker, all save the southern part of it is too far away for anyone who wants to spend all but his week-ends in that interesting city whose symbol is a steel-riveter, rampant. My farm is three hundred miles from New York; a brisk eight-hour drive: railroad connections abominable.

But for a writer, a teacher, a retired man of affairs, anyone who can take a two-month vacation, the place was appointed by the divine powers, and the only reason that I haven't gone into the Vermont real-estate business is that I have been somewhat occupied of late with sundry other forms of missionary labour.

For fifteen hundred to three thousand dollars, part down, you would, if you poked about long enough, find a hundred-acre farm with a solid old farmhouse of eight or ten rooms. It might have running water; it would not have a bathroom, electric lights, or a telephone. There would be one or two magnificently timbered old barns; one of them would make such a studio or minstrels' hall as to draw tears from Christopher Wren. It would be two-thirds of the way up a

mountain-side, protected from too shrewd a wind, but looking ten or twenty miles down a valley between hills chequered
with pastures among small forests of pine, maple, and poplar.
With luck, it would have a trout stream. There would be one
or two or three miles of dirt road, narrow, crooked, very decent
in summer, foul in early spring and late autumn. Five or ten
miles away would be a village almost as gracious as Litchfield
or Sharon. You can spend thirty dollars on modern improve-
ments—*i.e.,* fifteen for kerosene lamps and fifteen for a fine
tin tank to bathe in—and have a stoutly comfortable place, an
authentic home, for the rest of your life.

Your neighbours will be varied. Within a few miles of me,
these past few years, have lived such slightly unco-ordinated
persons as George and Gilbert Seldes; Alexander Woollcott;
Dr. Leo Wolman; Lynn Montross; Richard Billings, the great
railroader; Fred Rothermell; Louis Adamic; and a gentleman
named Calvin Coolidge. But, except at Dorset and Manchester, you will find no roar and flood of summerites. And
as to the natives . . .

They are a complicated, reticent, slyly humorous lot, and
I doubt if any place in the world will you find a citizenry
which so strictly minds its own business. If you come to know
them but slowly or not at all, on the other hand they do not
snoop; they do not pry; they have the reserve and self-respect
of an ancient race that feels too secure to be more than just
vaguely amused by the eccentricities of outlanders. Of a
millionaire New Yorker, a Rodin, or a George Bernard Shaw,
a Vermont farmer would stoutly say: "He ain't my kind of
folks, but guess he's just as good as anybody else, long's he
don't interfere with me."

It is a cool land, with ever-changing skies, this Vermont.
For me it is peace and work and home.

AMERICANS IN ITALY

1. Mr. Eglantine
2. Ann Kullmer

¶ *The following two pieces appeared in a series on Italy which Mr. Lewis wrote for the Bell Syndicate in 1948. The articles were published in many papers in the United States and Canada between January and May of the next year and attracted considerable editorial comment. Lack of space forbids the use in this book of more than two.*

These articles, with the completion of his novel World So Wide, *published a few weeks after his death on January 10, 1951, constitute his final printed work. For several months before his fatal illness he was writing something which Alexander Manson, the author's secretary-courier in Lewis's last months, revealed, in a* Saturday Evening Post *article, to be poetry. This material remains in the hands of the Lewis Estate, but there has been no announcement in regard to its publication.*

Mr. Eglantine is representative of a type, common in Europe, which Lewis knew well and abominated. In his many visits abroad he knowingly allowed himself to be fleeced time after time by the American expatriate grafter, just to watch the creature perform.

He had an almost pathological feeling about paying his own debts instantly and an equal hatred for the free-loader or dead-beat. Yet, as a student of humanity, he tolerated these leeches with an amused contempt and frequently kept a group of people fascinated for hours by his impersonations of the notable ones who lent colour to the European scene.

The second article, in a very different mood, deals with an American of another sort, and with an occasion to make a fellow-countryman proud. It tells the story of how Ann Kullmer of Macomb, Illinois, and Dorset, Vermont, conducted a concert at the San Carlo Opera House of Naples in the winter of 1948. She was the first woman, American or otherwise, to direct an Italian orchestra in a major presentation.

As stated earlier in these notes, Lewis's love for music came late in his life, and this is the only piece in our collection that reflects it.

1. MR. EGLANTINE

MR. VERNON EGLANTINE IS THIN AND RATHER TALL AND AS respectable-looking as an English muffin. He resembles a professor in a five-elm college, and that is what he was until that slight misconception of his interest in a girl student, when the college president is said to have chased him down the steps of Old Main and half-way to the library. Since then, he has prepared house organs for large and robust Cleveland firms, written verse for greeting cards, and translated scandalous novels from languages he does not quite understand into English which you'd better not understand. And for thirty years he has been a veteran of American artistic colonies in Europe, along with his latest wife, Mitzi, who is jolly and has large amounts of black hair, not often washed. Verny and Mitzi are usually shaky from ten a.m., when they rise, till ten-ten, when they have their first cognac.

They were insiders in the good old days of the Left Bank in Paris. Ten thousand Americans lived in Paris then and had their own bars and restaurants and newspapers. There Verny added to his literary art the art of sponging. His speciality was getting the names of rich new American arrivals from the local papers, calling on these innocents to ask, with all his skinny and stork-like solemnity, about a hypothetical uncle back home, and gratefully inviting the tenderfoot of the boulevards out to a fat lunch. Good old Mitzi always just happened to drop in at the restaurant and she got invited too.

Sometimes, with Verny's bright conversation and hints of how to see in Paris what could not be seen, the lunch was good for a hundred-dollar touch, so thankful was the cultural sucker at having this new friend to show him the soft and dusky underside of Paris. Sometimes it was only twenty-five—and a dollar and a half accepted cheerfully. Anyway, it was always a lunch—enough sordid solid sustenance to last the Eglantines for two days, so that they could reserve their cash for the more necessary provender of grappa and brandy.

When the magnificent luncheon bill was reverently borne in, on silver, Verny as host would look at it yawningly, and do a skilled and professional fumble. Oh! He had left his purse at home! Never mind; they knew and loved him here in this brocaded restaurant; they'd take his cheque. And he would actually, with the slow art of the old master, bring out a real cheque-book, but what do you think? All the cheques had been used up.

Sometimes the Eglantines had a quarter of an hour of warm pleasure in watching the downfall of the sucker, who ten days before had been a canny banker or salesman back home. Sometimes it was only five sly, exquisite minutes. But always, finally, the sucker paid for the lunch. Except that the Eglantines made it a principle that if he had 'lent' them, as it was called, over seventy-five dollars, they themselves would pay, out of the fistful of paper francs which Mitzi carried in her greasy black and gold handbag.

They felt that they were spiritually soiled by having thus to associate with American business-men, but they made up for it in their wonderful permanent friends of the Latin Quarter cafés: women with faces like athletic young men, young men with faces like petulant girls, and all the geniuses who for ten years now had been writing a non-objective free-verse play about Edgar Allan Poe. (After 1946 this play, all the hundred lines of it so far written, would be turned into an existentialist drama with Lord Haw-Haw as the hero.)

When War II came to make such annoying inconvenience to gentle people like the Eglantines, Verny and Mitzi escaped to England, where she washed her hair (early in 1941 that was) and he took to shaving and was employed by the government as an expert on American culture. Much later, they found that they should have returned to America, for their old friend Hank Hiller, who in Paris had never rated much higher than Anatole France, had gone to California and founded an academy of geniuses who stupefied America with admiration by spelling all the five-letter words with four letters, so that, reading them, young ladies in Bennington College became able to shock their ex-prospector grandfathers.

The Eglantines frolicked back to Paris in '47, but all the glories of their particular France, so nicely rotting like a decaying pear, were gone, and it was cold. They decided to take their combination of American enterprise and French culture to Italy, early in 1948.

Naturally, they first tried Capri, that lovely rock island of the sirens, which ever since the Emperor Tiberius has been a refuge for slightly frowsy genius. But they discovered there much better hobohemians and cadgers than themselves, Russians and Hungarians and Peruvians and Javanese, and they all spoke real spoken Italian. Verny did not speak it, no, not enough to call an Italian pussy-cat. He merely translated from it. And wrote articles on the young Italian poets. And Capri was so small, with so few boats, that nasty shopkeepers could get to you about that little matter of the five thousand lire for wine and cheese.

They moved then to the neighbouring island of Ischia, in the Bay of Naples, where the damp brethren were gathering, but all of these ingrates were inclined to keep their lire for themselves. Indignantly, they went on to Florence. They did find, in the Camillo and Sostenza, in Florence, such small, cheap, excellent restaurants, jammed with American art students and Russian mystics and Italian pianists, as in Paris had always meant pickings, but in disgust they also found that even the most arty-looking Anglo–Americans went regularly to church; that some of the English rather liked England, and some of the Americans still hankered after ice-cream soda and Grant Wood's paintings.

They were broke. Mitzi had to do baby-sitting for the wife of an American vice-consul, and Verny had to go to work and finish up his book on Romanesque Art: A Handbook for Normal Schools. He went so far as to walk nine whole blocks to look at the Tuscan Gothic church of Santa Maria Novella, which was the most intensive laboratory work he had ever done on the subject, and it took him seven cognacs to recover.

Then the good rumours came in. On the Ligurian Coast, below Genoa, in a bus-stop village where Ezra Pound had once lived, robed in purple petulance, the Boys and Girls were beginning to flutter in, and the beautiful realm of art freed from morals and oatmeal porridge would soon be established again.

To this village fled Verny and Mitzi, and the first person they saw walking down the tiny Corso was a rich and languorous American gent in Basque trousers and sash and rope sandals, and with him were a young lady in severe riding-breeches and starched white shirt, and another young lady in a smock so artistic and modern and novel that it might have been worn by her grandmother, who used to be the shock of the more advanced artistic circles in West Virginia.

The strangers and the Eglantines all looked at one another knowingly.

"Have a strega?" murmured the American gent.

Verny and Mitzi sighed and smiled and felt good—like a Hemingway hero after the seventh beer—and they knew that in Europe there would never be a time when Americans too sensitive to cope with high schools and tarpon fishing and gum and air-conditioning will not be able to find somewhere an asylum where the less-hairy Whitmans will sit together from 22.30 to 2 and tell one another how superior they are to all the Babbitts in Iowa and Ireland and Oslo and South Uruguay.

The Eglantines are still at that village on the Italian Riviera and every day they still say to each other, after borrowing lunch money: "I do hope this place won't be ruined by all these dreadful American tourists."

2. ANN KULLMER

TALL, GHOSTLY WALLS OF WHITE AND GOLD, SIX TIERS HIGH, lighted only from the rehearsal lamps on stage; the royal box surmounted by scarlet robes and a great gilt crown, all futile now, and in that box, listening, the ghosts of royal Murats and Bourbons. In humbler boxes, the humbler but greater ghosts of Bellini and Rossini and other Italian composers who, in this sacred, vast room, first heard their music given full life.

The San Carlo Opera House of Naples, built in 1737, and the Naples Symphony Orchestra rehearsing for the second concert of the 1948–9 winter season. On stage in flimsy chairs, a busy mob in sweaters and shirt-sleeves, very much like any New York musical group, with five pretty women among them—one of them the *Konzertmeister*. Then, striding out to direct them, no gaunt European male conductor, but a girl, and an American girl—the first woman, American or otherwise, ever to direct an Italian orchestra in a major presentation.

Ann Kullmer of Macomb, Illinois, and Dorset, Vermont, facing the probably approving ghost of Donizetti!

Not till the advanced age of six did Miss Kullmer complete her piano study and switch to the violin, and she was all of eleven when she won the first prize of the Detroit Conservatory, and a venerable fourteen when she became a member of the Indianapolis Symphony. Then off to Leipzig to study conducting, along with the violin, and nine years ago, at the hoary age of twenty-two in Berlin, she first conducted an orchestra.

Now, on stage, she comes out to the podium—a sturdy, energetic girl in work clothes of tan silk blouse and green skirt. She raps, and all of the ninety-odd musicians—some of them old enough to be her grandfather—snap into obedience. She has a proud, dark head, held high. Like other young orchestra leaders today, she conducts from memory, without a score, and does not use a baton, but moulds the music with her two strong hands, with arms that swing like in a walking race.

Conductor's baton, field-marshal's baton, king's sceptre, slave-driver's whip—all are gone now and, in what we call a mechanical age, the human hand returns to its bare magic.

For her Naples concert Miss Kullmer had not chosen an easy programme. It included the Second Sibelius, which had never before been presented in Naples, and Aaron Copland's *Rodeo,* with its mocking and intricate Wild Western American rhythms, which had not been heard in all Italy. None of her musicians knew a bar of either opus, and she had not merely to drill them—this foreigner, this young woman now first landed in Italy—but to teach them every step.

I still don't know how she did it, for, with all her knowledge of French and German, when she had taken the steamer for this tour she had not known a word of Italian except for such juicy musical directions as are printed at the beginnings of movements.

She learned it all, she said, from her little book and from her stewardess on the ship—in ten days! Yet here, in a language which seemed to be accepted by these shrewd professionals as Italian, she was pounding them, encouraging them, clarifying the tricky passages of old Sibelius, who is no friend to smooth amateurs.

And the orchestra loved it, loved her, and at intermission they jammed into her dressing-room to call her "Mæstra" with affection and to beg for her autograph.

That day I had seen three beautiful things: a monastery, brimming with utter peace, on a lava island-hill set against the rugged sulphurous slope of Mount Vesuvius; a rainbow over the Bay of Naples from the terrace of a restaurant on the cliff at Sorrento; and now the unity of artists from two distant nations in a common creation of beauty.

For the actual concert next evening, though Italian music-fanatics are not particularly welcoming to novelties like Copland, the vastness of the San Carlo was full, clear up through the sixth tier, from which the diminished features of students looked down as if from the roof of a tall apartment-house.

The bearded professors who had to be shown were there, and I picked out a round-faced and contemptuous youngish man, condescending to all the old stagers, as a music critic—even in the warm Naples early afternoon I shivered. And, higher up in station as they were lower down in ticket prices, were the hundreds of music students—all hard-boiled, ready enough to welcome a fellow artist among the American Barbarian Invaders, but quite as ready to hoot at Miss Kullmer if she and her Copland proved to be nothing but slick jazz novelties.

Now, before the orchestra, majestic in tails and white shirt-fronts, the conductor was equally formal in white blouse and dead-black skirt; and when her long arms stretched out for the first notes, the magic that is music and the stage and the hypnotised crowd came quick and sharp, and she already had won.

It was all an ovation: five curtain-calls for Miss Kullmer at intermission, seven at the end, and the mass rising in admiration for her, in fondness for her; and in that were both the monastery peace and the power of Vesuvius.

At the concert I sat with three American oil-men, very proud of "our Ann", though they had never before seen her, and with the officers of the destroyer-tender U.S.S. *Grand Canyon*. At the end, the executive officer-commander sighed: "I wonder if our being here and Ann's being here don't both have some new meaning in history? Some day her début here might mean as much as the Marshall Plan."

The doctor-commander reminded us that just across from the San Carlo is Naples's renowned Galleria—eloquently recorded in John Horne Burns's novel, *The Gallery*—and that there, under a lofty glass roof, in a private crossroads free from the rain and from the horrors of traffic, are practically all the liquor shops in the world, together with the spectacle of night strollers who are quite astonishingly ready to be friendly with such innocent strangers as we.

Seated there, drinking the Italian equivalents of 'cokes', we heard a stately couple at the next table give verdict, with a hand-wave towards the San Carlo: "*Si, benissimo—benissimo!*"

Next day, all the music critics in the Naples papers said that here had been no freak importation, like the unfortunate appearance of boy conductors in velvet knee pants; that Ann Kullmer's had been a directorial triumph: solid, massive, sure.

Is that history—this Illinois girl in an opera-house built forty years before the American revolution? If that isn't history, what is?

VI

SOCIAL QUESTIONS

Is America a Paradise for Women?
Cheap and Contented Labour

IS AMERICA A PARADISE FOR WOMEN?

From *The Pictorial Review,* June, 1929

¶ *This piece was the author's side of a debate with his second wife, Dorothy Thompson, Mr. Lewis taking the affirmative and Miss Thompson the negative.*

Friends who have heard him arguing any point which at the moment took his fancy will see in this as true a reflection of his voice and manner, under certain circumstances, as can be found—the hyperbole made convincing, the staggering general knowledge, the annoying facility for bending that knowledge to his uses, the intolerance (for the moment) of any contrary voice; and at the end, so often, a dizzying reversal of position in which he knocked all his own arguments out and left his hearers gasping.

WHEN OUR ANCESTRESS EVE STILL DWELT IN EDEN SHE COMPLAINED a good deal to Father Adam, and to all of the animals that would listen, about the dullness of the scene and the society. She wanted to live some place else. She was certain that all the men in all the Some Place Elses were gallanter towards women, and with lips apart she listened to the first gigolo who flattered her. But that gigolo was a Serpent and not a sound domestic adviser, no matter how well he danced in the moonlight, no matter how glistening his scales.

When she took his advice and was pushed into the Great World Outside which she had desired, she found that all the time, without knowing it, she had been in Paradise.

Eve's voluble belief that Eden was not Paradise did not keep it from being Paradise. And perhaps the fable is not entirely untrue for today.

I decidedly do not maintain that these United States compose or ever will compose an absolute Paradise for women—or men, or children, or any other breed of animals. But neither is any other country, and I do maintain that for the woman with imagination and eagerness this country presents problems and opportunities, presents a conceivable future, which are more stimulating than the beautiful peace of any other land.

I do not maintain that Mr. George F. Babbitt is any more uplifting as a husband than he is as a luncheon-club orator; I do not maintain that he makes love more exquisitely than the pretty Don Juans and Casanovas you see playing on the sands at the Lido. But I do maintain that Mrs. George F., if she has the stuff in her, has the chance here, and the invitation, to take part in creating a dramatic new world of industry, education, family life, and that her husband, poor clump, leaves her more free than any woman on earth to tickle her egotism with the flattery of the Don Juans between-whiles.

It would be the flattest sort of chauvinism to say that we have here all the European security of tradition, sweetness of easy gaiety, beauty of old marble—as yet. What we may have five hundred years from now no one knows save "the amateur ethnologists who have patented this Nordic supremacy myth", but now we are still awkward and self-conscious with newness, and we boast only that we may not quaver.

We can show nothing like an English drawing-room at tea-time, a French café looking on chestnuts in spring bloom, a German mountain-top with the knapsacked hikers singing, or the slopes of Capri in autumn sunshine as seen from the walls of Tiberias. No, we have nothing here save the spectacle of the very centre of the world's greatest revolution—a revolution that makes the Bolshevik upheaval seem like a mere national election and the French Revolution like a street fight!

We need not read history for our drama—we are in history, right now! The world is changing (for good or bad) from an ill-connected series of individualist businesses to a common-wealth of gigantic industries in which each individual has no more freedom than a private (or even a general) in any army in war-time.

Whether or not this loss of freedom is compensated for by an increased sense of importance in belonging to an organisation mighty and significant, whether one would prefer to be the lone trapper or the smartly uniformed corporal with his companions-in-arms, is not the question, for we have already been drafted, and, like it or not, we are in that war—the most exciting and dangerous war in history.

And women, hitherto the weeping stay-at-homes or the wailing refugees in war, have as much place in this one as any man. The woman teacher, controlling the education of a hundred men children; the woman wife, no longer regarding her man's business as a mystery, but as a plain job which she can understand as well as he; the woman uplifter or politician or salesman of real estate or publisher or author—she has exactly the place in this universal army that her brains and energy and ambition demand.

She is less secure than the lady of the manor, controlling her spinning-maids and the grubbers in the walled garden, four hundred dead years ago—but then, she no longer has to remain back home in the manor!

If Eve now finds Eden dull the world allows her to go out and make her own Paradise—and the women in America who have opened the barber-shops to women and closed the bar-rooms to men have done that remaking of Paradise to an extent which is slightly dismaying to low, ordinary men like myself—to such an extent that I wonder whether the question here debated should not be: "Is America a Paradise for Any-one *Except* Women?"

I doubt whether any of the reasons usually given so patly and fatly by most reporters of America as a female Paradise are really important. It is true that women here have more 'domestic conveniences' than anywhere else in the world—more electric flat-irons and toasters and refrigerators and dish-washing machines, more gas-stoves and vacuum-cleaners and oil-furnaces and garbage-incinerators. But then! For the women who are mistresses the servants are so much more expensive that the ruling class can have but a quarter as many of them as elsewhere in the world.

And for the women who are servants (it must distinctly be remembered, though discussions of women rather frequently forget it, that the wives of doctors and lawyers and authors and sales managers do not compose the entire feminine world)—for the women servants, their apparently high wages and their laboratory-like kitchens do not always make up for the fact that most Americans do not have the reverence for good cooking nor the respect for smart servants which is to be found in Europe.

And it is true that our women have more leisure than in Europe. Think of the canned goods which permit them to prepare dinner in five minutes! "Think of the increasing number of women in service flats whose chief daily task is to struggle out of bed and find the remains of yesterday's box of candy!" Yet this constantly offered reason why our women should be happy often means precisely nothing. It's not the heat—it's the humidity; it's not the leisure—it's what one may do with the leisure.

A man in solitary confinement in prison has complete leisure, yet I am told that he rarely gets any great ecstasy out of it. I am certain that a woman who has to work in the fields all day, but who works with her men-folk, who sings

252

with them, who laughs as she eats her bread and cheese under the hedge, who feels strong, and resolute, and significant, is considerably happier than a woman in a workless apartment who, afternoon upon drab afternoon, has nothing to do save play bridge, go window-shopping, look at a movie.

The third reason usually given for the paradisiality of America for women—that their husbands are so generous, so complaisant, so obedient—seems to me equally bunk, because most human beings would rather be united to spouses whom they must struggle to please, but whom they respect, than to weaklings whom they can twist around their fingers, but whom they despise. Whether they are conscious of it or not, most women would rather be married to a Napoleon than to a Mr. Pickwick—and it is precisely the amiable, vague, foolishly generous virtues of a Pickwick that have been exhibited as admirable in American husbands.

I seem to be arguing against my own thesis, that America is the women's Paradise. I am not. I am trying to dispose, or suggest ways of disposing, of foolish reasons for a wise thesis, because more debates are lost by the sentimental reasoning of the advocates than by the savagery of the opponents.

No, I do not present America as desirable for women because it gives them an easy life, but precisely because it gives them a hard life—a keen, belligerent, striving, exciting life of camp and embattled field; because it gives them a part in this revolution which (whether we like it or hate it) is changing all our world from the lilac-hedged cottages of Main Street to the overpowering, the intimidating yet magnificent bastions of Park Avenue; from the chattering court following a toy monarch in glass coaches to the hard, swift procession of industrial lords in 120-h.p. cars.

Women not only can take full part in this revolution—they are taking it, and such women, though they may long to return to the lilacs and roses and peace of Main Street, are certainly not returning. If they cannot utterly enjoy being warriors, they can never now enjoy anything less valiant.

Consider a woman like Miss Frances Perkins, recently appointed State Commissioner of Labour in New York—a position of considerable significance in a State where at least eight million people are classed as labourers or the families of labourers—a position considerably weightier than that of the King of Norway or Sweden or the President of the Irish Free State.

Miss Perkins has, with zest, climbed through all the grades from that of an unknown social worker struggling for fire-escapes on factories, through years as Her Honour the Judge in the Workmen's Compensation Court, to her present power. And she has managed to do it without any of that celebrated 'loss of femininity', for in private life Miss Perkins is a Mrs., an extremely good wife and mother, and the most entertaining of friends.

Consider Miss Mabel Willebrandt. Whether one admire her as an enforcer of prohibition or detest her as an evangelical politician and self-advertiser, one must admit that more than anyone else in the country she has won the right to be Attorney-General of the United States. Then consider a woman who was completely opposed to Miss Willebrandt in the late lamented campaign—Mrs. Henry Moskowitz, Al Smith's prime adviser and chief coach. If he had won, the credit would have belonged to her as much as to his own vivid self. And with them, view Miss Elisabeth Marbury, who is, both as politician and as producer of plays, quite the equal of any man rival.

And turning to what is sometimes known with amiable pleasantry as 'the art of writing', regard women like Edith Wharton, Willa Cather, Ruth Suckow, Mary Austin, Anne Parrish, Gertrude Atherton, Dorothy Canfield, Mary Roberts Rinehart, Kathleen Norris, Alice Duer Miller, Josephine

Herbst, Evelyn Scott, Katherine Mayo—at least as important as any equal number of males.

I could go on with women congressmen, researchers, actresses, heads of social settlements, editors, or women in business—developing narrow white tea-rooms into millionaire candy companies. I could suggest that Aimée Semple McPherson is, admire her or detest her, the most renowned figure in organised religion in America today, better known than Billy Sunday, S. Parkes Cadman, or Harry Emerson Fosdick, and more adored by her following. And the greatest religious leader of the decade before her was another woman—Mary Baker Eddy!

But these celebrated ladies I bring in only as a hint that, increasingly, the greatest careers in this country are open to women. But that fact, applying only to a few women of extraordinary vigour, or charm, or intelligence, or instinct for publicity, is less important than the fact that everywhere in America women have, if they care to seize it, a power and significance at least equal to that of the men about them.

It is most seen in the schools.

Actually, two distinguished English observers, Mr. Bertrand Russell and Mr. H. G. Wells, complain that the chief trouble with America is that women have too much control of our education, and thus, training our future citizens in the way they shall think or fear to think, have control of all our social life; that through the preponderance of women teachers in our schools all America is becoming feminised.

They politely hint that though the Typical American Business-Man, with his heavy shoulders, his large spectacles, his clenched cigar, his growling about poker and golf and fishing and the stock-market, seems to the eye particularly masculine, at heart, in his fear of offending the conventions, in his obedience to public prejudice, in his negative attitude that goodness consists not in doing fine things but in failing to do dangerous things, he is tied to the apron-strings of the women teachers of his boyhood; that he has become effeminised, without having the virtues of being frankly feminine.

Whether or not Mr. Wells and Mr. Russell are anything save ingenious, it is certain that in all our schools save a few private retreats for the rather wealthy, it is women who do nine-tenths of the direct teaching. The school principals, with their fussiness about ventilation and assignments in Cæsar, may be men, but it is women who day after day give, equally to boys and to girls, their concepts of courage, learning, decency, good manners, along with the less significant instruction in the details of algebra and the exports of Sumatra.

And when the boys and girls go home, it is mother—not father, as in England or Germany—who chiefly instructs them in the ethics of sex and cleanliness. And to make it all complete, on the Sabbath day it is women who, in Sunday school, teach them the eternal mysteries.

Women to whom Paradise is escape from responsibility, amorous flattery, and emulating the lilies of the field, will find all this rather grubby and irritating. But to women for whom Paradise is creation of life and thought, living life, this opportunity of having more power than was ever seized by any bandit dictator will be more satisfying than any condition of life that women in any other age, in any land, have ever known.

It is not alone the professional teachers, the home-determining mothers, and the religious instructors among American women who have power and the zest of activity. Everywhere in Europe, or in China or Timbuktu, for that matter, it is males who determine what books and operas and painters shall be popular, what social movements—eugenics or tenement reform or revised taxation—shall be considered momently important.

But in America these decisions are to an inconceivable extent made by our women's clubs. A curious situation, which will puzzle future historians, almost to frenzy. For ninety per cent of our male politicians, however billowing their frock-coats, however *basso profundo* their voices on the radio, however noble their hawk-like or Roman noses as depicted in the rotogravure sections, in private life use such brains as they may have only on the chess-like problems of political advancement.

Their utterances on the things regarding which they are supposed to be experts and representatives of the pee-pul, their opinions on prohibition, foreign affairs, pacifism, agricultural relief, and what not, are determined for them by the women's clubs back home.

It is the women, in these clubs, in their courses of study, their reading, their prejudices or lack of prejudices, who form the only really large and half-way co-ordinated 'body of public opinion' in these hustling but uncontemplative States.

And when all the male editors have produced their magazines, male publishers have issued their books, male authors have composed their arguments (on, for example, such a subject as 'Is America the Women's Paradise?'), when the male playwrights and producers have set forth their wares, and male critics have given judgment on novels, after this it is the women, the one sex in the country that really reads and meditates and talks to others about its reading and the fruits of its meditation, that decides what book or play, what magazine or article, shall be sufficiently approved—or vigorously enough disapproved!—to be allowed to live and have its being.

What brought prohibition to America? The Anti-Saloon League, the lauded evangelists? Not by a long shot! They do themselves too much honour!

It was the women of America, working for these past hundred and fifty years, diffidently beginning in the days when in frontier cabins they heard their men-folk yowling over fifty-cents-a-gallon corn liquor, rising at last to the women's temperance societies in all the evangelical churches, and the grim and powerful W.C.T.U.; it was the women at home, coaching their sons in the evils of alcohol and raising Cain if their husbands came home with a breath.

The women of America wanted prohibition, and got it. If they ever want any other incredibly revolutionary experiment—communism or universal church union, polygamy or vegetarianism, pacifism or cannibalism—they will get that, too, and all the walrus-voiced politicians and ingenious pamphleteers will be but megaphones for their small, invincible voices.

In fact, men have accomplished but one thing in America—they have, by some magic which one would suppose to be beyond their powers, kept women from knowing how lucky a human being is to be born a woman in these United States, to be born one of the ruling sex and not one of that pompous, waddling, slightly ridiculous, and pathetic race of belated children known as men!

But there are women, and many women, and extraordinarily intelligent and pleasant and notable women, who answer that this is all very well, and even perhaps partly true, but as for them, they do not desire this power, this influence. They want the things symbolised by the traditional beauty of Europe—husbands who are also charming lovers, children who are not automata to be filled up with feminised education, backgrounds suggesting two thousand years of building and passion and aspiration—who desire, in fact, to be not statesmen in step-ins, but to be *women*!

Well, if they desire gallantry, it is at least as much up to them as it is up to men to create among our hitherto somewhat stiff and embarrassed people, with our subconscious theory that the good Lord somehow made an error in creating

258

human bodies, the suave yet passionate atmosphere which raises Europeans above the level of shamefaced flirtation.

And I believe that it is precisely the reckless flapper, who is so much condemned by the long-noses for her wicked 'necking', who is, in an experimental way, beginning to create that atmosphere; I believe that as the New York of the '70s, the plush-horse New York of the Jim Fisks and the Boss Tweeds, has turned into a metropolis which in elegance compares with any European capital whatever, so a generation from now American social life, the easy and unembarrassed association of men and women, will have the richness known in Europe today.

And meanwhile, if our imprisoned Eves want Europe—why, they can have it!

Among all the nations of earth, only in America, Britain, Germany, and Scandinavia are the women allowed to go off travelling alone, at their own sweet wills, without having an infernal row kicked up by their husbands, fathers, brothers, and cousins even unto the seventh connection. And none of the three other lands gives to their women such liberty as does America. The English squire can, without hysterics, see his women go off to the Continent alone, but he expects them to stick to safe, canonical places—the nice quiet hotel at Vevey, or Cousin Ethelbert's at Hyères, or that really sweet *pension* at San Remo where you *never* meet any Americans or Italians or curious people like that.

But the American woman who feels that she must have European spice to her Yankee corn bread may go as she pleases, if her husband or father has money enough—or almost money enough—and he hears with equanimity, probably with too much equanimity, that she has stayed at a doubtful hotel in Paris, that she has gone to the Coliseum by moonlight with a count of the most dubious countishness.

If an Italian, an Austrian, a Frenchman, a Spaniard, heard

259

of such capers, his wife would jolly well be told to stay there in the Coliseum with her count, in rain and sleet as well as affable moonlight. But our American yearner, when she tires of gigolos and galleries, can come home at will, and at will resume her position as Lady Mussolini of the local study club.

I do not mean to say that any large percentage of American husbands have the money to permit their wives to indulge in such escapism. But they all have the willingness. And it is astounding how much American women in families of no great wealth do travel. The wife of the average small-town doctor or lawyer, with an income of thirty-five hundred dollars a year, expects to go across at least once. The wife of a man of corresponding income in Europe would be lucky if she were allowed to visit Aunt Marie a hundred miles away. In her family the money would be saved—for what? For her son, that he might show the smartness which in Europe belongs not to women, but to the lordly male!

In no other land, in no other age, have women expected to have their cakes and eat them. The joke is that they actually get away with it!

For every native American woman who sighs that she is a martyr to live here, there is a foreign-born American woman who gloats that she is lucky to have come.

We have a young Czech maid, six years in America, who saved enough money so that last summer she was able to go back to Bohemia to see her father and mother. She had a notion of remaining, but she returned in two months, and thus Mary explains it:

"Gee, I'm never going back to that country again. Say, gee, it was fierce. My Old Man makes my Old Woman do whatever he wants her to. She can't do nothing without he lets her. There was a fellow there wanted to marry me. He's well off, too, that fellow. But when I looks at my Old Woman, 'Nix,' I says, 'not on your life; I'm going back to America, where a woman gets what money she earns and don't get it took off her by her Old Man like they do back in the Old Country. Not on your life,' I says; 'even a cook is her own boss in America,' I says.

"And say, my Old Man, he don't need money none; he's got a mill, he's fixed good, but he keeps a-hinting and a-hinting about the money I'd saved and how a man ought to get what his daughter's made, and I says: 'Here's a thousand bucks,' I says, and say, he *took* it! And he didn't need it! Say! Do you know what the trouble with them Europeans is? They don't think about nothing but money!"

I had intended, with Rockefeller-like philanthropy, to present Mary's opinion to the next European who writes or lectures about Das Dollar Land and Uncle Shylock. But I donate it, instead, to all the Eves who find Eden insufficiently like Paradise to suit them, and who are unwilling to do anything whatever to make it so.

CHEAP AND CONTENTED LABOUR

¶ *This was originally published in 1929 as a series of articles in the Scripps-Howard newspapers, released by the United Feature Syndicate. It was republished as a pamphlet that same year by the Women's Trade Union League, in an edition of 25,000 copies. The pamphlet carries the sub-title 'The Picture of a Southern Mill Town in 1929.' Opposite the title page appears the following note signed by the Kiwanis Club of Marion, North Carolina: "This booklet presents facts and conclusions in behalf of the city of Marion that must needs command the careful attention of the whole great world of industry, commerce and finance."*

The text has been cut somewhat because of space limitations. Of all of Mr. Lewis's twenty-two novels, the unwritten 'labour novel' was threshed over by more people and more openly discussed than any other. Perhaps it is a fair question to ask if that is the reason, considering the author's temperament and method of work, it was never finished. As is generally known, Lewis enlisted the help of technical experts on various books, most notably Arrowsmith *and* Elmer Gantry. *For the most part he went it alone, retaining the freshness of the writing for the book rather than for talk.*

The following piece is considered important for this collection because it reflects what was in his mind in 1929, when he was most actively at work on the labour project. None of the note-books or partial drafts of the labour novel has ever been published, and this is the only available expression on the subject. True, it is journalism, but Lewis took the United Feature assignment to cover the textile strike, because at that time he was steeping his mind in material for the labour novel. What he learned there would be grist to his mill.

The account by Professor Ramon Guthrie of Dartmouth of his work with Lewis on this project, given at the opening ceremonies of the Sinclair Lewis Exhibit at the American Academy of Arts and Sciences in February, 1952, and republished in the Academy proceedings, is probably the most complete story that ever will be told of the ill-starred novel that never was written.

INTRODUCTION

THIS ACCOUNT OF INDUSTRIAL JUSTICE IN AMERICA TODAY IS A revision and extension of six articles on the cotton-mills at Marion, N.C., which appeared in the Scripps-Howard newspapers beginning on October 21, 1929.

Since then (this is written on November 25, 1929), two crucial things have happened, aside from court trials.

The chiefs of the American Federation of Labour have met in Washington to pledge support for an aggressive unionisation of the whole South, with special financial aid to the United Textile Workers, that branch of the American Federation of Labour which affects not only cotton-mill towns like Marion, but all cotton–wool–silk–rayon mills in the whole country.

But the second event is that the workers, especially in Marion, have become discouraged. They are hungry, tired, bewildered. They are sick of being shot down. Unless the whole country encourages them (and there are few more delicate and tactful forms of encouragement than dollar bills) they will crawl back into the slavery I have sought to picture here.

I

The history of the 1929 strikes at the Marion Manufacturing Co. and the Clinchfield Mills at Marion, N.C., is told here.

It is the strike in which deputy sheriffs fired upon textile mill workers with the unfortunate result that five, so far, are dead and more than twenty wounded.

Early in 1929 there was trouble at these mills. Three or four malicious workers said that wages just above the starving line were not enough.

The worst of these were two young men named Lawrence Hogan and Dan Elliott. I have met them both; to my simple mind they seem as fine, as magnificent young men as I have ever known.

Lawrence is a huge, square-shouldered Irishman with a quiet voice and a vast efficiency.

Dan is almost too sensationally good-looking. He looks like

Henry Ward Beecher, with his lion's mane, and my chief fear is that when the Church of God has time to hear about what is happening to God's children, they will get hold of Dan and make him a popular preacher.

These lads and a few others, sickened by conditions under which they lived, and having heard vaguely about a form of salvation known as 'the Union', in all innocence and ignorance asked the State Federation of Labour how to organise. An organiser was sent in and the workers flocked to the Union.

Committees were elected to interview Mr. Baldwin, manager of the Marion Manufacturing Co. The demands were reduction of hours to ten a day, without decrease in wages. Twenty-two of the most active complainers were fired. A strike was declared in both the Marion Manufacturing Co. and the Clinchfield Mills on July 11, 1929.

A certain amount of strike relief was provided by money sent down from the North. That 'relief' might not seem altogether adequate for people who live soft. In the way of food—and understand that this was the only food on which the strikers and their families lived during the period of the strike—it consisted of flour, salt pork, coffee, rice and occasional potatoes.

But at least a dozen of the strikers have told me that they were content, because this food is quite as good as what they could afford if they were working.

The strike committee was able to provide such old clothes as were given to them. As to houses, the mill companies did not eject the strikers from their cottages, which are owned by the mills. They are planning to do so, however, and when they do, we shall have the spectacle of penniless families being moved out on those red clay streets—families with their sick and invalid.

For Gastonia is in the same State of North Carolina as is

Marion. And here is what happened last May, according to a press report, when like evictions were carried out against like striking and otherwise seditious mill-workers in Gastonia:

"Striking members of the National Textile Workers Union were facing a new and pressing problem tonight as police deputies began carrying out eviction orders issued to-day against sixty-two families formerly employed by the Manville-Jenckes Co.

"The deputies began their dreary task at 2 o'clock this after-noon. As the chill of nightfall crept over the town, they had entered thirteen of the mill shacks, dragging the humble furnishings and cherished possessions into the street.

"The mill people, although reduced to a condition approach-ing absolute poverty by the five weeks' strike, offered no resistance to the officers. In most cases they stood by passively while their homes were emptied.

"Some, however, spoke bitter words, while a few of the women wept as they watched their belongings dumped into the gutter in front of the place where had been home.

"For two families the eviction was a grave matter. Illness failed to stay the hand of the officers, although the order pro-vides for special consideration of those families thus afflicted.

"The families of Henry Tetherow and J. A. Valentine were evicted, strikers said, contrary to orders of Magistrate Bismark Capps, who signed the eviction writ. Valentine's four-year-old daughter was said to be seriously ill with smallpox, against which this State has no quarantine laws."

Well, then, there were the Marion strikers and their families, who, without having to work, were receiving enough food to keep from absolutely starving; who had $10-a-month houses and such old clothes as people happened to give them.

With such luxury as this, foreigners would probably have gone on loafing for ever. But these strikers were authentic one hundred per cent Americans, and they wanted to get back to work. So on September 10 the strike was settled on this basis:

The hours were to be reduced to fifty-five a week; wages were to be increased at the pleasure of the Marion Manufacturing Co.—and since then they have honourably complied with this by increasing wages five per cent, which must be a tremendous help to a man making less than $13 a week—and there was to be no discrimination against men who at that time belonged to the Union.

It is the third clause, regarding discrimination against Union members, which has created trouble. Union men say that in the Marion Manufacturing Co. all Union members have been discriminated against. The employers say that it is just a coincidence.

A telegram from John Peel, from Marion, has just come to interrupt me. It says: "Carver one of wounded died noon." That makes six, instead of five, who were killed by the volley of the sheriff's deputies.

I saw Carver in the hospital.

He was very thin and yellow; he looked under-nourished; he was very courteous to me, a stranger.

He is dead now. He is one problem that we need not solve in Marion. Isn't it unfortunate that the nimble guns of the sheriff's deputies did not get all of those misplaced 600 who work for the Marion Manufacturing Co.! Then, like Mr. Carver, they would none of them have any more problems.

To continue where I left off when the telegram came in, the employers at the Marion Manufacturing Co. say that it is just a coincidence that they have not re-hired the men who were most prominent in Union affairs—that it is because these men have proved, upon scientific investigation of their careers, not to be so brilliant as a mill-worker ought to be if you are going to force a salary of $13 a week upon him.

Whichever of these sides is right, there arose discontent among the workers who had not been taken back into the mills. So Bill Ross, left in charge of the strike for the United Textile Workers Union, planned to call a strike in the Marion Manufacturing Co., presumably with the thought of a later strike in the Clinchfield Mills.

The date of the calling of the strike was vaguely set for October 2, because Mr. Baldwin, president of the Marion Manufacturing Co., had been called away and the strikers, in their inconsiderate way, waited until he returned. They wanted to see if he would not rather settle the whole business instead of having another pocket edition of hell on earth.

But on October 1 the superintendent of the mill, Adam Hunt, worried by the rumours of trouble, called in Sheriff Adkins, who brought with him some eleven deputies.

Accounts differ enormously as to what happened in the mill that night.

There is an assertion, current in Marion, that the sheriff and his men drank too much corn liquor. I have seen the sheriff's men. I do not believe that they needed corn liquor to start shooting. They look like hard-boiled movie sheriffs.

There is also discrepancy regarding what incitement was given that night to the workers to start trouble in the morning. One version has it that the mill foreman so taunted the workers, so badgered them and told them that they dared not quit, that, without any orders whatever from the malign, foreign labour leaders, with Bolshevik names like John Peel, they began to walk out voluntarily at one o'clock in the morning.

The day force at the Marion mill goes on at seven. It is a very curious thing that the workers—despite the charm of their company-owned houses—usually get to the mill and stand there gossiping long before the whistle blows. I have seen them do so, at noon.

It may be quite true that from six to seven on the morning of October 2 the crowd of mill workers gathered early for a wicked purpose. But whether they were wicked or good, whether they inclined to the Bolsheviks or the Rotarians, there they were at 6.45.

You had there a brick building, not particularly large, employing only 600 men, with a decent grassy yard in front of it; you had a narrow road, and across from it the building which combines the company office, the post office and the company store.

What happened then is a case for the sovereign State of North Carolina to decide. I have sat for hour on hour in the court-room at the feet of Judge Harding, sitting as a committing magistrate, and I have tried to make out from the witnesses of both sides just what did occur.

I have heard somewhat conflicting testimony.

I have heard that Sheriff Adkins shot down two men, and I have heard that he never even had his pistol loose from its holster.

I have heard that the crowd of strikers were an angry and heavily armed mob, with sticks and revolvers, and I have heard that there wasn't a single gun among them.

But so much is certain: The superintendent of the mills, Hunt, gave an invitation to all the strikers who wished to work to enter the mill. From the strikers there were cat-calls and curses. Tear-gas was thrown by Sheriff Adkins and his men.

Then the shooting started.

The forces of law and order—naturally, I mean to say the forces of the sheriff and the mill owners—say that the shooting started from the middle of the road, from amidst the force of strikers, and that the sheriff and his eleven deputies, faced with a murderous mob, had to shoot in return.

On the other side the workers insist that there were no guns and very few clubs among the strikers. They point out that among the eleven deputies and the sheriff, the only injury was a scratch on the cheek of one of the deputies, whereas among the working-men, there were four—then it was five, and now, since the telegram about Carver, it has become six— who were killed and twenty wounded.

To an outsider, it seems astonishing that if the strikers were armed and belligerent, none of the deputies was wounded, and *all but two of the strikers were shot in the back,* as though they were fleeing from trouble instead of starting it.

Astonishing!

This shooting of twenty-five or thirty workmen brought the whole affair to a temporary end, and the strikers are now seeking for justice from . . .

Where do you get justice?

Since I wrote this, a North Carolina jury has made a Christmas present of final exoneration to such of the deputies as Judge Harding did not release in the first commitment trial, and mill-owner Neal has announced that this makes everything cheery and splendid.

II

This is the story of Old Man Jonas.

When Sheriff Adkins threw tear-gas at the strikers, Old Man Jonas, the striker nearest to Adkins, attacked him with a stick. Adkins was broad, fat, strong, about forty years old, armed, and supported by the majesty of the Carolina law which he represented. Beside Jonas was the distinguished constable, Broad Robbins, aged perhaps fifty, but as powerful and menacing as a wolf. And Old Man Jonas was sixty-eight, and so lame with rheumatism that he had to walk with a cane—the cane with which he struck the sheriff.

One would have thought that these two proud and powerful guardians of law and order would have been able to control Old Man Jonas without killing him. Indeed they made a good start. Adkins wrestled with him, and Broad clouted him in the back of the head. Jonas fell to his hands and knees. He was in that position when he was shot.

The Court has decided that Adkins did not shoot him.

Someone shot him—a lame man, sixty-eight, on his hands and knees, in the dust.

The general shooting and the flight of strikers had now begun. If the fleeing strikers did any shooting at all, they would have had to shoot high; they couldn't possibly have shot that beaten and wallowing man.

After the riot, Jonas, wounded fatally, was taken to the hospital with handcuffs on, was placed on the operating-table with handcuffs still on, and straightway he died on that table . . . with his handcuffs on.

I come now to the trial—the commitment trial, corresponding to a Grand Jury hearing, of Sheriff Adkins and his men for murder. There was a rather curious mix-up of attorneys, for in this case, as Sheriff Adkins and his men were on trial for murder, the defence counsel were mill lawyers—the mill lawyers were not attorneys for the prosecution, as in the trial of the Gastonia Communists at Charlotte.

I feel certain that Judge Harding has been desirous of getting at the truth. But I hope that I shall never be on trial for my life—unless, like Sheriff Adkins, I have these attorneys defending me—before such an array of attorneys as those representing the mills, and, by the quaint custom of North Carolina, therefore representing the State, which is, apparently, following its mill-owning Governor, quite willing to be identified only with the mill.

Of course, the court-room was filled with people, plain ordinary people, but since I have been in Marion I have learned that ordinary people count so little that they are scarcely worth describing.

They were a bunch of tall, slim mountaineers, the men mostly wearing overalls, the women in their best gowns— made in 1900 or earlier—and their girls and boys in rather smart clothing.

For be it said that, however horrible the houses of the mill workers of Marion, the boys and girls are buying good clothes. Some day they may wish to have flivvers and decent food. I wonder what will happen then? I wonder if they will go on being satisfied with less than $13 a week wages?

III

The crux at the present moment in Marion is the **Marion Manufacturing Co.**, locally known as the Baldwin Mill. **Mr. R. W. Baldwin** is the president and general manager. He is a small, bewildered man who dashes about.

On my first morning in Marion he sought me out to give me his version of the strike trouble. And, as one who has every desire to be completely fair, I wish to repeat that version, which is this:

Bill Ross, the local strike leader, threatened a new strike several days before the shooting.

That is all of Mr. Baldwin's version—and fair enough, too.

We have, out of the three mill owners in Marion—Miss Sally and Mabry Hart and William Neal—two who assert that they are not unwilling to have conditions changed. I do not think that they will disagree with the theory that every worker in America has, according to our present standards and according to our protestations of unprecedented prosperity, the right to a flivver, a radio, and a house which will keep the wind out on a cold night.

But behind all of these individual manufacturers there is the powerful Southern Textile Association, the manufacturers. They have their mills in the South because of that famous supply of 'cheap and contented labour'.

If Mr. Hart or Mr. Neal were to deal with the workers' union—if, by the most poetic imagining, Miss Sally were to do so—there are a number of things that the manufacturers' union could do.

I wonder if Mr. Hart is courageous enough to fight them, on behalf of justice?

He will be judged by what he does hereafter.

There is another element, less organised than the textile manufacturers, which is quite as important in controlling the decisions of the manufacturers.

This is, in Marion and every other mill town, the local body of respectable citizens.

They do not wish any labour trouble.

They do wish the Northern manufacturers to bring their plants to the South.

They do wish to sell their lots, to find new patients for tooth extraction and appendectomies.

Northerners have wondered why the respectable shop-keepers and professional men of Marion and like Southern mill towns are not enamoured of the celebrated Ford theories; why they do not support the workers' demand for more wages so that they may get more from the workers.

In the first place, in these towns, the mills control the banks, the banks control the loans to small business-men, the small business-men are the best customers of the professional men—even when the latter are professional men of God—and so the mills can back up the whole human train, down to the clerical caboose.

Second, the South, more than any other part of the country, retains the idea of the Gentry versus the Lower Classes—i.e., the Poor White Trash—with the negroes not even in the social system. It doesn't take much to feel that you are Gentry. Owning a small grocery, as does Sheriff Adkins, will do it. But once you are in, you must fight, kidnap, kill, anything to keep from being charged with seditious sympathy with those unruly monsters called the workers. To keep those monsters in check, clergymen will leave their Bibles for coiled ropes, physicians will leave their scalpels . . . . or, better, refuse to care for wounded strikers . . . till they get their money.

It was a mob of men like this, professional men and police-men, who kidnapped the labour organisers at Elizabethton, Tenn., only eighty-seven miles from Marion, put them across the border and told them not to return.

It is a mob like this that will have something to say to Mr. Hart and Mr. Neal if they recognise the Union.

Before I leave the owners I want to deal with one aspect of this whole Southern mill problem that is not too well known. This is the supposition that in some curious way all of the mill owners are Southern gentlemen, while most or all of the discontented workers are Bolsheviks or some other kind of discontented foreigners.

The fact is that a very large percentage of the ownership of the Southern textile mills is Northern.

As for the strikers, the quaint thing is that they really are one hundred per cent Southern and American—including the foreign agitators whose foreignness is readily indicated by such names as Peel, Hogan, and Elliott.

I want to switch quickly now—it is such a quick switch on the typewriter, but so distant in social values—from the owners to the strikers.

Here is the strikers' headquarters. It is only a few feet behind the mill, on a plot which by some mischance does not belong to the company. It is the basement of a little store to which the workers have, very curiously, been going instead of to the company's store. Under this store the strikers have for their headquarters a room perhaps three times the size of an ordinary New York hall bedroom.

This is the only place in which they can meet, except for the little sloping plot of ground which is their regular site for mass meetings.

On this little plot there are eight new sawbucks. It was on these sawbucks that the coffins of the four men killed in the sheriff's defence of Americanisation rested before the smashed bodies were taken away to a place where there is no argument about the best method of running Southern textile mills.

Yet they are stubborn and unreasonable, these strikers. At the 'dugout', as they call their headquarters, I met a widow of sixty. Her clothes, I should judge from the glass buttons, were made in 1870. They may have belonged to her mother. But, naturally, she had put on this, her best costume, when she went to the 'dugout'.

I was introduced to her as she was going home with a sack of flour from the strike relief over her shoulder. I was told that she had no one to support her, because her older boys had gone away and were having enough difficulty taking care of themselves.

She had worked in the mill for many years. "But now," said she, "I can never work there again. I can't go across the blood of our murdered boys at the mill gate. I don't know what is going to happen, but I reckon that it's time for the Lord to take care of me."

That was an old woman, in old-time clothes, going along the road with a sack of flour over her shoulder. She believed in God. But in the modern and efficient America there is little place for old women who believe in God.

And there was another man in that dugout. A man with quiet eyes. I do not find many men with quiet eyes in New York.

This man's name is Dan Elliott.

I have already referred to him as one of the strike leaders who discovered striking even before the 'foreign' agitators came in. I hope he will leave Marion immediately. Marion is not a very healthy place for men with such foreign and Bolshevik names as Dan Elliott.

IV

Perhaps the strangest thing I found in the dugout, the headquarters of the strikers in Marion, N.C., was that there was absolutely none of the corn liquor that has made the Southern mountains famous. These men were serious. They were not drinking. They were not even particularly angry.

Oh, there were men among the strikers, not among their leaders, who did seem to be angry. There was a brother of one of the men who had been killed by the deputies of Sheriff Adkins. He said, rather gently: "This court proceeding ain't the end of this here."

There was another who said: "I'd rather murder 'em up than have 'em murder us up."

But mostly they were so quiet—so quiet. They went away from the hovel of the strike headquarters with their flour over their shoulders and said nothing.

After the battle with Sheriff Adkins and his men, the wounded strikers were taken to the Marion Hospital. Now this is supposed to be a community hospital. At least, when they were building it, the workers in the mills were invited to contribute to its building, and most of them did so. But when the men who had been shot down by the sheriff's posse were taken to the hospital, they were informed that they could not stay there, after their first emergency treatments, unless they paid.

These men had no money with which to pay. So there was a somewhat unpleasant situation in the hospital.

Bill Ross, the local labour leader, had to telegraph to New York to beg money so that the men would not be turned out.

But all of that has been solved now, because most of the men who were taken to the hospital after the little fracas with the sheriff are dead.

I want to describe what I myself have seen of living conditions in Marion, N.C.

From the court-house in which the sheriff and his deputies were on trial there is a view which recalls Italy. If you disregard a few littered back-yards in the foreground, you can lose yourself in that smiling vista of hills and valleys, with a distant group of houses that are obviously plaster Italian villas.

Well, they aren't. They are houses in the East Marion mill village and, seen closer, they are atrocious.

It is about two miles from the town of Marion to the two mill villages which, along with the farmer trade, support Marion and glorify it.

Marion itself has a bookshop, two movie theatres, and shops in which gents can get furnishings. But the 100 per cent American mill operatives do not often travel that long two miles—partly because they do not own motor-cars, and partly because they haven't much to spend in the way of furnishing gents. On a wage which averages less than $13 a week you furnish yourself and your family mostly with overalls.

No, the town of Marion proper is left to merchants, lawyers, doctors and the like.

But, going out the two miles, you come to East Marion and to the mill of the Marion Manufacturing Co., which makes plain white cotton cloth, the sort of cloth that is used in cheap pillow-cases. The mill is the centre of the village, and to its six hundred employees it is the most interesting thing to be seen. Its clamorous shuttles, its dirty floors, its roar and utter ghastly fatigue take the place, for some six hundred men, women and children, of the quiet mountain glens from which our civilisation has rescued them.

Since the first strike at Marion, these six hundred are working only fifty-five hours a week, but in the good old days, before agitators came to disturb the peace of this idyllic village, they worked twelve hours a day or twelve hours a night, and had no time to think about such un-American ideas as how to get more than $13 a week.

With wages so low, everyone in the family over fourteen or so has to work in the mill, from dark till dark. Where there are younger children, the oldest—often it is a girl of eight or nine—has to wash the dishes, make the beds, try to clean the house and sweep the porch, and amuse the still younger slaves all day long.

In the Baldwin mill, the floors are not very clean, the toilets rather unpleasant. For the young girls, and all such women workers as do not chew snuff, there is a fair degree of sickeningness in the fact that the snuff-chewers spit voluminously into the drinking-fountains and the linty space behind the looms.

The Marion Manufacturing Co. provides houses for its employees. I have examined these houses with considerable care. They are rented to the employees at the incredibly low cost of twenty cents per room per week. That means that a four-room house rents for $3.20 a month on the basis of four weeks to the month. Their water supply comes from old-fashioned hand-pumps, with not even enough pumps—usually there is one pump to two houses, of which each holds from two to twelve people.

In one glimpse, on a visit to Marion mill villages, you can see that none of the houses has running water—or, therefore, toilets.* The houses are all of them up on stilts, with no wind-breaking foundations whatever, so that if there were any water-pipes, they could be seen.

For toilets, there are ill-built privies and, of these, one often serves two families.

The houses are of the cheapest and flimsiest construction. I have tried to prise the clapboards apart, and have found that it could be done with my little finger.

A four-room house, in which twelve people may be living, is just this: it is a box with an unscreened porch. It has three living-rooms and a kitchen. In each of the living-rooms there are, normally, two double beds. In these double beds there sleep anywhere from two to five people, depending on their ages.

I have been in a mill-worker's house in one of whose rooms was a striker wounded by Adkins's men; just out of the hospital that morning with a bandaged leg, unable to move. He sat trying to look cheerful in front of a fireplace roaring with two handfuls (literally) of coal. In the two other tiny rooms that I saw there worked and talked and played five or six assorted adults and children. The kitchen was papered with newspaper. But I did not see the fourth room. In it, in her coffin, lay the aged aunt of the striker. She had died that morning, but they were so harassed, so crowded, so familiar with death, that they did not think to tell us about it until we were saying good-bye.

In the kitchen is being cooked the family food, which consists largely of flour biscuits, hominy, fat-back—the cheapest sort of salt pork—and coffee which will be served without cream or sugar.

The sheriff, Oscar Adkins, who was a grocer up to the time

* Since these and the other unkind Northern articles on Marion have been written, Mr. Baldwin has, with fanfares for his excessive generosity, announced that he has begun to dig sewers and instal running water in all his mill cottages.

he was elected sheriff, told me that the mill people insist on eating the finest of food.

"Why," he said, "they eat Palace flour, *and that's good enough so that I eat it myself.*"

I want, therefore, in fairness, to give the report of the other side—to say that there are authorities who assert that these one hundred per cent Americans eat flour good enough for Sheriff Adkins. But I must say that their babies, under-nourished and dirty, playing about in the blazing red mud, do not look as though they ate food good enough for Sheriff Adkins.

Governor Max Gardner, of North Carolina, himself a mill owner, has said in a recent report on the Carolina textile industry that North Carolina has been grievously misrepresented in the matter of wages, because a part of the mill workers' pay is taken out in houses—such admirable houses as I have just described—which are provided by the company at a low rent.

And it is true that the rent is low. In Marion it is only twenty cents a room per week. That is low, isn't it?

But unfortunately it happens that precisely such bonny homes, owned by private persons and let for a profit, in Marion rent for $10 a month, so that all that the mill is giving to the workers in the way of free rent, to be added to their earnings of from $5 to $15 a week per person, is $6.80 a month. And when you divide $6.80 a month among two to twelve people living in each cottage, it is not a tremendous increase.

Governor Gardner's own mill in Shelby, N.C., is among the model mills of the South. The houses which he himself gives to the workers are not at all the type I have described. But, nevertheless, mill owner and Governor though he be, I suggest that his arithmetic is a little twisted.

And I suggest that he, who has done nothing as yet about appointing a committee to investigate conditions at Marion, might go there and try living in one of those pasteboard boxes under which the wind howls in winter.

If a man is to accept the responsibilities of so high an office as that of Governor of the State, it would seem to me to be *noblesse oblige* for him to share the lot of his humblest constituent.

There was a time, before we became modernised and efficient, when kings prided themselves upon their willingness to bear sword and share meat with their humblest subject.

It is doubtless too much to expect anything so quixotic from the Governor of a State. But if Max Gardner will go to Marion, with his family, and live in one of Baldwin's mill cottages all winter, and work, under normal conditions—and this, of course, implies that all of his family also will work—in the mill, then I think he will before spring understand much about the need of unionisation if the Carolina situation is ever to be solved—and Carolina to be saved.

It must be stated that, in addition to this tremendous decrease in house rent, the worker at Marion and other Southern mill villages gets free electric light. So far as I have been able to find out, this free electric lights costs the company $3 a month per house, at the most.

I should think it would cost very much less, because when you have worked from ten to twelve hours a day—when you are looking forward to arriving at the mill at six-forty-five each morning—you do not ordinarily sit up very late reading detective stories and consuming electric light.

One of the most important things about the mill-cottage situation in Carolina is that every prosperous and reasonable man to whom you talk about it, North or South, says: "Well, perhaps their houses aren't so good when you take it from the standpoint of people like you and me. I guess we wouldn't like it so well to live there. But you gotta remember that the folks in those houses are just down from the mountains and, to them, these houses are a luxury."

In the first place, this comforting theory happens to be entirely inaccurate. The mill cottages are not better than the mountain log cabins of Tennessee and Kentucky and the Carolinas.

I asked several minor officials of the Marion Manufacturing Co. wherein the cottages are definitely better. They said that the mill cottages were superior to the mountain log cabins in three respects—in that they have electric lights, in that they are painted, and in that they have board floors instead of floors of beaten earth.

This, of course, comes down to exactly one advantage—that of the board floors. Electric lights are of no particular value to men who work from ten to twelve hours a day and who do not sit up and read. They would be quite well served by kerosene lamps or by candles. And the flimsy boards, however well painted, are decidedly less good material for houses, for protection against summer heat and winter cold, than honest logs.

v

The mill cottages at Marion are lined with thin tongue and groove lumber. They are painted, inside and out, in drab colours. They are not altogether appetising. But when the worker leaves his cottage for his long, careless hours of leisure, he has the privilege of seeing the other features of the East Marion mill village, provided practically free by the Baldwin Company.

Passing down the somewhat lava-like roads, the worker comes to the free public features of the town. They are a really well-built public school, in which every teacher is under orders from the mill company, so that no teacher is ever likely to criticise the company's policy; several churches, in which the preachers have one-half of their salaries paid by the mill company, so that, by a curious coincidence, they too have nothing whatever to say about the gay little incident of killing six men and wounding twenty.

I do not think that if I were a Minister of God, if I had the inconceivably high position of being in the confidence of Almighty God Himself, I would care to have half of my salary paid by the Marion Manufacturing Company.

There are two other public places to which the mill workers may go in Marion. One is the company store. This store, which is supposed to serve a community of six hundred workers and such members of their families as are not in the mill—which I would judge to be the children of under five and the old people over ninety—is about one-quarter as large as the country store serving the village of one hundred people two miles from my home in Vermont.

But that is probably a conscious and thoughtful act of the Marion Manufacturing Co., because when the average wage of all workers in the mill, including foremen—or 'overseers' as they call them in the South—is less than $13 a week, they do not need a very large store to take care of their trade.

And there are several other stores in the community, though they are not quite so large and handsome as that belonging to the company—which company store, by the way, is not co-operative.

The final public feature of the East Marion mill village is the building variously known as the Y.M.C.A. and as the Community House. It touches me more than a little to think that when Baldwin had this built he must have felt that he was being authentically generous.

It is a handsome building, of brick, with a classic façade. It contains as good a swimming-pool as you can find. If the whole of East Marion were as admirable as that swimming-

282

pool, then you would have the paradise which God must have intended when He constructed these glorious hills, and then left the rest of the job to the Marion Manufacturing Co.

But aside from the swimming-pool and the bowling-alleys, there is nothing whatever in the Community House to comfort people after they have worked from ten to twelve hours in the noise and stench and linty air of the Marion Manufacturing Co.

No, I am wrong. There is a library. I have examined its books with some care. I do not know who assembled that collection, but I think that he was somewhat unwise in presenting these books as the final solace for people doomed to the hell of that life.

I noted a book about Life among the Brahmins. I noted the *Everyman's Pepys*. I noted particularly a book about Linguistics, by Professor William Whitney, published in 1867. It must be a consolation to a woman like Mrs. Roberts, whose seventeen-year-old son was shot down by the deputies, who is a widow with young children to support, to be able to go to the Company Y.M.C.A., and read, perfectly free, a book on Linguistics published in 1867.

Since the first Marion strike in July, this building has been closed to the public. It is now the headquarters of the State militia. That library-room is now the office of the major commanding. So I am afraid that Mrs. Roberts must find consolation for the death of her seventeen-year-old son elsewhere.

Oh! And there is one other public place, but it is only partly provided by the company. That is the government post office, at the rear of the company store. In most parts of these United States it would be assumed that a post office was a 'United States Government Post Office'. But that is not true in Marion. During the first strike the State militia, who came in to keep peace, forbade the strikers to go to the post office for their mail, or for any other reason.

In my innocent days I was told that the United States Government is supreme in the United States of America. But I have learned a great deal in my few days in Marion, in the fair State of North Carolina. I have learned that the militia, under the orders of the State Governor, Max Gardner, has such power that it can close the office of the mail department of the United States Government to citizens of the United States.

There was a time in the days of Jefferson when this would have been regarded as an act of rebellion and of treason. But such days have gone now, in this age of efficiency.

VI

The labour situation at Marion, N.C., is not impossible to solve.

Marion is only forty miles, by an excellent and beautiful mountain road, from Asheville, to which a hundred thousand or so of tourists go with bright, open, inquiring minds every year. They must be intelligent, for otherwise they could not afford to stay at Asheville. And there are other resorts not far from Marion, with the distinguished universities of Chapel Hill and Duke, full of learned men, at no vast distance.

Well, then! If every tourist who visits these resorts, and every student and professor at these universities, will drive to Marion and Clinchfield and look around, there will be no more labour trouble, because there will, after enough of us have looked at them, be no more of East Marion and Clinchfield.

I am told that the Marion Chamber of Commerce desires publicity. I want to give it all the publicity I can. I want to add to the much-hymned glories of the South the spectacle of Marion—the spectacle of genuine Native White Americans, undefiled by non-English blood for ten generations, living and working under conditions as bad as those of negro slavery before the Civil War.

I want no one to take my word for it, still less do I want anyone to take the word of those malign foreign agitators who recently have, for reasons mysterious but certainly evil, been stirring up disorder in the fair State of North Carolina.

But I do want every autumn and winter visitor to Asheville to drive over—oh, an hour will do it; an hour will take them from luxury to inferno—and see for themselves the houses and the people of the Marion Manufacturing Co. and the Clinch-field Mills.

But if the Asheville tourists drive over to Marion, I beg that they will not stay too long—I beg that they will return to their hotels by daylight, for in Marion they will be afraid of being shot if they make too many inquiries.

The first night I was there, a pleasant gentleman went around town looking for me with a gun.

In the dining-room of the hotel you look about to see who is listening to you before you talk. When you go to bed you wonder whether or not you will be pulled out of it before morning by a mob of realtors, bankers and clergymen, as happened in Elizabethton.

But perhaps the tourists will stay, for surely it is evident that the gallant American motorists would like to experience everything that happens in this one part of the country where the predominant population is of one hundred per cent Americans.

I am told that one hundred per cent Americanisation is now quite the choicest condition in the world. Well, then! In Marion there is a population of only about one per cent of foreign-born; in the mills there is practically no labour that does not come from what is laughingly known as 'pure Anglo-Saxon blood'. And the mill village illuminatingly shows what we can do to such undefiled peoples; what the contrast is between the treatment in these United States of pure stock and of those foreign elements whom we must keep out of America by a constantly revised immigration quota.

I am afraid it will not be enough for the Buick-aristocracy to see the entertaining show of the one hundred per cent Americans living in misery and under the shadow of mortal fear unless they see it with softened hearts and softened eyes and softened pocket-books.

For certainly their peers in Marion itself are not particularly moved—certainly the well-to-to Marion fellows of the men who did the kidnapping in Elizabethton, Tenn., do not seem to be stirred to angry pitch by the sight of horror.

Of course!

I know just how much is to be expected of the respectables of Marion. They have deliberately made it clear that they are ready to fight for the mill owners. Here is a pamphlet just issued by the Kiwanis Club of Marion—Kiwanians elsewhere, especially at their next national convention, are invited to consider the frankness of their brothers at Marion.

A handsome pamphlet. Coated paper. Photographs of lakes, mountains, luxurious houses. In these quotations from it, the impertinent interpolations in parentheses are mine; and I have italicised certain sinister—openly and cynically sinister—lines:

"This booklet presents facts and conclusions in behalf of the city of Marion that must needs command the careful attention of the whole great world of industry, commerce and finance. For Marion has earned an established place in this broad sphere of affairs and occupies in its civic relations a secure position of honor, respect and shining promise.

"And Marion's voice would address the ear of that impelling spiritual power whose name is called by men—Achievement. To those who possess this vital urge, Marion's message is clear, frank, simple and straightforward. A single word gives it expression: Come!

"Come to Marion where there's courage. Where there's opportunity. Where there's help and co-operation for every worthy man and woman. Where there's wealth to gain. Come to Marion—now!

"If you would live richly, locate your home in Marion and join a most delightful company of neighbors, cultured and hospitable, sociable and sincere.

"And for children, Marion is an ideal happy home town, with a fairyland around it in which they may frolic and grow sturdier through all seasons of the year."

(Happy fairyland, where an eight-year-old girl frolics on bare sun-bitten red clay, after only seven or eight hours a day of washing, combing, feeding, quieting her four smaller brothers and sisters, with no older person there to help. Happy Kiwanians, dreamers and poets of the Vital Urge!)

"Clean and substantial pavements, modern lighting and all the conveniences of urban life place Marion well in the van of the most progressive cities of the New South—a South that is rushing toward a destiny of extraordinary wealth and glory.

"And Marion aspires, through the liberal education of its youth, to speed the dawning day of universal training and attainment.

"These tax rates are not only exceedingly low, but will almost certainly remain so under State laws and supervision that sharply limit the taxing powers of counties and municipalities.

"*Stocks and securities of non-resident corporations are entirely exempt* in North Carolina. Resident corporations are assessed under a fair and liberal system.

"*Taxation in Marion is deliberately intended to invite investors and investments. Careful study and consideration will assuredly reveal the promise that new capital is guaranteed the absolute minimum of cost from taxation.*

"Labor in McDowell county is plentiful and willing, and of a most intelligent, loyal and desirable kind. *Under no more than reasonably fair treatment of its help,* every factory or branch of industry is certain to be able to secure adequate, satisfactory and contented labor."

(Was there ever a more extraordinary expression of Marionian and Kiwanian ideals than that "no more than REASONABLY fair treatment"?)

"Marion cordially invites the inspection of firms and individuals who may wish to investigate its desirability for any line of business or industry."

To such an open declaration by the Marion business-men that they will assist Capital to choke Labour, can there, on the part of workers, be any conceivable answer save the most militant and universal and immediate organisation of trade unions? Can there be any conceivable policy for neutrals save hearty assistance to that labour organisation with sympathy, with pen, and with money?

"This nation cannot survive half slave and half free."

INDEX OF NAMES

Thompson, Francis, 198
Thoreau, Henry David, 16, 181
Thurston, Katherine Cecil, 79, 176
Tiberius, Emperor, 241
Tilden, William, 173
Tinker, Chauncey Brewster, 177
Tolstoy, Leo, 156, 158, 166, 172
Tschaikowsky, Peter Ilich, 69
Turgenev, Ivan, 69, 156–8
Twain, Mark, 8, 17, 115, 135, 143, 172

UELAND, Brenda, 232
Undset, Sigrid, 10
Updegraff, Allan, 177

VALENTINE, J. A., 265
Van Doren, Carl, 20, 66, 115, 118, 136, 139
Van Doren, Mark, 139
Van Dyke, Henry, 29
Van Loon, Hendrik William, 180
Vesalius, Andreas, 36
Villon, François, 10–11, 98, 225
Voltaire, François Marie Arouet de, 36
Vorse, Mary Heaton, 77, 81

WALPOLE, Horace, 77
Walpole, Hugh, 77, 184
Walter, Bruno, 36
Warwick, Countess of, 165
Washburn, Claude, 232
Washington, George, 62
Waugh, Evelyn, 172
Wells, H. G., 10, 14, 16, 29, 70, 77, 116, 158–66, 172, 255, 256
Welty, Eudora, 198
Werfel, Franz, 36
Wescott, Glenway, 139
Wharton, Edith, 11, 122, 135, 139, 152, 172, 254

Whistler, James McNeill, 35, 61
White, Walter, 129, 132, 133
Whitlock, Brand, 11
Whitman, Walt, 8, 16, 18, 77, 146, 181
Whitney, William, 283
Whittier, John Greenleaf, 181, 182
Wiegand, Karl von, 106
Wilder, Thornton, 19, 139, 142
Wilkins, Roy, 132
Willebrandt, Mabel, 254
William the Conqueror, 227
Wilson, Edmund, 136, 137, 139, 140
Wilson, Ruth Danenhower, 129
Winchell, Walter, 136
Winter, Alice Ames, 232
Winterich, 157
Winters, Yvor, 137
Wister, Owen, 11
Wolfe, Thomas, 18–19, 139, 158, 172, 181, 198
Wolff, Maritta, 172
Wolman, Dr. Leo, 237
Wood, Grant, 199, 242
Woollcott, Alexander, 180, 237
Wren, Christopher, 236
Wright, Dr. Louis T., 44
Wright, Richard, 128–9, 131, 133, 172
Wright brothers, 61
Wylie, Elinor, 139, 142

YOUNG, Marguerite, 195–6
Young, Stark, 148

ZACHARY, R. Y., 197
Zangwill, Israel, 79, 176
Ziegler, Eddie, 110
Zola, Emile, 69, 124, 143
Zweig, Stefan, 36